Music
IN EVERY ROOM

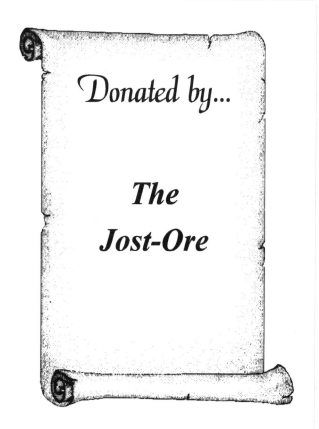

Donated by...

The

Jost-Ore

Music
IN EVERY ROOM

❖

Around the World
in a Bad Mood

❖

JOHN KRICH

THE ATLANTIC MONTHLY PRESS
NEW YORK

For El Zabeth, proofreader of dreams—
and for the six hundred thousand

Earlier versions of several sections of this book appeared in *The Berkeley Monthly,*
Black Messiah, and *Bump City* (published by City Miner Books).

First published in the United States of America in 1984 by McGraw-Hill
Book Company

First Atlantic Monthly Press edition, April 1988

Library of Congress Cataloging-in-Publication Data

Krich, John, 1951–
  Music in every room.

    Reprint. Originally published: New York: McGraw-Hill,
c. 1984.
    1. Krich, John, 1951–   . 2. Voyages around the
world—1951–   . I. Title.
G440.K93K74 1988   910.4'1   88-3445
ISBN 0-87113-194-3

Published simultaneously in Canada
Printed in the United States of America

Design by Grace Markman

The Atlantic Monthly Press
19 Union Square West
New York, NY 10003

FIRST PRINTING

CONTENTS

NEAR NIRVANA

NEAR EAST

NEAR HOME

---- ❖ ----

AUTHOR'S NOTE

EVERY ACCOUNT of a journey celebrates an event that can no longer occur. The Bicentennial year has passed, with no particular effect on the course of our nation; holders of U.S. passports are now free to nose about China, and are likewise excluded from diversions, noble or ignoble, in Afghanistan and Iran; changes in the official portraiture of all three countries have been thorough enough to make a case for history as a form of amnesia; new generals with ever more unpronounceable names rule Thailand; Mrs. Gandhi's "emergency" was met by an emergent opposition and eventually by Mrs. Gandhi herself; Mack Schreiber has switched networks and beats; the narrator of this book and Iris no longer keep company. Facts, historic or personal, are fleeting as the bad mood of the title. As I make my way once again around the world's girth, this time on paper, I trust my readers will skirt the obstacle of details that have since altered and offer me a ride on their imaginations.

—J.K.

"...The alternative is inescapable: either I am a traveler in ancient times, and faced with a prodigious spectacle which would be almost entirely unintelligible to me and might, indeed, provoke me to mockery or disgust; or I am a traveler of our own day, hastening in search of a vanished reality. In either case I am the loser—and more heavily than one might suppose; for today, as I go groaning among the shadows, I miss, inevitably, the spectacle that is now taking shape. My eyes, or perhaps my degree of humanity, do not equip me to witness that spectacle; and in the centuries to come, when another traveler revisits this same place, he too may groan aloud at the disappearance of much that I should have set down, but cannot. I am the victim of a double infirmity: what I see is an affliction to me; and what I do not see, a reproach."

—Claude Lévi-Strauss, *Tristes Tropiques*

"Continual Hot Shower! Meticulous Bedding! Sanified W.C.! Music In Every Room!"

—Indian hotel handbill promises

NEAR ESCAPE

HARD TRAVEL
AND SOFT TRAVEL

D AY ONE. Iris and I are real vagabonds now, no locomotives but our legs to pull us along. Our first steps take us across the gravel patio of the Kathmandu Guest House. Our packs are heavy with equipment we've rented for the sake of moving light. With free hands, we clutch the permits to trek. Available at a nominal fee, they must serve as passports to Himalayaland, letters of introduction to Yeti and Yak. Is that why we keep them in view, bearing them like amusement ride tickets to be punched, scorecards to be filled out with logged mileage? Our names are somewhere inside the gray booklets, above dotted lines printed faintly on coarse parchment specked with the pubic hair of serfs. The script is ancient, the regulations indecipherable, as befits good bureaucratic forms. His Majesty Birendra, King of Nepal, grants us this license to get lost in the hills.

For the moment, I'm following Iris' lead, trusting she knows how to keep us on the right path. There's nothing to it, she insists, except distinguishing down from up. I still harbor hopes for a sudden ankle injury, or change in the weather, or the arrival of some urgent telegram, to keep us confined to the farthest mountain outpost of civilization. But I've been promising Iris this monumental stroll ever since the word "Asia" first appeared in our dinner conversation, long before we abandoned the flatlands of California. It's one of the main reasons she agreed that we see so much more of each other in order to see a little more of the world. We make a good team. Reared in small-town Texas, Iris looks for sustenance in unyielding landscapes; a New York City kid, I feel safer in the wilderness of back alleys. She scours Asia for symbolic guidelines in the creation of what she calls a "new mythology," while I'm on the trail of a liberating *realpolitik*. Tribal refuges, the ruins of Mohenjo-Daro, top her explorer's shopping list; I find my stirring vistas amidst the slums of Calcutta and Bangkok. She likes dark meat, i prefer white. And though I'm suddenly regretting my prior willingness to don the outdoorsman's role, I know that I only become obliged to Iris so that I can keep pledges to myself.

Before scaling real or psychic heights, summits measured in attitude, the expeditionaries need to stop for a solid breakfast. A local impresario, who calls himself "K.C.," plays scratched Jefferson Airplane records in his basement café and orders his eight-year-old chef to fry us some eggs. They're practically all he offers besides the monstrous birthday cakes that satisfy the sweet tooths of hash-heads. K.C. looks like a shorter, kindlier Pancho Villa.

"And how much high you will be roaming?" he asks. We answer timidly. Every Nepali knows that the Helambu trek is for toddlers. Just a four-day jaunt to the fringes of Sherpa country. Up around 11,000 feet—too low for worries over arctic blasts or altitude sickness. Yet we're not sure we can make it. Requiring breakfast is our first show of inexperience. It arrives some hours after we order it. We can hear the eggs crackling over the electric hot plate, yet somehow they don't cook.

The late start gives me an excuse to coax Iris into a taxi that takes us as far as paved roads go. We're in Sundarijal, last settlement in the north end of the Kathmandu Valley, having cut several miles from the first day's suggested walk—which turns out to be what our friend Mack Schreiber, cribbing from Chairman Mao, would term "a good thing, not a bad thing." Past the proverbial dusty row of huts, the thick granite rim of the valley's soup bowl rises. The mimeographed itinerary we're carrying, thrust at us along with boots and sleeping bags by a mellifluous Kathmandu outfitter named Pasong, leads us to a series of stone steps to get us started. Then, the handout reads, "climb for two or three miles." It means climb, not walk.

The monotony of chiseled staircase gives way to the trail. My fears about being able to follow it are immediately made foolish. These two-lane furrows are the true highways of Nepal. They were here before the Red Army or the U.S. Corps of Engineers decided Nepal needed their "aid." They are the worn thoroughfares of a mountain nation—a pedestrian nation. These main arteries are necessarily flooded with the self-regulated traffic of the country's teamsters, the superhuman porters who truck along in convoys. They will be our companions and our pacesetters. In shorts and muslin tunics, cloth caps tilted jauntily, and bare feet—rubbing the salt of humiliation into the blisters our borrowed boots are already giving us—the porters lug bundles of chopped wood, canned goods, blankets and cloth bolts tied to straw saddles on their backs. They plod at a constant rate over these first quiet folds of peak. Our strides look quicker, but we're soon left behind by one caravan and passed by the next. They stop only for day's end or a cigarette. Ascent and descent are parts of one unvarying motion. Thirty miles is an average day's work. And the trails have been built for these billy goats: no snake-curves or banking to blunt the climb or give it grades. We go up and still up. The shortest distance between two damnable points.

The body waits for an end to steepness. None comes. *Nux vomica.* With the help of our sheet and its maps and their estimated times for getting from rest stop to rest stop, Iris plays the taskmaster. We must reach the village of Pati Bhanyang by nightfall or sleep outside. Kathmandu is as hazed-out behind us as the high peaks ahead. As our mimeographed sheet cautions, April is the month of poorest visibility in the mountains. We can only hope the author is wrong about this and right about everything else. The hills we can see are bare. We push on the path's starting blocks toward the sun. The water bottle that had seemed so cumbersome on our many train journeys is now far too small. Two hours up the first incline, we've finished our rations for the day.

The trail winds sideways through a rung of wooden shacks

that is the first man-made notch in the great rise. We've conquered the first 1,500 feet on schedule. A young woman standing beside a bark yurt *cum* shack, beckons us in for *tchai*. We can't resist refreshments or the woman's pigtails and dimples. Our packs come off, leaving welts that make us feel they're still on. Cooling down in a dank kitchen, crowded closer than we'd like to a fire, we get liquid and shade. The tea is syrupy sweet and thrice-brewed: meant to power trekkers like truckstop java. A little girl plays by the hearth that both supports and blasts a black kettle. Without inhibition, she swipes my gray Mao cap. Mother and daughter laugh easily as she tries it on. Iris and I drink too feverishly, inhospitably. The father peers in the doorway. He squats beside me and inspects my wristwatch. I let him try it on, too. He seems to know what it is, but is not sure of the value. I show him how many rupees it's worth with a triple flashing of ten fingers. He's impressed, though I've underestimated to discourage him from keeping the toy. But that thought's in my mind, not his. Theft is an act of envy; this farmer's face holds none. He has nowhere to sell a watch, no reason to use it. He follows the twitch of the second hand, but has no concept of the pressure it measures; he has no itinerary, no appointments, no place to get by nightfall. No twentieth century. He and his wife do not even ask us to pay for the tea, but we do. We teach the little girl how to wave goodbye.

Our respite from the sun has only made it stronger. We are reaching the ridge, the edge of the soup bowl. The huge hillock is rounded off by winds roaring down from Tibet. Such exoticism is no comfort. The ascent's sheerness has been blunted, and with it a clear sense of what's ahead or behind. The path holds steadily to its ken. The earth here is almost white and crumbles as our tread grips it. Scrub forests surround us now, not quite high enough to shade us. Iris is excited to see her first rhododendron bushes. They are not flowering. We should be able to see the full chorus line of Himalayan peaks when we reach the top of the rim. But we won't. The spring haze continues to smother views. The top of the ridge may also be a mirage. We reach it only to glimpse another ridge. The benefits of the glucose tea wear off. We start taking rest stops before our booklet tells us. Neither of us speak. We will find words, we will picnic, once we reach the top.

I am lost in the first hallucination of the trail. How quickly it coalesces! But I can't shake it. My thirst, spiting itself, manufactures the ultimate vision of all homesick Asian travelers. In a fresh-scoured Formica kitchen, not a hovel with cauldrons, I approach the white glazed Frigidaire of the hep-u-sef suburban all-American home. I have never lived in such a place, except vicariously, through television's eternally prosperous models, but I know it just the same. I open the icebox door. Within, enveloped by gleaming enamel, sits the imperialist bounty: a rack full of thick glass and stainless steel pitchers, frosted over and beading up and uncovered so I can peer lustfully into them. And I can have anything I want! Freedom of choice is great when there's something to choose from. Shall I try some plain, old-fashioned uncontaminated ice water? I can see the chunks of ice from the freezer floating in it. Nothing will ever be cold enough for me. What about some lemonade, or Kool-Aid, or Hawaiian Punch? I don't care, I'll take it. Pass it my way. I crave all that hydrolized purple alchemy. Next to the punch, there's orange juice, and doubly thick tomato juice—the mother's milk of vegetarians. And then the wholesome hormonal stuff itself. Builds strong bodies twelve ways! Where's the strength from all those sour swallows forced down me as a kid now that I need it for this hill? I'm just a crazy fool dreaming of six-packs and sweet homemade libations in the midst of parched nowhere! We've made it. No one in the settlement at the crest offers a pit stop. They just stare and shoo us on. Just out of town, Iris and I squat at the edge of the trail and suck oranges like monkeys.

We compare notes. Prematurely, but independently, we've concluded the emphasis of our march will be less anthropological than athletic. It is not the cultural challenge for which we've been hoping, but we're game to meet it. That is, Iris is game and I am sure not about to go back down that hill just yet. Climbing, Iris now concedes, will not take us into untamed wilds but into the country. She argues that's just dandy. It's fitting that the lure of nature should bring us closer to the social fabric of Asia. After all, Asia is a peasant continent and, for us, this peasantry's been unglimpsable as the snow leopard.

Porters pass us while we eat. They are gruff, concentrated, not as curious about us as they might have been fifteen years ago when Nepal was first opened to the world. Yet they always break into grins and polite replies when we have breath enough to call out "*Namaste!*" This is the greeting of a pious sub-continent, the "God-be-with-you," and the password that gives us entry to the daily, working etiquette. As for nature . . . to love nature, I'm finding, one must love the finely striated turds (so much like Pillsbury pull-aparts) left freshly ahead of you by the livestock on the path you both must travel. To love nature is not necessarily in the nature of man, just as he does not love his own nature. Out here—Himalayan foothills, bigger than your average feet—there's a struggle with that natural world which breeds appreciation but not fondness. The porters who know all about it seem solitary and intent—but not ennobled. Man here is alone and coughing. When he huddles with other men, they are nothing more than men together coughing, with children, born of her, coughing. So cry *"Namaste!"* The trail is long and God had better be with you because someone sure should.

Aren't such rigors just what I'm after? The climbing leaves time for self-examination, encourages the anesthetic of detachment. "One man cut adrift from the customary! . . . Our hero unshackled from the coercions of duty or cash!" These adventure book phrases have no bearing on why I decided to head off around the globe. If anything, they depict the sort of stationary rover I'd been at home. The occupation "world traveler" sounds so much more impressive than anything I'd held down previously, even though the job is secured with a charter ticket and fake student ID! A refuser, an "underachiever," a coddled dropout—at last glance, a twenty-seven-year-old paper boy, holding down a weekend delivery route for the meager benefit of an obscure leftist organization—I want from the road what I'd never found by staying put: participation in the most common forms of distress. Travel, for me, does not offer the prospect of flight, but rather attachment, be it to next trainload, busload or boatload. Every journey, not just in the Himalayas, has a chance to become a forced march, commanded by the primacy of next meal and next bed. The more distance I cover, the more surely I'll be restricted. With any real luck, I may be permanently thrown off my individualist course. Rambling, my lot will be shared. And while I may not exactly "meet my fate," I can at least be in position to sneak up on it.

Lo, I will be Magellan with toothbrush! I can find myself only in disaster. Too bad this doesn't hold down my alarm at a change in terrain. We are now on the exposed backside of the big fold. But skipping downhill is no easier. New blisters form where our ankles are jammed forward in the boots. We careen across half-mile knolls, rock bosoms covered with the soft tendrils of silvery grass. This time, it's the wind that gives G-force resistance and tries to drive us back. These blusters come from a place, so close by, where summer doesn't exist. Why can't we have a peep at those icicle heights? The sun moves over the rim of the valley to join us, and the hills turn golden. This isn't Nepal, it's the Scottish Highlands. We come to our first pure spring, pouring down over the slope of the crest. We drown ourselves in it, but don't drink. Our handout warns that there might be a field of cow patties right on the other side. Though we can hardly stand to, we carefully fill our water bottle and dump in the customary dose of iodine. We poison the water to match our poisoned systems.

A few solitary journeymen overtake us in silence. They carry carved walking sticks and sacks of candy from the city. No more caravans for the day; the porters are already bedding down. They are wise to escape the gusts of sunset. The ridges are purple, their folds an angry blue. With our heavy packs, we are thick sails, blown taut with each breeze, tacking from side to side of the trail's surface. But we must keep going, keep being buffeted, because we're two hours behind schedule. Just when I'm considering panic, Iris points to our resting place, cries "Ahoy!" like an explorer sighting Atlantis. Pati Bhanyang is below us, a huddle of roofs clogging a single spur that crosses a crevice between two enormous mounds. We skitter down a last hill's sharp cleavage. The handout says the first house on the left offers lodging. There aren't any "Vacancy" signs flashing. No electricity, no plumbing, no transportation but human legs. The first house we pass is the only one separated from the town's single street, a natural bridge to which commerce clings, a glacier-formed *ponte vecchio*. This first house is too large, too foreboding. We decide it's the wrong one.

Suddenly, the Nepalese version of a Swiss hot cocoa lady leans out her second-story window and calls. She motions us around the back of the house, then up a set of folding stairs through a trap door at the back of a first floor that's used as a stable. Ground level is for goats. The upstairs, divided into four large rooms, looks unoccupied, but this informal innkeeper guides us to a particularly bare one. Just straw mats covering a mud floor: the suite reserved for the trekking trade. We set down our packs, inspect the damage done to feet, ankles, skin. And this is only day one! I'm not moving another inch, but a young girl leads Iris to a washing place through a grove of birch trees in the back yard. It is getting dark so smoothly, so effortlessly, and darkness means a quick end to the Nepalese day. No electricity out here, no reading lamps. One candle is all that's provided to postpone this organic finish.

Out the window beneath which I've dropped my bedroll, I watch Iris return through the trees. Their white barks grow isolated in the darkness. But from what I can see of my partner, she looks ecstatic. Her eyes dilated, her tread firm. There must be some high country fur trapper in Iris' lineage. She's the same stubborn, self-made woman I've known all along, the diehard dreamer and feminist, yet she's sparkling now, like the night air in these mountains, a trifle mad with that stubbornness. Who the hell is she really? And why do I follow her to the ends of the planet so I can breathe down her neck? I wonder only when I'm too fatigued to find out.

And what are the two of us, taken together? Hardly just "postal employees," as our passports state, though that's how we'd raised our traveling fund. Would a budding writer and a reluctant psychologist be any more accurate? Surely, we're not merely ex-radical comrades, since neither of us put much stock in such terms. Technically, we're lovers, but neither of us has ever been sure enough of that to speak the word "love." Indeed, there are moments when love seems more distant than Johore Bahru, than this Happy Trekker Motel. Yet I'm hoping to prolong our ill-defined state through this trip, woo this lady once and for all with a guidebook's bounty. Iris is my journey's first and last destination, and as such, has to enforce its haphazard tests.

She climbs back up to me just in time for the evening meal. We've been warned it will be meager. The cocoa lady brings more tea, with a mound of basmati rice, scooped from an iron crock that, as Iris observes, "has seen better days." A muddy dal, or lentil paste, serves to moisten the rice: the "pot liquor" in Iris' oilhand argot. A few dabs of hot curried spinach and potatoes are offered as a condiment, a precious chutney. The long hike and unsullied oxygen have their predictable effect upon our appetites. We eat with our hands for the first time, using the right hand only, just in case the old woman is watching. Fingers and mouth tingle together. Everything tastes like it's tugged from the earth.

An emaciated French couple arrives just in time for supper. They are veterans who know all the rituals. I notice at once that they're in shorts and rubber sandals. They carry no packs or unnecessary weight, foisted upon them by some Mister Pasong. And they've walked all the way from downtown Kathmandu (if there is such a thing)! The flush, and ache, of our first outing's achievement pales when the Frenchmen casually describe past and future exploits. They've just finished a month-long pilgrimage to the Khumbu Glacier, complete with malnutrition and frostbite. For them, this route is a leisurely skip through *Les Tuileries*. We are glad the twilight hides our blisters, our sore calves, our immense and rigid boots.

Soon as the four of us have settled cozily on the floor, the man of the house slips into an antechamber. He is a phantom we will hear through the night. We know of his presence by his habits. Smoking acrid tobacco through a water pipe, or "hubble bubble" as the more onomatopoetic British call it, the husband follows his draws with vicious coughing. After phlegm is brought forward, the cycle is willingly continued: more bubbling, more retching, more bringing forth. I hope there's a spitoon.

"Ze Brahmin . . ." the Frenchman whispers.

Now it is clear. In the nights ahead, it will become clearer. Where there is man, there is caste. The house of the Brahmin is nearly always apart from the rest of the town, is the largest, is ordained to accommodate visitors. The Brahmin doesn't do it for pin money. He's top dog, and apparently the only villager whose status cannot be lowered by sustained contact with foreigners.

"Ze tuberculosis . . ." the Frenchman whispers again.

I nod a thanks for the diagnosis, though it's spoiled my slumber. Now I can't help but listen more closely to the native form of insomnia and the equally native disease that accompanies it. Are both catching? Iris, game trooper, has gone to sleep at once. But I can't shake my usual anxieties, geographic and not-so-graphic. Disfigured by culture shock, I am the monster who must go on stalking private demons, must keep guarding a familiar mental terrain—even in the unfenced Himalayas. "The envied wanderer, shrewd enough to skirt allegiances!" No, I am the only Abominable Snowman in these parts. Or perhaps an abdominal snowman, since I'm better at bellyaching than chest-thumping. Some poor devil inside me keeps asking, "What am I doing here?" The answer can only come through learning not to ask.

I lay throbbing on the straw mat, out of whack like the Brahmin. I hear him gagging and suffering, hear the water aerate his life away. Through the night, the two of us labor side by side, trying to turn the clear air dirty, to narrow our wide expanse.

❖
TEN THOUSAND LI

I T WAS A typical Mission-style spread, with tiled roof and adobe garage added on. Just one of a dozen suburban haciendas, bay view included, along a tract so freshly poured that the ground cover—aptly tagged ice plant, vintage freeway landscaping—wasn't high enough to mask the computer driven sprinklers. Yet, like everything else in California, the street where this instant mansion sprawled was permanently slanted. This ridge of prime real estate slid away from its own continent, just as "lifestyles" along America's self-proclaimed cutting edge tilted toward the influences of the Pacific rim. Having come West, young man, there was no farther to go but East. History had been revealed as a tipped scale, increasingly weighed down on one side by those original cultists, first sensualists, pathbreaking mystics, renowned extremists, model beatifics, exemplary holistics, the billions of Asia. In this curiously unpeopled, unencrusted setting, we sought one of them.

"Are you-all sure this is the place?" Iris asked, still gunning the spunky VW that she kept in the pink with her own set of wrenches.

"*Insh'allah*," answered Mack Schreiber from the back seat. But just in case Allah wasn't willing, as he'd learned to spout on a recent stint in Pakistan, Mack checked the directions jotted in pictographs on the back of his reporter's notebook. "I'd expect nothing less from Lin Hua."

"You mean, the bigger the house, the better the . . . what's it called again?" I asked.

"Fêng shui. It means 'wind and water.' And the size of where you live has no effect on it, just how you arrange the furniture. What I meant was that there's no reason a self-respecting geomancer shouldn't make out all right. Lin Hua would never take hard cash for his services, since that might sway his predictions, but he accepts all gifts and charity, deluxe room and board. . . . See!"

Jutting from the garage at the end of the driveway were two Lincoln Continentals, with customized license plates that read "YIN" and "YANG."

"Those must belong to Lin Hua's benefactor. I've got his name here. Y.K. Chu. . . . Probably a shipping magnate."

"Do you think he uses one car for good and one car for evil?"

"I think we've arrived at the moment of decision," Iris announced, ignoring my question. It was just like her to have jumped at this chance to have a consultation with Mack's former Chinese tutor and current internationalist seer. Iris already had one trusted oracle, appearing in her dreams as an ageless Indian squaw, shrouded in sun and ceremonial garb. I should have known she would employ similar means to make up her mind about going to Asia with me. Now she turned to ask, "Scared of what you might hear?"

"No. Just scared that you might believe it." Personally, I preferred to check my itinerary with a travel agent, not a fortuneteller.

"Don't worry," advised Mack. "He may not volunteer anything. He doesn't just perform on command."

Getting out, I had to wonder what Mack was after as well. This was his first leave after two years' work in Hong Kong as a tenderfoot China watcher for one of the networks (radio only, as he was still a little too hirsute for on-camera work) and from what I'd seen, our old pal from the antiwar days had to be losing his Marxist marbles. Was this the same manic, sniffly nosed imp who'd made it his daily practice to sing "The East Is Red," in its triumphant entirety, while skipping across our college campus to Twentieth Century East Asian History 110, or, more likely, a meeting of the People's War Defense Committee? Who'd been busted at Sikorsky Helicopter? Thrown ice cubes at General Westmoreland? I was aware that he now conspired in the less tolerant realm of diplomats' double-talk and thirty-second satellite feeds. Still, I hadn't expected him to so readily swap the stirring prison homilies of Uncle Ho for the evasive riddles of some Taoist-for-hire.

"Do you really have faith in this dude?"

"After living in Asia," Mack confessed, "you trust nobody, but you believe everything. Just in case."

Nearly sprinting toward the front door, Mack reminded us that every multinational corporation in Hong Kong shared his new-found caution. They all sought the opinion of a geomancer before positioning and building skyscrapers. Lin Hua himself had been a consultant to the Bank of America, just as he'd guided thousands of mere mortals who wanted their tombstones angled to insure the proper fêng shui through eternity. Next, Mack emphasized his point about this modern medicine man's powers by repeating the story I least wanted to hear. It seemed that this Lin Hua had only once withheld his blessings from a friend of Mack's. She was a young English anthropologist, most respectful of the Orient's rites, but Lin Hua had gotten rid of her as fast as he could. Refusing to hand out the usual lucky charms, he had merely warned the girl about a dangerous lack of chi—the universal breath that moved through everything which possessed spirit—and within a week, she'd been asphyxiated by a faulty water heater.

What if this human ouija board pointed evil tidings toward us? Or simply refused to open the redwood portal on which Mack rapped? But the door swung back at once—had Lin Hua divined our arrival?—and we were greeted by the first of our journey's many stereotypes: a chubby man with monastic crew cut, black slacks and flat Tai Chi slippers, a blue padded Mandarin jacket, complete with cuffs that nearly covered his hands and looked like they'd sopped up too much sweet-and-sour gravy. Was it possible for us to see the individual beneath the anticipated composite, the caked-on layers of stereotype and inadvertent disguise? All that was missing were the pigtails, as once sported by those compatriots of his who'd come here to build the railroad and been misunderstood ever since. Lin Hua bowed, ever so inconspicuously, while barely looking at us. For Mack, he had a jolly, embarrassed cackle—which could have been his way of demonstrating that there was a good deal of childishness left in anyone or anything holy.

Still, there was no air or piety, no posed quietude, to this contented hen who led us, by clucks, toward a white couch, then tumbled, one leg tucked under the other, into a rattan armchair. The geomancer and Mack Schreiber set about at once, in Mandarin and without formalities, to exchange the latest word on shared acquaintances back in Hong Kong. At first, Mack paused to translate for us, but the stories of other pupils married, moved back to London, expelled from Taiwan, were at once too complex and mundane. Anyway, there was no need to interpret Lin Hua's jolly savoring of Mack's news. Their chatter gave me time to look around the most un-Californian of sitting rooms. It was devoid enough of "personal statement" to be a hotel lobby. Across an expanse of white pile carpet was a mock fireplace, flanked with panels of smoked mirror; one potted Dieffenbachia here, one jade Chow dog statuette there, much purposeful emptiness. The alignment of furnishings was harmonious, tranquil, classically Chinese— and, thanks to Mack, I now guessed that this interior decoration was not guided so much by aesthetics as by the considerations of fêng shui. This grand room seemed not to be meant for current household use—women's voices trickled in from a remote kitchen wing—but for soothing and placating resident spirits.

Gossip exhausted, Lin Hua rose, chagrined and awkward as a blind date. The rest of us imitated him, though it didn't look like he knew what came next. Did he also wring his hands at the Bank of America? The geomancer didn't fuss like an ordinary host; ignoring protocol, he waited to be guided by hunch. Shifting weight, casting about, Lin Hua's eyes still evaded ours, as if he were afraid of what he might see.

Mack filled the silence with an explanation of how the three of us had first met. What was the Mandarin word for "affinity group"? Or for LSD?

When Lin Hua started cackling, Mack told us, "I said we were once members of the same commune. That we tried to go amongst the workers and peasants."

He continued on merrily, summarizing recent history without any apparent fluency problems. Careening through the low and high tones of the language he'd set out to master when he was fourteen, our old pal showed a side of himself that was more whimsical and less driven than the clawing journalist. He'd even picked up the stuttering "ha, ha, ha" that wasn't a laugh in his adopted tongue, but an indication that he'd learned to listen as well as speak. We witnessed Mack's performance with awe and delight. Finally, after watching him showcase his skills in small talk with a thousand bow-tied Chinese waiters, we were getting to see him do more than find out which bean curd dishes were most highly spiced.

He stopped to assure us that he'd just told Lin Hua about our effort to decide if we should embark on arduous travels. Just then, Lin Hua stared up at Iris. Now he surmised all he needed to know from one look at features half-pretty and half-craggy, part-cheerleader and part-Eskimo, framed in hair tirelessly long and parted down the middle, a face that would look the same at sixty as it had looked at six. Could he tell that this lady didn't need makeup to keep her cheeks ruddy, her eyebrows sincere, her lids sleepily padded, her nose pugged, her dimples five fathoms deep? Maybe all he had to see was that chunky smile, lips pulled far up the gums with a "Ping!," so persistent and involuntary on Iris' part that it looked like a permanent deformation.

The geomancer reached out with both cuffs and took Iris' hands. The gesture was most spontaneous, and a trifle chilling. But Iris took it as a compliment. She turned demure as any latent Southern belle. Willingly, she let Lin Hua lead her toward the marble staircase to the second floor, and, presumably, his fortunetelling lair. With a nod, Lin Hua indicated an alcove through a stucco arch where Mack and I could wait.

We made ourselves at home in a thoroughly American den, complete with picture window overlooking the bare yard, built-in bookshelves to either side, couch upholstered in tartan plaid. The coffee table was as well stocked with magazines as a doctor's foyer. They gave me the feeling I might be about to hear some dreadful diagnosis.

"She'd better not back out now," I couldn't help muttering.

After all, I'd already given up a life of principled indolence to join Iris on graveyard shift at the Oakland Post Office. That was one employer who took anyone—no experience necessary, no dress code enforced—so long as you scored high on the civil service test, and we calcuated that three months' union wages as Christmas "casuals" would buy at least twice that amount of rambling on open shop continents; maybe more if we could learn to

hoard our rupees or turn otherwise ascetic. Starting out by visiting
Mack in Hong Kong and ending up in Europe, Iris and I could
be Marco Polos in reverse. Plying the trade routes, we wouldn't
so much loot the world—or seek looting's pale, modern equivalent: the bargain. We hoped to let the world loot us.

"How are you two getting on anyway?" Mack asked the over-
riding logistical question, partly to distract me and perhaps as a
reminder that he recalled those days in the "commune" when Iris
and I had laid our sleeping bags beside other partners.

It may have been because we still saw our association as an
effect of rebound, a cozy and predictable permutation, that I had
to answer, "Shaky."

"But she's considering the trip . . ."

"Sure. Why not? Except last week, I slipped and called it the
trick. Iris caught me on that right away."

"Doesn't she want you to have something up your sleeve?"

"I don't know what she wants. All I know is she's issued an
ultimatum. Total fidelity on the trip. But when the trip's over,
we're over."

"Then go slowly." I couldn't tell if Mack was making a joke
or talking Oriental.

"I don't think the worst Indian train will be slow enough."

"You've got too many ghosts following you around." Now he
really sounded like the geomancer. "That's why you should make
her come to Asia. Past lovers can't follow you there, or compete
with the multitudes."

"True. And we'll have to stick by each other for the sake of
the journey. Here, we renew our contract one week at a time.
For two years, the relationship's been 'temporary.' "

"A typical Berkeley ploy. The long break-up method. You
can't really part 'cause you've never been together. . . ."

"Are you advocating arranged marriages now?"

Before Mack could answer, we were joined by a gentle, elderly
man, his bald head spotted with experience. He was so unpre-
possessing that I thought he might be coming around to empty
the ashtrays. Then I realized this was probably the aforementioned
Y.K. Chu, proprietor of the Lincolns and the rancho and who
knew what else. His identity was confirmed by the Hong Kong
tailoring of his pin-striped suit and his offering of sesame candies.

"Please, please don't arouse yourselves." This businessman was so deferential to the business Lin Hua was conducting in his house that he did not even bother to introduce himself. Instead, he asked, "Have you seen the videotapes?"

Before we could answer, he'd opened what I'd imagined to be the liquor cabinet, revealing the Betamax, monitor and video camera that were his favorite toys. In a flash, Mr. Chu had switched on his very own closed-circuit broadcast: no cockfights or acrobats or more acrobatic hard-core acts, just Lin Hua, in more modern garb, clutching a pointer, before a thoroughly defaced blackboard. No subtitles either, so Mack had to explain that this was one of the master's lectures on the I Ching—and that the many smeared slashings behind him were the various hexagrams that charted every nuance in the combination of universal elements. "Mountain with thunder is the Corners of the Mouth." "Mountain with wind is work on what has been spoiled." "Lake with fire is revolution." It was a world-view in chalk.

"His first class at San Francisco State," our host informed us. The murky quality of the picture told us Mr. Chu had been the cameraman. Clearly, he saw no conflict between new technology and old teachings. This broker or developer or cotton waste king got so rapt that he could not help settling onto the couch with us to watch this thousandth repeat broadcast of Lin Hua strutting his stuff. He tittered along with the few nervous students present at the taping, for the seer's explications, like his predictions, were delivered in a style that was off-handed, intimate, consciously droll.

I couldn't follow any of it, and neither could the restless teenager who appeared in pursuit of his old man. Here was the number one son and heir of the household, the first of this family's American-born generation, milk-fed and already taller than his dad. He wore braces and granny glasses and a demonic T-shirt that read, "Black Sabbath—West Coast Tour." Unlike his less prosperous counterparts in Chinatown, this kid looked thoroughly assimilated, an Asiatic Beaver Cleaver. Yet, like his father, he seemed to treat the presence of a geomancer (and clientele) in his house as commonplace, the obligatory boarding of some spinster relative.

Oblivious to the guests and the mystical algebra on the box, the intruder started up in a tinny California rasp, "Come on, Pa! When are you gonna fix it?"

"It" turned out to be a ten-speed bike, and the answer was "Patience." In Cantonese. While Mr. Chu and Mack exchanged

opinions on the latest Kowloon shopping malls, I tried to pass the
time with my countryman. At the very least, we could talk baseball.
But did he have favorite players when none of them shared his
race? The name Carl Yastrzemski popped out at once, expertly
pronounced. I should have known better; there were hardly any
Russian Jewish intellectuals in the big leagues either, but that had
never stopped me. A moment later, the boy went off to play and
I went back to worrying.

The intricacies of The House of Arousing and The House of
Keeping Still hardly kept my mind off the proceedings upstairs.
Why had Iris been chosen, not me? The dirty old man! And what
could be taking them so long? Perhaps Lin Hua understood more
English than he'd let on, or could decode the confessions of his
nervous customers into some spiritual Esperanto. Might Iris be
telling him about our curious "agreement"? About her extensive
readings in Joseph Campbell and Harlequin romances? About the
conflict she felt between monogamy and independence, between
becoming a Jungian therapist and a kimono maker? Or how she
collected both guiding archetypes and swaths of handloomed fabric
for the clothes she planned to design, which she called "the robes
of my Indian woman." I was pretty sure Iris made no mention of
Lin Hua's competitor in the harbinger biz, or another recurrent
dream image, where Iris was put in an elevator that could only go
down, and found herself delivered to a basement crowded with
black cleaning ladies. This was never a nightmare for her, just
another purgative, one more means to cleanse the guilt bred of
an all-American lineage that led back through a great-granddaddy
Indian agent who tried to unseat Sitting Bull and greater-
granddaddies who kept people of color in their basements and
made them pick cotton. More likely, the communion upstairs was
intuitive, just the way Iris liked it. A whole lot of intuitin' goin'
on.

Whatever had transpired, I could hear them coming down to
join us. Y.K. Chu stood, and we followed, so that it seemed we
were a jury waiting for a judge to enter. If Lin Hua held the
verdict, it was announced by Iris: smile and dimples more exag-
gerated than ever, one hand curled around her new mentor's arm,
the other clutching a scroll. Lin Hua, too, was like a silk-encased
Cheshire Cat. He said nothing before plopping into the nearest
chair, but Mack nodded at me reassuringly. While he and the

fortuneteller slipped right back into the conversational mode, Iris came around and snuggled close on the couch.

"See what he made me!" she whispered. In her lap, half unfurled, was a sheaf of rice paper, freshly graced with a single Chinese character. A fluid blotch with long tail. "It means 'tao.' That much I understood! And he had more gifts, like Santa Claus. One for each of us. . . ."

In her palm were two Ming subway tokens, stained brass hexagonals, with square stamped out in the middle. Around each had been tied a length of red ribbon.

"They're ba gwa coins," Mack explained, peering over. "For good luck."

Luckiest of all, for Iris and Mack, was that they could put credence in such ancient guarantees. I was still plagued by the notion that the success or failure of our expedition depended on reading all the guidebooks, taking the full series of gamma globulin shots. But the two of them may have been right: there was no more way to prepare for a trip around the world than to influence the course of a jet.

"Do these things work on airplanes?"

"Except on UBA," Mack chimed in. "That's Union of Burma Airways. Also known as U Betta Ask. Again."

"Come on!" Iris urged. "Take your coin. And don't lose it!"

"I won't."

That was the trouble with blessings: one slip-up and they turned to a curse. The irrational, like the rational, entailed responsibilities. But apparently, Lin Hua's gifts did not guarantee a good outcome. They were merely an indication that he'd sensed "positive forces" enough in the two of us for him to reinforce. Now Mack was asking for advice about a decision he'd have to make on his return to Hong Kong, concerning the offer of a new correspondent's post from another network. On the nearest available cocktail napkin, Lin Hua had Mack make a quick sketch of his apartment. Soon enough, he suggested the placement of a standing mirror in one corner, the blocking of a window with a rubber plant, so that Mack's reasoning might be aided by the better dispersal of chi through his digs.

I was relieved the two of us hadn't been asked to do the same. That would have gotten sticky, since Iris and I, on the verge of sharing so many hotel rooms, still kept separate homes. It was complicated enough that we'd just been given a "Godspeed" for a journey that carried an emotional death pact. How could any good fortune be attached to such a leavetaking? Was it in the going, the returning or in never coming back? Maybe this clucking soothsayer knew more than I thought.

With thanks and profuse bows, we said goodbye to him. Lin Hua brushed aside Iris' admiration for his calligraphy with another schoolgirl giggle. It was strange: this man had nothing, short of everything, to say to us. At the door, he pulled forth his business card, should we ever need him again. It was bilingual and called Lin Hua a "scholar of Oriental philosophy." But how many scholars could list mailing addresses in Hong Kong, Taipei, Honolulu, Manila, Seoul and now San Mateo?

Through Mack, he invited us to join him later that night, after another lecture, in a Grant Street restaurant.

"Oh goody!" And Mack led us away from the door with one last aside, "You've got to see Lin Hua holding court! The food is always primo, not to mention the ladies who flock around him. Miss Chinatown and her hand-maidens. I don't know how he does it."

"Lucky coins, I suppose."

"Don't play the cynic," Iris cautioned. "He's the real thing."

Checking one last time to see if he really was, if he'd ever really been there, I caught Lin Hua still assessing us, still grinning.

"We'll be there!" Mack spoke for us while Iris and I waved. "*Insh'allah!*"

Too bad Iris and I wouldn't get the chance to appraise the geomancer's stable of chi-endowed consorts or share his banquet of aphrodisiac shark's fin. We had other obligations. On the third floor, foreign parcel post, Iris had to heave boxes into hampers marked "Palembang," "Pondicherry," "Surabaya Dis." On the first floor loading docks, I had to shove my own willing charges down battered, silvery chutes, move the mail along in one huge, brown volume while I stood still. Just as booze, bad marriages and car payments held the others around me to their place beside the insomniac conveyor, in this satanic realm where another shift just meant the sun didn't get any overtime, so I'd struck my Faustian bargain with the East. When the leadman on my crew shouted "Gentlemen, make yourselves scarce!"—suggesting we take the opportunity to hide from our supervisors in the swing room or grab an hour's snooze in a musky trailer that provided stuffed number three sacks for pillows—I was comforted to know that I'd soon be making myself scarcer still. At her station, Iris could remind herself that she'd soon be following her packages on their way.

"It's all decided, then?"

Iris answered with a wink and got behind the wheel. Now that we were on the road to Mandalay, California sped past us like one long exit ramp.

Our drive ended near the campus we'd once looked upon as a center of international revolt. Yet Berkeley's "free zone" had become a giant leech. The Telegraph Avenue ragamuffins, who'd once looked for discipline and guidance to the "oppressed peoples," going so far as to paint the sidewalks with Vietcong colors, now peddled those same peoples' handhewn articles to weekend guerrillas at the going rate. The world beyond, it seemed, was no longer worth liberating; it was just a giant crafts fair, an inexhaustible source of pretty things. But each blanket, pendant, and sandalwood incense stick was a clue to a puzzle that had to be pieced together; the world's collective unconscious showing itself in free trade's shopwindows.

How Iris and I longed to dive in! It didn't matter that we knew little more about where we were going than we'd gleaned from Ravi Shankar records and video footage of Tet offensives. It was enough that the Bicentennial year was beginning and that the revolution it would celebrate was not ours. Like Berkeley itself, our past rebellion had tied us all the more closely to what we'd sought to topple. So long as America stalled, we were stalled; so long as it was unchanged, we could only change by getting out.

"A journey of ten thousand *li* begins with a single step!" Mack Schreiber proclaimed, citing the Little Red Book. Or was it Lao Tzu via Lin Hua?

For now, that single step was reporting to our nocturnal duty. And if, in the automat glare of that perpetual night, I was suddenly overcome by fear of what was ahead, fear of Pathan bandits and Bengali swindlers and sudden dysentery in a public place, of what would become of my contract with Iris, I had only to reach under my Oshkosh B'Gosh smock, down inside my jeans pocket, and make sure I was holding new money. I could fondle that charmed coin with sash around it and emptiness through it, the best currency a prospective traveler could earn.

NEAR CHINA

Music:

❖

THE HIGH PRICE OF SZECHWAN CHICKEN

HONG KONG is the bargain basement of the world. Through the barred windows of Mack's high-rise cell, we can check for shoplifters amidst Kowloon's clearance sale. Already laden with spoils in newspaper satchels, waves of Cantonese housewife commandos stage their attack. Ejected from Piccadilly double-deckers, they head straight into the department stores serpents' maws. They waddle toward sidewalk tables heaped with textile trade shards. They cram into cubbyholes already stuffed with black market cassettes, Sonys instead of penny candy. They line up to pluck prizes from the glazed shooting galleries of pressed duck and fish tanks underoxygenated as the sidewalks.

Down Hanoi Road, the advertising runs horizontally, jutting at right angles from storefronts to make bridges in pictographs. Reaching around trees, the neo-neon forms trellises of words. The sign just beneath us belongs to a joint that serves, "Fresh Chinese Noddles." Whatever those are, we can usually sniff them. Mack's thousand-dollar-a-month cubicle looks over an inner courtyard behind the kitchen, providing us with the panorama of a procession

27

of cooks stealing time from their woks. Bony and fatigued in smeared aprons, they draw so hard on cigarettes that you'd think these were death row smokes. Then each haggard stir-fryer clears his chest in turn—an overture to the heaving and spitting that is Asia's congenital soundtrack. Ceaselessly, they serenade us with a song of sputum.

Is this all there is to living above a Chinese restaurant? At first browse, this town offers too many deals and too few obstacles. We want more than this watchband world that's mainly wound-up, mostly practical, all pricetag, part pidgin, half wholesale and two-thirds under the table. Searching, we shuttle between Kowloon and Hong Kong sides, traverse and retraverse the invisible boundaries between mislabeled First and Third Worlds. Where's the Second, and what is it, when the Third was here first? The banks and hotels built by the Brits are gray and seamless. Hand-tailored suits in concrete, not worsted. In the Chinese neighborhoods pillars that support walkway overhangs are whitewashed, then festooned with brushstrokes in fire-engine red. This combo is old as the clash between purity and lust, spirit and blood, worker and compradores. Old as the tableaus seen in transplanted Tang Dynasty streets: a fish peddler brushing cornstarch veneer on his pile of curried octopi; a woodworker on haunches, hammering with hands that seek their task without prompting; nimbler old men kneeling at curbside to the bowl between their knees that hold customary diet of broth, noodles cushioning oily greens, barbecued knuckles dotted with impudent mustard; gentle goat-beards sharing a pipe and newspaper, lunchtime philosophy, visceral brotherhood; alleys stacked with warehousemen's pallets and round-hipped apothecary jars, uncut sugar cane; stores that offer only dried butterflies, silkworm tonic and antler power; all surveyed by impassive bookkeeping girls who are mute but for the appreciation they show with a mounting ovation of abacus clicking. From these first forays, Iris and I emerge image-stuffed, dumb and wise, envious and anxious, dripping, gooey, Shanghaied, changed.

Night provides no refuge. Swaying bare bulbs turn each lane into aisles of impromptu shop, each green of British gardens into fields for competing entrepreneurial tag teams. If what they offer is duplicated a hundred times down the block, that doesn't deter these tabletop merchants. At every stall in every gutter bazaar, there's just enough action to earn tobacco, rice paper, holiday tangerines. Customers or no, each wheelcart chef tosses his ingredients endlessly. Here, every man is his own supply and demand. Underdevelopment, as we should have known, as we still have to learn, is really an overdevelopment of need: too many trying to sell to too many who cannot buy.

Yet few seem so poor that they can't pick out their own live carp for supper or pick a winning horse at the races. Iris and I find that out when we're trapped in a riot for the few remaining grandstand seats at the track that's misnamed Happy Valley. Not only do few of the bettors look happy, but the hills on all sides are covered in the Chinese cemeteries' crazy cross-hatching. The tombstones aren't in neat, Presbyterian rows, but tilted to join nature's chaos and catch the proper fêng shui, we know. Before the afterlife, before the last exacta, there's time to gamble on "Empress Wan," to make one last stab at good fortune—which, the Chinese wisely admit, will take a man farther than talent. Where's that geomancer to give us a tip when we need it? Our gray mare finishes out of the running. "Sometimes lucky, sometimes no luck," murmur the denizens of Happy Valley. And Hong Kong itself is but a long shot, lease expiring. It's one big bookie joint operated under the nose of the Maoist vice squad. It's a gamble against the future but the lines at the wager windows keep getting longer.

Where do the winnings go? Some get dragged up the peaks to estates whose walls are capped by broken glass; some get invested in Rolls-Royces that come by the bushel; some pay to erect a statue of one's diminutive self, as in the case of Doctor Aw, inventor of Tiger Balm—that Asian Ben-Gay, which makes the Asiatic claim to soothe all manner of soreness, even spiritual— who's immortalized himself in business suit, overlooking the porcelain phantasmagoria of his Tiger Balm Gardens. Lesser bankrolls buy gadgets that get smuggled out to appliance-hungry relatives in the mother country. One day's parimutuel provides helpings of Szechwan chicken devoured in galleys of sampans moored in the dark. Here, pleasures are not so much savored as hoarded.

In this materialist enclave, there's little argument about what people want, and only infrequently about how to get it. The Brits run a high volume, low overhead trading post; they offer one prized rock's worth of real estate on which cling the addicts of property. Hong Kong, divided into two cultures, remains a solid-state colony. Shake it like a digital nine-band dream-bar clock radio you want to buy—and let the buyer beware! Tickle those transistors. Turn this model upside-down. The circuitry won't come loose. There's no rattle.

Where everything comes duty-free, nothing comes free of duty. Six days and sixty hours are the average work week, a perennial version of the Christmas overtime that's got Iris and me here. Only these workers aren't planning any jaunts. With the tacit approval of their Communist confreres, they remain prisoners of the "balance of payments," unprotected, democracy's coolies. Inside Kowloon's fabric factories, nearly naked men breathe cotton candy air, place bare feet close to the cutting edge of the presses. Their comrades must fit the huge bales into truck trailers—a Chinese puzzle solved by overexertion. Their sisters sew Parisian names and pricetags into blue jeans, trapped in a sunless, surfless riviera of sweatshops.

Though barely in Asia, we're acquiring a heightened sense of all cities as stationary fronts in a war. Factotum against peon, colonialist versus tong, banking cartel aimed at politburo: a tussle goes on for souls by the millions and paper money by the trillions. But each side seems so enlivened by their maneuvering that none are eager to impose the stillness of outright victory, all aim for mere upping of stalemate. The result, if there's any, is to be found in the gradual, gnawing "betterment of man," usually measured by square feet of housing per occupant, nearly unrecognizable when it arrives, certainly unknown by those who are its martyrs. Even the beggars of Hong Kong, those human filings drawn to the sidewalk magnet, lying face down in strategic placement, seem to be answering a distant command by offering themselves for trampling. These are foot soldiers who have fallen in place. "Sometimes lucky, sometimes no luck." They, too, are members in good standing of an army on yet another long march.

TO THE BORDER

THOUGH HONG KONG means "fragrant harbor," it is a gateway to nowhere. Speaking with an Etonian accent, scheming with Horatio Alger zest, it is still a creature dependent for its life's blood on a communist umbilical. Mack Schreiber, too, was here only to chart blips in the parent cardiogram. China was the pot he was being paid to watch, and, according to our host, it was always at the boil. Monitoring Radio Peking 'round the clock, he managed to glean such earth-shattering items as Chou En-Lai's absence from a party congress, the medicinal uses of seaweed, rumors concerning the latest captive pregnancy. Above the mild-mannered correspondent's desk was a poster that proclaimed, "WE WILL LIBERATE TAIWAN!" And Mack identified with the "we" of Red Guards and militant pandas, not with Hong Kong's "capitalist roaders"; indeed, he was useless in the local Cantonese dialect, despite years of copying out ideograms.

Like Mack, Iris and I couldn't do much with the ancient Confucian lingo that the refugees carted about. We were more fluent in the rhetoric that had been developed to serve a new faith across the border. As radicals, we'd once taken a cue from the Cultural Revolution, scoured the plodding homilies of Mao's Little Red

Book for justification of our urgent need to turn the world topsy-turvy. It was to this land of perpetual change that we had to make our pilgrimage, whether or not it really existed.

There were reminders all over Hong Kong that it did. For one thing, this haven was only allowed to exist so it might serve as a conduit of foreign exchange for the Bank of China. For another, many of the department stores where Hong Kong clothed itself (in quilted, proletarian jackets) and fed itself (with preserved ginger and thousand-year-old eggs) were supplied and supervised from the "mother country." The bargains provided were not for interlopers, but for frugal refugees: underwear, dish towels, dried mushrooms. Still, Iris found bolts of raw silk to send home; I outfitted myself for the journey ahead with a gray Mao cap to shield me from the Hindu sun and all other revisionist hazards. I couldn't resist a pair of "Forward!"-brand high-top tennies, or miniaturized "Yangtze" shortwave radio, which would keep me in touch with Peking's latest ideological shifts, as well as those in the standings of the American League.

What these stores really sold was another social order. The Communist-run retailers functioned as a soft-spoken advertisement for a People's Republic that simply banned such nonsense as inflation and consumer fraud. Leaving behind the chaos of night markets, one entered the quiet and comforting orderliness bred by central planning. The clerks were the backbone of this merchandising fifth column, living exemplars of the new way. Happily identical in floppy blue smocks and matching engineers' hats, they waited patiently behind oft-dusted counters. Since no profit imperative goaded them on, they did not pester, barter or hawk. They spoke only when spoken to, and when they did, it was in Mandarin, the official government dialect, the language of China's avowed unification.

This gave Mack Schreiber a chance to talk back. And there were other opportunities for him to keep his hand, or tongue, in. There were plenty of ways for us to get at the Maoists and them at us. One was the movies. There were nearly as many Communist products in the cinemas as there were in the stores. In one plush palladium, we joined record crowds to view a documentary of China's "Second National Games." Clutching king-sized Cadbury bars, Mack and Iris and I cowered in the dark, wondering if our decadence was about to be castigated. Through the coming attractions of grunting kung fu masters, we yearned for a good dose of "criticism, self-criticism."

We also held hopes of being entertained. But this extravaganza, with its volunteer cast of thousands, was long on action and short on plot. Beginning, middle and end were one cheery continuum with a single moral. "The people will win still greater victories over ill health!" The narration was strident, the subtitles in shorthand. "With Mao Tse-Tung Thought, lack of health among masses is mere paper tiger!"

On screen, in thick yet finely grained colors, the aforementioned masses merrily executed jumping jacks and deep knee-bends as far as the lens could discriminate. The camera moved away from Peking Stadium for a montage of calisthenics before a little red schoolhouse, a rural commune, an immense foundry. Fitness was an ancient ideal, but the workers and peasants were coming to know it for the first time. They were turning it into a weapon. The body was a commonly owned resource, and you kept up maintenance on the thing as much for your comrade's sake as for your own. In the new China, each biceps, each ligament was collectivized.

Gymnasts, cyclists, even ping-pongers had been left on the cutting room floor so this film could feature those who were able to beat the West at their own games. Chinese basketball didn't need "big men"; the Szechwanese champions shot with the accuracy of pint-sized Meadowlark Lemons. The "Peking Red Sox" had farther to go, and the subtitling cadre needed to work on their fundamentals. "Fair strike!" was the translated call. "Batsman makes four bases. Home ball!" The pitchers looked like they'd been studying training films of Robin Roberts and Early Wynn, smuggled in from Taiwan. But the stadium's immense flashcard sections outdid any such mania attempted at Notre Dame. Cheering units of placard bearers carried off split-second changes that would have shamed Busby Berkeley. One vast, tumescent cartoon depicted the People's Liberation Army locking loins with the burning promise of steel furnaces. For a finale, the coded colors burst into a spring garden of China's "thousand flowers" in bloom.

The politburo reminded their renegade audience that this fertile epoch would last "a thousand years"—unfortunate Hitlerian claim. Mao himself provided the leadership that won those battles, not to mention the rain that watered the plants. (If anything, his

imminent death would but free him to devote more of his spare
time to these tasks.) And though there was only one Chairman in
China, there were always too many duplicates of everything else.
A hundred records had to be broken; a thousand motorcycles had
to fly through hoops of fire; a million peasant sportsmen primed
themselves on the starting blocks of the classless future.
The athletes before us weren't just jocks, they were sprinting
dialecticians. They made our eyes bone tired. Did Marxists always
have to point forward, lunging for progress' tape? Was the human
race really in a race where none of us could afford to look back
over our shoulders? This time, I wanted the Chinese to be a bit
more Confucian. They were much too busy denying that suffocating
legacy of charting "the middle way." Yet there had to be one
somewhere—because man was neither the capitalist ape we knew
too well, gripped by the territorial imperative, nor the proletarian
demi-god being presented, with his nose to the communal grind-
stone and his eyes on the latest banner.

Beside me, Mack tried to stifle his giggles. I knew what was
making him laugh, yet wished that he wouldn't. It was a little too
convenient for the former "East Is Red" crooner to be changing
his tune. A good dose of skepticism was just what permitted him
to uncritcally pursue his professional ambitions. But he could hardly
be blamed if the serpentine course of Asian politics did such a
good job of breeding such skepticism. How could he, or any of
us, remain loyal to a party line that changed quicker than the latest
character posters could be torn down? This China in the grip of
the so-called Gang of Four was everything we'd said we wanted,
but not the way we wanted it. At college, we'd supported all calls
for the "ascendancy of politics" in every area of common life. Now
that we were actually witnessing the results, we couldn't help but
be chastened. Slogans like "Friendship First, Competition Second"
were still worthy of our endorsement, but were they enough?
Furthering the irony, China's socialist realist lingo didn't have
enough riddle, enough inscrutability for Western ears. We weren't
used to accepting truths from official sources. We needed to dig
it up ourselves, to do our own homework.

Still, Hong Kong's expatriates offered a standing ovation. Yet
another irony: where the colonialists in knee-pants were keeping
most everyone duly employed, the Communists had been put in
the uncomfortable position of making appeals to the spirit. And

they pulled it off admirably. The awesome discipline and optimistic vitality on-screen beckoned all family members back into the fold. Iris and I, too, could not help but be drawn to this imaginary fiefdom—which existed so few miles away—where tasks of common good were so clearly defined and fiendishly set upon. After the movie, we got Mack to pledge that he'd take us as close to China as we were allowed to get.

But first, he took us halfway. Some fledgling Sinologist had invited him to a party at the spanking new university built by the British in the New Territories. We went along, catching the 7:08 PM commuter train from Kowloon to Canton. And though it was obvious to all that tracks once laid were bound to be used, we had to get off far before the final destination. Instead of disembarking in the brave new world, we found ourselves at a railhead without discernible town attached, and rode a shuttle bus up rolling hills to a Hong Kong-style campus, completely vertical in white turrets. An instant "ivory tower" if there ever was one: insulated by height and distance from the shanty towns, sweatshops, typhoon shelters.

Following the thumping of a stereo, Mack led us to the right dorm, where the exchange students were dutifully working their way through several cases of San Miguel beer. The music was old (early Rolling Stones), the dances dated, the boys wore button-down shirts and had just started to grow their hair over their ears; some imported Wellesley girls were also in attendance, the sort who can't help always looking like they've just come out of the shower. I even spotted a few surfers, their vigor preserved in Man-Tan. (Sounds Chinese.) As with most exiles, temporary or otherwise, it was hard to tell if they'd been forced to miss their own epoch or if they'd lent circumstance a hand while no one was looking. I chatted with several young missionaries, earnest and conciliatory and thick-eyebrowed, happy with whatever sort of convert came their way. The color bar was broken by a pair of Chinese sweeties, modeling their best party dresses, who sat in a corner, holding each other's gloved hands. Smeared with mascara and inferiority feelings, their eyes called out for rescue by any foreign gentlemen.

Mack introduced us to the inevitable Peace Corps contingent, who were a bit more worldly. Most of them tried to act jaded as good sahibs, not so much to downplay their do-gooding assign-

ments as to affect that seen-everything, done-everything callous-
ness which would mark them as true "Asia hands." One of them
was an already plastered and mischievous wisp of a thing named
Tim. His stringy blond hair was brushed back and curled around
his ears, revealing features effeminate and precise. At once, I
recognized in him a rival very like the rivals romantic coincidence
had thrust at me in the past. Tim's attractiveness was made of the
opposite stuff as mine. He was dazzling, flighty and aloof. There
was nothing solid, therefore nothing disagreeable about him.

"You're from Berkeley, really? Do they still wear flowers in
their hair?"

"They never did," Iris answered.

"Oh. I wouldn't know. I've been stationed in the Land of Oz."

"Where's that?"

"Gujarat. Turn left at Bombay. . . . Can I get you guys some
nice warm brew?"

A few dixie cups of the same brought out an easy intimacy in
Tim. He knew you before he knew you, or tried to make you
think so. I was jealous of such skills because I never pretended
to know anyone. I was getting jealous, too, because Iris was getting
more giddy from her serving of San Miguel than I thought possible.
She was awfully enthralled with Tim's sample of fluent Gujarati,
and I felt the need to drift off. After Mack occupied me with an
analysis of Madame Chiang Ching's virulent opposition to the
Stanislavski Method, I returned to find Iris and Tim fled. To a
bedroom? No, just the kitchen, from whence they emerged one
innocent moment later, grappling playfully for control of a brown-
tinted quart bottle.

"Gimme that, you Southern cracker . . ."

"Gimme that, you burned-out liberal . . ."

Tim matched Iris in showing fondness through one gruff crack
after another, and I knew she missed out on such tussling with
me. All too suddenly, too absurdly, I was fearing abandonment.
It didn't matter that when Tim asked for a dance, Iris signaled
"No" with a toss of the head so honest, so nonobligatory, that I
was touched. It was too late.

"Get over here, will you?" I heard myself whine. I grabbed
for Iris, Neanderthal-style. She chuckled fondly, more flattered
than fettered by my attention. In the nearest corner, I whispered
some variant of "How-could-you-do-this-to-me?"

"But I'm not doing anything!"

"Remember our bargain . . ."

"I remember."

"You know me. You know I'd rather be handed over to Afghan cutthroats, I'd rather get malaria, than be left . . ."

I'd raised my voice, and the others could hear. My possessiveness was now common knowledge to a group I hoped knew nothing of me. My outburst had been historicized. I got Mack away from the only other journalist and told him it was time to go. The whole party seemed to watch our hasty exit. Tim waved at the door.

"You-all come back now, you hear?"

Once outside, on the train back to Kowloon's stunning density, I turned dreadfully contrite. Iris just slept on my shoulder, infraction dismissed, but I could hardly wait to apologize. I kept asking myself: How could I have lost perspective? What made me so quickly come up against my personal border?

Next morning, the three of us went the rest of the way to the other one. On this raw January Sunday, we weren't the only folks making a trek in the direction of the colony's international peephole. We shared another recycled London bus with plenty of land-starved Chinese, making their weekend emigration to the New Territories. Leased from the Communists until 1997, this vestigial chunk of farmland was grafted to Hong Kong out of sheer pity for the high-rise millions. It was a rundown back yard, combed and frisked for each remaining speck of the pastoral. The winding roads had their moments of high adventure, but like the railroad lines, they were all cul-de-sacs. Agriculture appeared limited to the traditional Chinese greens and the New Year's ornamental peach blossoms. The just-budding pink stems waited shyly in obedient rows, still in the ground yet already wrapped for delivery, and against premature bloom, in sheaths of tissue paper that fit like expensive stoles.

Overworked and overrun, the New Territories suffered from too many people stubbornly overstaying their time on the land. The rural setting was squalid, disordered, lacking in placidity. Tones ranged from lozenge green to mortal brown; the farms were lots, the villages, ghettoes. Even on the holidays, British bulldozers scooped landfill toward inlets of the South China Sea. More space was needed for housing, for labor-intensive industry, for country clubs. The new earth resembled a muddy webbing between the mainland's spotted fingers.

Our bus passed the university's twenty-story sentinels. I shuddered to see them in the daylight. I was still smarting over the knowledge those party-goers, those "others" now had of me. Across the aisle sat a shriveled old Chinese in even older garb: curious fur hat like a velvet magician's box atop his shaved skull, black slippers to match, a ring on every finger, a mother-of-pearl cigarette holder on which he casually teethed. Did this living receptacle of folklore and superstitions and wisdoms care what any "others" thought of him? Could this journey be my means of achieving such serenity? Or was that serenity just a more complete form of surrender to "circumstances beyond one's control"? It would have been nice to think that some Eastern belief or Eastern vista would lead me to a "dissolution of ego"—to let go of ambitions, of proving myself, of hurrying, of Iris! —but I wasn't expecting it. And the selflessness I'd seen in the face of this old man, and already so many others, merely looked like a more thorough form of self-absorption. Still, the one, perhaps the only, advantage to the life of a traveler was that destructive emotions could be disrupted through a break in the channels of habit through which they customarily flowed.

We reached the end of the line. On a dirt main street that divided the last colonial settlement in two, a mini-bus waited to shuttle chicken farmers out to their tenuous homesteads. But we carried no chickens and our new driver didn't have to ask us where we wanted to get off. He stopped in the middle of a rice terrace, then pointed, with fatigue, toward the frontier. We had to walk the last half-mile down a road elevated above the flooded acreage. For the first time, the eternal Asia came into sight: implacable water buffaloes in harness, no less implacable women planting the slender and drooping shoots, knee-deep in the muddy pools. A black viper writhed across the path, briefly sharing the high ground with us. The bus' whirring motor faded, and for a moment, there was no American echo.

We headed up the back side of a shaded bluff. The square yellow bunker of the border station was outlined against a murky sky. Some hundred feet before the top, just near a turn-off that tickled around the bottom of the hill to a striped gate with a "RESTRICTED AREA" sticker, we came to a parking lot and viewing area. A busload of Japanese businessmen arrived right behind us. They moved in tight formation and identical blue suits, ready to attack with cameras strung like amo belts across their chests. Children rushed up to them and us, bearing sodas direct from the coolers that lined the way. Were we allowed to continue on, they could have hoisted a sign: "LAST COKES FOR THREE THOUSAND MILES." We took them, though they turned out to be less than cool. Iris and I had yet to learn the Asian custom of squeezing bottles to test their temperature before they got opened.

An encampment of souvenir hawkers blocked our way to the "scenic viewpoint." And what souvenirs! Lin Piao on People's War next to Bruce Lee martial arts magazines. Jiggling, naked lady dollies next to dog-eared post cards showing the Gate of Heavenly Peace under a virginal winter snow. Every artifact served to remind us that a border, artificial as it may be, achieves real, often shocking results. On one side of this barrier, the next generation grappled with Brylcreem and bowling alleys and Dylan's "Blowin' in the Wind." On the other side, their counterparts coped with self-criticism and penance in the countryside and "The Helmsman Sets the Ocean Course." The difference between a three-year-old Chinese peasant and a three-year-old British tyke was more like three centuries. If the young of both lands, of all lands, were busy proclaiming their solidarity and obvious sameness, while the old of both lands were feverishly multiplying irreconcilable differences, both were proved right by junctures like this. On the one hand, it seemed a cruel hoax that countries should exist at all, quarantining in cages the "family of man." On the other hand, it was a profound relief to have someplace to peer out toward where you knew there were others—those pesky "others" again—who were unlike yourself. After all, human beings happen to be terribly varied. It's one of their few redeeming qualities.

We knew we were nearing the ridge, the outer limits of the "free world," when droves of rapacious peasant ladies stepped forward to rent us binoculars. Trying to entrap us, these part-time peddlers haggled over the price before we'd even made an offer. There wasn't much before us that we'd want to magnify. Across the no man's land of paddies, a patchwork of shallow tureens mirroring a blank sky, flew the first red flag. It was too indistinct from our position to give off any of its customary connotations: alarm, uprising, *sangre*. Clustered beyond the flag was the first red town, just more catty-cornered bamboo roofs. A hazy valley sloped toward a far-off range. Beyond that range, out of sight, was Canton, home of chow mein, the Pearl River Bridge, all things and beings Cantonese. The small but imposing mountains had a faintly bluish tint similar to the mysterious rock formations in the fabled Kweilin Gorge. (Nixon had been permitted to see those formations, but Iris and I weren't, not yet.) The haze's blue pigmentation was somehow ineffably Chinese, as commemorated in rice paper watercolors through the dynasties. That blue could belong to no other place.

This was the other side of the world, the spot where you landed when you fell down the proverbial well. But how did we drink from it? I wanted a snapshot of Iris with China as hickory-smoked background, and she went along diffidently, eschewing anything "hokey."

"Come on. You're just a tourist like everyone else!"

"No, I'm not. I'm a stranger. . . ."

Mack was more than eager, and for his pose, he ran to get one of the red chapbooks off the souvenir table. He held the volume high. Its title, "On Dialectical Materialism" was printed too small to show in the picture. Mack's fist, clenched and raised out of homage to the good old days, was in sharper focus.

"Down with Confucius! Down with Edward R. Murrow!" He looked younger suddenly, relieved of the pressures of new allegiances. "With Mao Tse-Tung Thought, foreign correspondents will win greater air time!"

"We will liberate the evening news!"

"The Nielsen ratings are just a paper tiger."

"Dig tunnels deep, store grain everywhere, and never seek hegemony!"

That was Mack's current favorite, because it lost everything in translation.

"Now we can blackmail you," Iris teased. We had photographic proof of this cub reporter's "nonobjectivity."

By habit, abstractions stood out more clearly to our eyes than the actual terrain upon which they were tested. The symbolism was highly visible, even if China wasn't. Out there, beyond, were those busybee one billion, building their utopian hive; over yonder was that threatening neighbor called the future (also known, in China's case, as the past). This place and its standards hovered, geographically and spiritually, close to each of the befouled countries we'd be visiting. Somehow that knowledge made it easier for us to leave behind the purist China that had once inspired our slogans and our gripes; made it harder for us to look closely at the ground on which the line between a real China and us was drawn. When we did, we saw worms in honest nightsoil, clods of dirt we could not turn, fields we still didn't know how to work.

Mack and Iris and I came back down off the ridge, on the lookout for more snakes. Everything we couldn't stoop toward and pan with our own hands fell away and lost meaning. Even last night's covetousness and contrition was wiped clean. The border had shown what a border must show: that our worst fears are finite, contained by something grander.

Snapshot:

❖

RHINESTONE COWBOY

THE CALIFORNIA BAR opens. The door lets in the green light of Wanchai evening. The door is thick and padded. Little brass thumbtacks hold a quilt of shiny oilcloth to the door. It's very exclusive to have a padded door. It makes the sailors think there is a great secret behind the door. And Wanchai is a place for sailors. And all the bars have padded doors. A solid vault door separating outside from inside. No in-between allowed. Outside are sailors swimming in the Wanchai sea, green with neon. Because of the door, the sailors can't see inside unless they go inside. The bar has no window. There is only a glass frame on the outside with red and green light bulbs around it that flash on and off. Inside the frame, glued to a plywood backing, there is a picture of a well-endowed blonde wearing only a cottontail. It is cut out of a 1964 *Playboy*. Next to it, there is a hand-lettered sign: "WEL-CUM TO THE MEN OF USS ENDEAVOR." The *Endeavor* has been mothballed. There are no blonde bunnies inside the California Bar.

Some of the sailors don't know this, and open the door. Some know it from previous shore leaves, but they go inside anyway. Some are relieved there are no naked girls, though they never say this. They find wooden booths along walls painted black. They find a dart board that is rarely used, always easy to hit. They find a jukebox that is always lit-up. They find some girls, too. There are three sisters here, and they are always dressed. You can tell they are sisters because the sailors call them "sister." Also because they really are. The girls talk to the sailors if the sailors buy them drinks. If you come to the California Bar very often, if you make buying your drinks here a habit, and if you learn to call all of the sisters by their first names, there is a place upstairs where one of them will go with you. But first she has to have lots of drinks, and then she has to get permission from a fat, jolly Cantonese lady behind the bar. This lady runs the California Bar. She isn't related to the three sisters, but she does have two sons. One is very big, big as she is wide. He stands by the padded door. He clears the tables and sometimes clears the bar. He makes sure there isn't any trouble. And there is the boy.

The boy takes empty glasses off the counter, sloshes them in soapy water, pulls at his mother's apron, hides behind his wide mother, watching the door opening and closing, the green light surging in, the green hint of an outside that remains far away. The boy is not only a Mongolian, he is a Mongoloid. The sailors can't always tell at first. The sailors aren't all that observant, not about people who aren't girls, who aren't naked or potentially so. Besides, the whole family has that flattened look Mongoloids have. It's like they're made of clay, and the clay is melting. They all smile, too, further flattening their noses and cheeks. Even the boy's big brother smiles when he throws you out. But this boy only smiles when he's hiding behind his mother. And he's too big to do that. The sailors who notice, and notice the boy, like him. They call him Leroy, because they think his real name is Lee. Leroy Lee, they call him. Once he's sure that they like him, they can coax him away from the sink and his mother. Then they can teach him how to shake hands. They teach him the soul-shake and the power-shake. Leroy's stubby arms barely reach over the bar. "How're they hangin', Leroy boy?" Sometimes he has to be coaxed several times. But once he starts shaking, he doesn't want to stop. The sailors hands are warm. They have a relationship to him. His hands tell him that. The shaking makes him know it. Like the outside and the inside, there is his weakness and their strength. Their weakness and his strength.

Leroy speaks your basic Cantonese, but he does better with English. He sings English. When the English is singing on the jukebox, he doesn't mind leaving his mother so that he can stand next to it. And sing. He sings with feeling and feels all his insides shake. He follows the words by sound, memorizes them by their sequence. He doesn't know what they say, but he knows what they mean. He knows the songs are the songs of the sailors. Of their place. They have brought them from their place. The songs are like the sailors, loud and great and big, very happy or very unhappy. Moaning and laughter. No in-between allowed. Just the pulsing of jukebox bass. The on/off of Wanchai's green light. The California Bar is Leroy's body, the jukebox is his heart. He doesn't know why, but when he hears the beat of his heart, he forgets about his eyes and his mouth and his belly and his Cantonese cock. He doesn't know why, but he knows the sailors' songs are his songs. "A rocket man, a rocket man . . ." He is never lonely. Leroy has the entire U.S. Navy for friends.

Leroy doesn't want to go to America, the place they come from. He doesn't even want to go outside. Why should he? The outside comes inside to him. That's easier. America comes tramping to him. All kinds of Americans: skinny and wide, frightened and tough, weepers and celebrants. And all kinds of colors: deep wooden or peeling pink of a permanent seasick pale. Generally, they are good at darts. They play darts much longer than Leroy can sing. They have a few beers and fall off their stools. They make a lot of noise when they fall. Afterward, they are very quiet. And all the nights in the California Bar have been quiet since the end of the Big War. Not enough sailors. This worries Leroy's mother and the three sisters. But it doesn't worry him. The sailors don't stay for long anymore, but Leroy recognizes each of them when they come back. He knows the rhythm of the harbor. He keeps track of the sailors, moving in packs like minnows. They are restless, looking for something. Leroy doesn't know what the sailors are looking for. Leroy never dreams, except when he gets tired of rinsing glasses and goes to sleep. He knows who he is, not what he might be. The sailors' dreams spill all over the bar.

Leroy hums to himself when he hides behind his mother. He feels how the humming tickles his tongue. He sways. His fingers slosh in gray water. No bubbles, no green. On the other side of the bar, a petty officer with thinning hair and waxed red mustache is hazing a seaman on his first tour. The poor kid has put on his best threads to come to the California Bar. They are loud. Plaid checked bellbottoms. Last year's styles bought in last year's port. The drunken officer is telling him so. He is giving it to the kid. No class. No soul. Shoes your grandma wouldn't wear. And what's that fool cap for? Everybody else on their stools joins in. He had a lotta nerve to go around lookin' that way. A disgrace to the service, they say. They say, a Wanchai hooker wouldn't take you in those duds. Would you take him, Tina? Tina is one of the sisters and Tina isn't her name. She drapes her arm around the petty officer. He is one of her boyfriends. He's spent a lot of money on her. Only the two of them know just how much. He doesn't want the other sailors to see all the money, but he wants them to see her sticking by him. He doesn't really want anything else. Tina knows this. She calls him Charlie. She doesn't even look at the poor recruit. She says, I got my man, Charlie. Everyone at the bar laughs. Leroy's mother shakes with laughter. Leroy feels like the harbor is shifting.

The seaman droops in his beer. Two years, he mutters. Two years and four months to go. The petty officer and his pals move on to darts. Tina plays, too. She keeps them drinking. She runs back and forth to the bar, though it's not easy in her black pumps. Don't you guys change the score on me, Tina calls. She pinches Leroy's mother with excitement. The money is coming in. Leroy sees the bowl behind the bar filling with circles of metal. The same circles that go in the jukebox. The jukebox plays Tammy Wynette. The Stylistics. Tony Orlando and Dawn. "When you're hot, you're hot. When you're not, you're not . . ." Guitars strum, rev up, wail. Back-up voices out of nowhere lilt. Leroy doesn't know how the metal starts the machine. He doesn't see how so many people can get inside the machine. He can't tell if the guitars are electric, only that they must be machines too. He crouches near the jukebox always lit-up, always warm like his mother. He bends toward the source of the sound. He asks the sailors to play the one about the rhinestone cowboy. The one with most of his heart in it is about the rhinestone cowboy. Leroy's tongue is heavy in his mouth. The sailors don't understand. They can never make out his request the first time. If the sailors care, they ask Tina what he wants. Tonight, they ask Tina. Then they reach in their pockets for more circles so they can play the "Rhinestone Cowboy." Selection J-6. They watch Leroy start to sway. Then he sings. Low at first, but building up quick. All of him trembling. His feet leaving him. His air leaving him. His mother looking at him, admiring. All of the sailors looking at him. If he looks at them, he laughs. They make him close his eyes. Then he's lost in the song. He's right inside it. And there aren't any words. There's no cowboy. Or any America. To the sailors, it sounds like Leroy is wounded. A spaz. Off-key. No natural rhythm. But plenty of guts. To himself, Leroy sounds like the universe. Gongs ring inside him. He doesn't know if what he's doing is going by rules but he knows it's right. He senses a command in the music. He follows it like a wish. Not because it's the sound of the big place it comes from, or the sound of money going in the jukebox, or the sound of the sailors' hearts, or the sound of anything Leroy knows or has ever known. It's the sound of the harbor, and better. It's the man who sings when they put the coin in the slot becoming the man inside Leroy. The sound outside just like the sound inside. All in-betweens allowed. Singing makes him know that the music will outlast why the music is there. Why the sailors were there. The music was the reason the sailors had to go home, and had to leave home, and had to sleep sometimes just like Leroy did. The song stops. Leroy doesn't stop seeing sunlight. He can't quit seeing a long, long place with only sun and no people and just Leroy running every direction with no padded doors to stop him. He's back in the California Bar. Leroy runs to hide behind his mother.

What would Leroy's mother do without the American? What would Leroy's brother do? What would the three sisters do? And what would Leroy do without the rest of them? Leroy had an aunt and uncle who lived on a boat in the Typhoon Shelter. Once Leroy slept on the boat. It made him sick. The earth wouldn't stop. The harbor wouldn't stay in one place. They woke him up early. They took him out on the boat until everything moved or was light. Leroy had to stand in one place, holding string. The string cut him. Then fish came on the boat. They were funny and happy and shining on the boat. Then they stopped, like the music. Leroy got sick from the smell. Leroy's mother was not there. He was sent back to the California Bar. He slept on straw again. He sloshed dirty glasses. He saw the sailors swimming and swam in the noise again. He heard his heart again.

Another selection is on the jukebox. New music that goes too fast. Leroy is afraid. He can't sing or sway along to this. This music means trouble. Leroy's command to get behind the bar. "It ain't me, it ain't me, I ain't no senator's son . . ." The dart game is over. Someone cheated on his score. Now no one remembers the score. The sailors don't remember their drinks. Stools are falling like the tombs of ancestors. The floppy green cap gets ripped from the head of the seaman. Tina screams. Leroy's brother lets the front door take care of itself and strides toward the middle of the fighting. Bare forearms locking. Sailors whooping. Even the music fighting itself. Sailors singing along, more timidly than Leroy, "It ain't me, it ain't me, I ain't no fortunate one." Leroy's mother moving down the bar to the beat. Leroy trying to stay behind her. Leroy not wanting to see. So it won't happen. Leroy's mother clearing all the glasses in case the trouble gets worse. The music louder, but not loud enough to match the hollering. The petty officer helps Leroy's brother. He's an honorable brother of the sisters now. It's his bar now, too. He and Leroy's brother clear it. The loudest sailors leave only with coaxing. Sailors protesting. Sailors harmonizing. Sailors without a harbor, swimming away. Carried off in the green light.

The beat of the front door, thwapping. Is this the Big War? Is this tonight or last night or every night? Is this what the bar is for, what Tina is for, what Leroy's mother is for? Leroy tries to find her and hide. Why does the music get so angry? Who is it punishing? Leroy is scared though somehow he feels it is too late to get scared. He hears his heart but it's not making a song. The shouting stops. The door flaps no more. The green light is gone, and doesn't curse them. The music's ejected. Selection Q-8. Another coin slides into the chamber. It is sliding down his chrome gullet. Leroy hears the metal falling every time, falling into the pit of himself. Then the man sings. Then America knows how to be beautiful.

THE REAL MACAO

MACAO came to us before we came to Macao. It was one of those reverberating locales regularly rebuilt on Hollywood lots. A free port for spies and gun runners and damsels in distress, Macao, the movie backdrop, was an inexhaustible source of atmospheric decrepitude, the fountain of age. Its chief exports were murky quays, posh gazebos, and conniving Chinamen. Here was a setting invulnerable to ideological swings: forever sexy, forever evil. In this cozy roost, free enterprise was unbridled by Christian conscience—if Babbitt did wrong, the yellow man shrugged and looked the other way. Every known definition of merchandise changed hands and only a born sucker couldn't make something off the deal. This Macao was boffo box office, a place where all plots were plausible.

Robert Mitchum and Jane Russell starred in one *Macao*. The times were expansive, wide-bodied; so was the screen, newly stretched. Mitchum and Russell were so wide-bodied, they practically came with fins. Bob and Jane made goo-goo eyes at each other across rickety, shadowy sets crammed full of rubber plants, jade statuettes, and carved bamboo screens. Bob and Jane toyed with inscrutable croupiers and aphoristic thugs; they stumbled through opium dens and smugglers' caves, guided by their grand American common sense. The haze cleared just in time for the triumph of decency and fair play. Bob and Jane, the hardboiled habitués of the Orient, were revealed as hapless victims of fate who pined for Indiana and found their happy ending in a one-way ticket for home.

Leaving Iris and me to live the remake—which could be done without script, in a single weekend. Leaving us to shoot this one on location—easy enough to find, since this city-state perched on a silty silver of the Pearl River delta was but two hours' hydrofoil ride from Hong Kong. Leaving behind the reel Macao for the real McCoy Macao, still the self-styled "Las Vegas of the Orient," but urbane as a youth hostel, malevolent as a game of marbles.

What a welcome relief from Hong Kong's commercial throb! Checking into the Hotel Bela Vista, we discovered that it was an abandoned ambassadorial mansion. Better yet, we were its only guests, free to romp through the obsolescence. One era of white man had gone, and we became its rightful heirs simply by signing our undistinguished names in the guests' register. Our room was a suite, with ceilings that brought the heavens indoors, impish cherubs stenciled along the moldings, and a bear-sized bathtub where we wrinkled our white skin in the privilege of hot water. On a balcony big enough to accommodate an entire ruling junta, we sipped dão, which was not Lao Tzu's invention but Portuguese red wine. We were on the wrong continent to be sampling the grape, but it went down more easily than ever after so much jasmine, chrysanthemum and dishwater tea.

From the Bela Vista's deck chairs, we followed the long sweep of ballustrade, promenade and breakers that traced Macao's arched outline in the guava green South China Sea. Taking our own *conquistadores'* survey, we plundered the place with our starved eyes, wooed it with our sinning hearts. Why was it that we could feel so instantly ensconced, so guiltily at home on this six-square-mile anachronism, this colony nobody wanted to claim, this banana republic without bananas? Here, for the taking, was a cut-rate hideaway, where we might go on being exactly who we were without being noticed. But what were we if not carpetbaggers? When a round of jiffy-pop explosions went off along the water-front, casting off puffs of gray powder that skimmed the jade waters and seemed to trace the outlines of sharks beneath, we took these to be the first salvo of a revolution aimed against us. The barrage never let up during our stay. Whether this was just because of the Chinese New Year, or whether the citizens always helped rid their firecracker industry of its surplus, gentle Macao was in love with the noise it could make.

We rode rented bicycles to the source of Macao's name, the shrine of the sea goddess Ma-Kwok, and found out that Hollywood wasn't all wrong. The smoke of incense and the bluer discharge of the crackers met us along back alleys and shrouded the boulder-strewn entrance to the blazing red temple. Children and priests in feverish tandems strung packages of the poor man's dynamite from the limbs of holy trees to the scalloped overhang of the central pagoda. The shrine's courtyard looked decorated for a high school prom, only these paper stringers went off, a gatling gun's worth, leaving a special kind of prayer ringing in everyone's ears. A permanent smog encased the temple grounds which rose in winding stairs toward a harbor-commanding promontory. All pathways were littered with festive red shrapnel.

Confucian worship appeared hectic, casual, lunatic. Leaving our bikes with the beggars at the front gate, we tiptoed toward inner sanctums and found off-track betting parlors. Unfrocked priests, calm as undertakers, poker-faced as bookies, handed out yellowing bookmarks across a receptionist's counter. Worshippers then pinned these prayers to the back wall of a nave, the calligraphed streamers looking like handicapping sheets on the next life's exacta and futura. Before granite altars, bursting through the ground like lost ships' prows, old women in black tunics threw joss sticks and fortunetelling stones with the hopeful concentration of pros at craps. Others left offerings of lettuce and pork charbroiling over a slow fire of more incense. Theirs were hungry gods, and noisy gods. In the temples and casinos, the Macaoans tested their destinies. In the streets, they conducted uprisings with toys.

On our bikes, we climbed a higher bluff to the old fort. This was one of many colonial ramparts which defended the indefensible, overlooked the long since overrun. This day, the battlements had been scaled by Hong Kong day-trippers. Mom posed Dad for pictures, Dad posed the kids. A snapshot in these parts was invariably a formal, everyone smiling shot; the Asian photographer did not yet value the spontaneous moment. But Iris and I were alone at the nearby mansion of the current, and last, Portuguese governor. This final paternalist outpost had been all gussied-up, its authority ridiculed by a paint job that was all pink and rosy, with stucco flowerets forming a daisy-chain around the upper story. One butler-cum-doorman stood watch at an equally feminized gate over the tumbledown and badly terraced estate.

History seemed to hold Macao at arm's length. The city's European edifices were like broken swords in the ground, blunt end up. The Cathedral of St. Paul, an imitation Toledo, was built in the seventeenth century by Japanese converts going for baroque. A steep climb up hundreds of marble steps led to a wedding cake facade, stuffed with saints. Behind it, the wind. Instead of the customary three walls, encasing altars and favorite saints, there was an unobstructed view of nearby China. The cathedral burned down a hundred years ago and the ostentatious front was all that was left. It looked so formidable, this entry to ruin, this Magritte portal opening onto clouds.

Macao was the continent's oldest colony, coveted by Vasco da Gama in 1497, and as such, had plenty of time to evanesce. Here, the Portuguese ambience, pasteled and peeling, served as the medium through which filtered the greater serenity, the profound seniority of China—which meant this was neither Peking nor Lisbon, but some way station halfway in between. The rusting grillwork balconies, crowded with potted palms, the stucco tenements overburdened with rainbows of laundry, might have worked as a Tennessee Williams backdrop, the French Quarter of anywhere. The green shutters, always drawn, had to be the shutters of Venice. And the tree-lined, untrafficked avenues suggested newsreel pictures of Hanoi. But Macao had dug no pavement bomb shelters, staged no war of liberation that could not be fought by time, won with patience. No longer of use to the Portuguese, this carbuncle city now helped the Chinese take from the West the things they did not publicly admit to needing. What did the poeple of Macao need?

Looking for an answer, we did innumerable laps around the same cobblestone tracks. An easy job, since this place was too small to get lost in. We coasted and gripped the handlebars through unabsorbed bounces. We quickly learned the rules of this two-wheeled road: when to pass, and when to panic. Our bicycle tour passed doorways the size of cupboards that hid workshops and garages where wheel reshaped wheel without the aid of electricity. One-legged men grappled in peace with their infirmity, and the dogs had lost the habit of snarling. Lizards leapfrogged from one overgrown baronial garden to the next. And homelife spilled out everywhere, in harmless disputes and dirty undershirts. These streets were a bed, one common and sagging mattress.

Bicycles returned, another bottle of dão in our bellies, we set out to try the transplanted Portuguese cuisine. After our regimen of noodles, we were happily reintroduced to the mysteries of the potato. Strange Indian dirt food, half-hard, half-wet, half-hot New World potato! Seared in peanut oil, crisped and cratered, here was a sweet and sour without sauce. Much of what came with it was undistinguished. "Tournedos" turned out to be thawed Australian beef covered with a Béarnaise sauce the consistency of silly putty. The Chinese seemed to think the distinguishing quality of so-called continental food was that it be served with pomp on silver platters. In Hong Kong, too, a beef stew would be mixed from its component parts at the table, just like a Caesar salad. Ketchup from the bottle got a personalized pouring. Yet the old waiters in Macao's plutocratic inns did it all with a practiced disdain made famous by their colleagues in Kosher dairy restaurants. After two helpings of flan, there was nothing left for the evening but to try our luck.

From temple to casino, pray to play. We could make the transition without a false step, as did the Macaoans (that term makes them sound like some intraplanetary race). It was the gaming room that got all the hushed reverence. Chinese in the presence of their cash-quantified fates—amen! The floating "Macau Palace," a double-decker boat house, embellished Mandarin-style, was where life got serious. Hitched permanently to its seedy port, close to a floating village of junk-dwelling squatters, next to a warehouse that reeked of drying cuttlefish, the casino was a grounded Mississippi steamboat, crowded with Black Barts. Few tourists here, just high-rollers in bow ties and busted old men with wispy beards mumbling to themselves. The boat's innards were so crammed with broken losers and vengeful intents that familiar games of chance looked deadly and alien. The roulette wheel's dancing balls spun out like shrapnel.

Finally, we'd been thrust into the movie set we'd been seeking—except this place had served for that earliest atmospheric standard-bearer, made by von Sternberg and starring Marlene Dietrich. Black suits, black ties, black hair, captivated black eyes on the dice's black defeats. Attention was riveted on the quick-handed dealers, who were all mobile-eyed ladies in bellhop suits. What did these cookies do when they got off work? Sharpen knives with their teeth? Iris and I skidded across the lacquered floors, adrift, slightly seasick. Peeking at myself in a saloon-length mirror bordered by a dragon fashioned in teak, I was startled that so unscheming a fellow could be found in such a place, cast in this virulent film noir. That wasn't Mitchum or Gary Cooper, ogling the action from the back of the pack. How could I stride forward to make my fortune or wreak havoc on a dope ring when my clothes were so creased from suitcase folding, my hair so frumpled by the harbor winds, my mug so freckled and goofy and guileless? And I had been thinking Macao innocent! But the shock wasn't just that I was too caucasoid, too raw—or that my glasses were crooked. For a few turns of the Macau Palace wheels, I was actually lost in looking.

Our stroll back to the hotel took us through the Cape Canaveral of fireworks. Ducking the paths of backfiring projectiles, Iris and I skirted the waveless sea, extinguisher of Macao's fire. Rocket launchers sent baby warheads toward unknown enemies in the shallows. Gunpowder creampuffs lingered in the shallow night sky. Sparklers lay stockpiled on the sidewalks. This ongoing racket added to the difficulty I was having in focusing on the internal dynamics of this curious "backwater." Didn't it secretly strive to be a "frontwater"? Or was progress and change merely my warped ambition for it? Everywhere I looked, Macao seemed to be reminding me that our whole planet was but a tiny galactic backwater, and that most of what the West labeled change was merely repetition: one flume of smoke following another.

If Iris and I had really believed that, we could have ended our journey right here. We could have stayed in the casino's entrails until dawn. We could have clung to our handlebars forever. We might have sat on the Bela Vista's balcony, lazily tracking the pyrotechnics, nursing the wine, working for a decade or two on the project of having no project.

❖

LUNAR NEW YEAR

E ACH TIME we got in bed, we were still at home. And we weren't staying under the covers later and later because of some lingering disorientation, but rather to hide from familiar terrors. I'd been expecting more affection from my traveling companion, and the more I wanted, the more she recoiled. On its first run-through, my "trick" wasn't working. Now that she'd climbed out with me on this journey's limb, Iris was acting as though she didn't care if it snapped. Diffident, she climbed further up the tree to establish her own nest, delineated a portable piece of territory marked "no entry." She was moving about in a deepening trance. On the eve of the Lunar New Year, I could only hope that tonight's celebration would sway all Iris' branches. Hong Kong, roaring in dragon's drag, would have to wake her.

The calendar may have been lunar, but the ambience was solar. Not only did Iris and I get to start the new year twice this January, but we were at the beginning of a nine-month summer. It was the heat that finally roused us and made us head for the beach. To get to the water from Mack's place, we first had to get across the water. Shielded from the Pacific by one puny crag and a buttressing ring of skyscrapers, Hong Kong harbor was a choppy tureen. The fabled junks were now outnumbered by oil tankers. Where were the steamers we sought to hop for rides into the sunsets of Jakarta and Singapore? Iris and I had spent the last week pursuing this Conradian fantasy, making the rounds of shipping agents, studying the notices of cargo transfers in the *South China Morning Post*, even going so far as shouting dockside pleas at captains on the bridge. But such tramp traffic wasn't permitted anymore, a matter of insurance, a casualty of regulation. The only passage Iris and I could book was crosstown on the Star Ferry. It only cost a nickel and was smoothly accomplished by venerable deck hands who glided about in those heeless rubber shoes so favored by Bryn Mawr dance majors. The pockmarked, baggy faces of these urban sailors sprouted incongruously from Buster Brown collars; their all-knowing fingers were scarred from tying too many slip knots.

At the bow, Iris' short chestnut hair blew back. She'd cut it because of the heat; I'd shorn mine because longhairs weren't admitted to some of the countries along our route. Iris wore the green silk jacket I'd bought her. It was embossed with the ancient motif that stood for "Double Happiness." Why didn't that describe us? Her puppet eyelids, the only lazy part of her, drooped wrinkleless over sharp eyes. Iris may have been a daughter of the Lone Star State, but the Chinese had been taking her for one of their own. I almost got a rise by calling her "My Eurasian beauty."

Next, we caught a double-decker for what was referred to as the backside of Hong Kong Island. It was really the front side: a glorified boulder that dared to meet the sea head-on. This was Hong Kong, too: granite turrets, protecting limpid coves from the oceanic brunt; ridges soaring from the water, green and slinky as Anna May Wong cheong-sams, valleys upholstered in underbrush, basins of leaf plummeting from the roads. There could have been plantations tucked in the creases that built toward the sheltering summit, coffee and spices abounding, if Hong Kong had been meant for agribusiness instead of the people business. At the end of the line, last stop for the tired red Charing Cross local, there was a single boomerang of sand, sandwiched between Her Majesty's radar station and a royal golf course, at the village known as Shek O.

We shared the winter seafront with an outing of sixth graders. Iris and I waded into the surf, groping for dolphin rhythms. There was something wrong with this unseasonal swim; the tides seemed to sweep backwards. We were picnicking on the dark side of the moon. But the schoolkids, good children of Cathay in blazers and kilts weren't impressed. When we staggered out and toweled off, they surrounded us, playing ring-around-the-rosy. Skipping in the sand, thrusting flat hips, teasing in guttural Cantonese, they sang a nursery rhyme with challenging intensity. We couldn't understand the song, but thought we heard one of the boys mutter a phrase we'd learned to decode "*Gwei lo.*" Translation: foreign devils.

Iris and I ran a foot-race to the headlands. A stone path, hewn from the breakwater like steps up a pagoda, took us to one immense gallstone, polished by the tides. Waves drowned the smaller, companion boulders, then withdrew with eery resolve. Hitchcock might have set a murder here.

"Is anything wrong?" I was finally asking. I didn't really want an answer. I stared at Iris' sandaled feet, watched them grip the boulder through rubber soles, rise against the wind, seem to depart on their own.

Iris said, "I dreamed that I was blind in one eye."

In night's brave mirror, she'd found a reflection of our timid days. "It's not me, then?"

"Isn't there enough it could be besides you? If I trust what the dream tells me, then I've been unhappy because I'm learning to see. . . . You know how one bunch of South American Indians define depression? They say it's when the soft-shell crab tries to grow a new shell."

"So that's why you've been so crabby."

"Watch out for my claws!"

And I told her, "You're strange."

"Am I? Am I really?" For Iris, the Pollyanna from birth, this was the greatest compliment. She put her arm around mine at Shek O.

"Which eye did you lose, crab? Left or right?"

"Does it matter?"

"Could be a political statement."

"You know my politics."

"Either that, or you want to look at the world without having it look at us."

After all, what would it see? A couple that was going to have stories to tell, but had already decided not to tell them together. A pair that had taken passion off their itinerary, but stood kissing on a most scenic, and slithery rock.

The New Year's parade hardly mattered now, but we left the beach before dark and made yet another pass through the mercantile free-for-all.

"*Gung hay fat choy!*" The traditional greetings were strung everywhere, even across the brown glass humidors of the English banking houses. There was nothing seditious in these banners, just a generalized wish for "good health, get rich." The Chinese knew happiness was a by-product, more likely to occur given the other two conditions. Potted kumquat trees, solstice symbols, pushed the merchandise out of the display windows. Though we were in the mood for a nuptial banquet, even the restaurants were shut down. We'd chosen to renew our appetites at that one brief moment when all the world's Chinese waiters took a rest.

Did we really hold our festivities in the Hong Kong branch of Lindy's Delicatessen? How else could two travelers guarantee "good health, get rich" when we were bound to spend money and get sick? We didn't know how to count our blessing on an abacus. We weren't even sure if our year in Asia happened to be the Year of the Rabbit or the Rat. Fortunately, we hadn't been warned that this year after the Vietnam War's end was claimed by the dragon, foretelling political upheaval, earthquake and much turmoil under heaven.

If there was a parade, Iris and I never found it. We stumbled on no 40-foot monsters screwing their way toward eternity. We did not get to peer under fiery shrouds at the club-footed shuffling of a dozen right legs battling a dozen left. We missed the fat businessmen passing in limousine review, the mock Ming princesses, the spastic flitting of paper bumblebees. Turning corners, we stumbled on occasional solitary drummers in white headbands, fierce soloists pounding with mallets to protest time's passing. Lost in back alleys, we listened for the clashing of Secret Society gongs. We heard only old men offering us young girls and the slapping of tiles on enamel tables in mahjongg parlors high above the dead garage of Kowloon streets.

At last, we were alone, back in bed—this time willingly. Once

again, we were in our own country, silently speaking our own
language. Other people, other places, would have to wait. We
made love like a real, old-fashioned couple. If someone had peeked,
they might have mistaken us for newlyweds. Iris was fiercely loyal
to the honeymoon suite. She didn't want to drain our juices on
Mack Schreiber's sheets. I fetched the *South China Morning Post*
to put between her legs.

NEAR VIETNAM

SHADOW PLAY

IRIS AND I were stalled in the bell-tinkling traffic of Jogjakarta.
Another rickshaw pulled alongside and a zoot suiter in the
carriage called out, "Australian?"

"American."

"America. Very good. Hello to you!"

"Hello."

"Married?" He got right to the point.

"No."

Our inquisitor disappeared, his lane of bicycle stalled. We
could hear him berating his driver until he was once again pedaling
parallel to ours.

"Friends?" the young dandy resumed.

"Yes."

"You live in same house?"

"Yes." There seemed little harm in the truth. It was making
him so happy.

"In Indonesia, never!"

He dropped back, then surged once more into view, a persistent Kinsey researcher.

"You sleep in same room?"

"Yes."

"In Indonesia, never!" He was incredulous. "In the same bed?"
"Where else?" He couldn't translate that phrase, so before he
fell behind for good, I added another "Yes."

"In Indonesia, never!"

In Indonesia, what then? So far, we'd found a country in stasis,
a people in a political state of grace—where the military took full
advantage of the masses' tropics-induced tolerance, where the
snoozing, sensuous body politic had rolled over in its hammock
one too many times, crushing alternatives. Where the ghosts of
six hundred thousand slaughtered Communists lurked. Where jeeps
and lorries, paregoric-colored convoys, made up the occupational
force called the government. Where banks and barracks were indistinguishable. Where patronage flowed from neo-Fascist pillbox
ministries, complete with Dixie colonnades, and even the cinemas
were impregnable bunkers. Where whole pages of *Time* magazine
were blacked out. Where children scorched bulging plantains over
open fires, where fathers scraped about in sandals and bathrobes
from sleep room to eat room to card room across cockamamie
family courtyards large enough to be called hamlets. Where mothers fanned their ample Micronesian forms, their faces so round as
to not possess shadow, adjusting their one-piece batik gowns on
the way to fetch rainwater for lemonade and feed the parakeets.
Where life looked idyllic, until all the evidence was in, and we
realized these people had nothing to do.

Hong Kong's precise social clockwork had jammed with equatorial rust, strewing human coils and springs everywhere. While
the most fawning Chinese might have called me "mister," here I'd
become boss. But I felt like a stumble bum. Crossing the hemi-
spheres had turned low winter into high summer. Iris and I were
now paying for our show of geographic nonchalance. If we could,
we planned to stagger across the sauna bath of Java and jump in
the ocean's cold shower at Bali. Yet we were so unprepared to
feel this unprepared! O, Java! O, dread coffee bean sprung to
indecipherable life! Was Krakatoa brewing again? Was that the
source of this everlasting steam?

Iris and I had to adjust our thermostats, and our expectations.
Indonesia was the first lesson in "Seeing the World Through Asian
Eyes." Jakarta had proved a city hiding from itself, a collection of
peasant towns divided into monotonous blocks. The impressive

boulevards carved cordons sanitaires in neighborhoods of squatters. Close to the national nerve center of Merdeka Square—merdeka meaning freedom, freedom from the Dutch—the streets were unpaved and the shop windows empty. Restaurants ladled out "Padang-style" curries to disguise the condition of what little meat was on hand. Though this was the capital of the world's fifth most-populous land, one third-rate tornado, one efficient collection agency could have boarded up the whole shebang.

Our first Asian train ride was not just measured in miles skipped, but in scenery skirted. Eight hours on a slatted, second-class bench turned inevitably into sixteen, but where were the volcanoes, the rain forests, the monkey habitats? Plains of paddy flat as Kansas hypnotized us, and except for the locust waves of oval-eyed boys who raced through the aisles at each stop—their cries too grand for their banana leaf catering—we saw nothing to justify our decision to take the journey in the day's heat. It was only at night that there was anything much to see and that was the one creature who made sure we could see it: the firefly. And not just a few, mind you, like those stray kamikazes we used to chase and lunge for in the cool twilights of our frigid North American youth. Our train passed through a miles long firefly tunnel, a throbbing cloud of loop-the-loop current. Pattern within strafing pattern, glow subsiding to glimmer replaced by glow again, these "lightning bugs," as Iris called them, did seem to crackle, conduct, and drain the darkness of its power. Interrupted only by the black-out of banana groves, we sifted for hours through the rice fields' astonishing electromagnetic harvest. Outside, out of reach, we found our first show of Asian abundance. Nature's generator was doing just fine, even if the lights in our slumbercoach never came on.

Jogjakarta, the "cradle of Javanese culture," had turned out to be one glorified main street, the Malioboro. It was combed in klaxon-ringing swarms by glorified bicycles, the becaks that hauled an upholstered, fringed passenger seat which doubled as the drivers' homes at night. How could someplace so ancient look so temporary? The most solid edifice, and the oldest was the prince's candi, or palace, a pavilion of spindly pylons. The local university was laundry-bedecked, its enrollment largely of chickens and roosters. Downtown "Yogya," as we learned to pronounce it, consisted of two covered uneven boardwalks, that had the feel of a pacifist Dodge City. No poker parlors or saloons here, just tinder boxes containing batiked surfer wear, hippie hangouts serving fruitwhips beneath creaking ceiling fans, one drugstore for every sick citizen. There were certainly enough horse-sized antiflu capsules being displayed, but "enough" was a word that Iris and I would soon stop having cause to use.

As for the loesmans, or "guest houses," where the pedal cabbies took us, they were no more than designated corners of those sprawling atriums in which the Indonesians sat out lifetimes with a minimum of disturbance. The inns' plaster dividers made a gallery for pin-ups of American rock groups who were vapid enough for export: the Spiral Staircase, Suzi Quatro. Masons' mishaps let in malarial moquitoes like the *Titanic* let in water. A nail driven into the wall served as a closet. Sheets? Sometimes washed, always stained. Telephones? The whole province was lucky to have one. Brotherhood was the only item in great supply, which wasn't so bad, except that the main time it got called into action was over the toilet, the squatter, the flushless hole—where guests learned to love the look of the next guy's worm-riddled feces as they loved their own. And when hotels down the road beckoned us with flyers promising "MUSIC IN EVERY ROOM!" we were amazed when a single radio rasped in the common courtyard.

It was enough to turn anyone into a tourist. Even the all-natural Iris, who grudgingly conceded that where the present looked so unmomental—and the future positively eager for corruption—the best way to make contact with something we could label "Indonesian" was through the monuments of the past. She was the one who usurped my guidebook and proposed an outing to the twelfth-century temple of Prambanan, some twenty minutes ride from town. Before we'd reached the bus station, another of the Malioboro's charming sycophants was at our heels. Like other practitioners of his amorphous trade, he made a dashing figure. The padded shoulders and baggy cuffs of the white linen outfit they all favored did a particularly good job of highlighting his long legs and sprightliness. Wavy black hair streamed down the back of his collar. A flowered tropical shirt went underneath, another Carnaby Street hand-me-down that seemed to find its best use here. The popular fashions were at least straining to be up-to-date, even if the popular history wasn't.

"First time in Yogya?" he called. "You would perhaps like to come with me?"

"Where?"

"Where? Why, all about. On seeing of sights. Prambanan and Borobodur temples."

"No, thanks," Iris fibbed. "We're leaving today."

"And why so soon you go to Australia?"

"We're not from Australia. America."

"Oh, America, I like. Rock and roll. Suzi Quatro. You live in California, yes?"

"How did you know?"

"All Americans from California. San Bernardino, okay? I meet doctor from there. With Polaroid. He took pictures. Was guest in my house. . . . Please wait! I show you! I am Datak."

We stopped to see the smudged pictures and introduce ourselves, but we still weren't sure what he wanted.

"And where did you learn to speak English so well?"

"At university. You want to see university?" English was the universal language of wanting.

Iris looked at me, beginning to waver, but then Datak made a mistake. "Very good batik work at university. Good prices. Friends to Datak."

"We don't want good prices. We want to see Indonesia."

"Okay, miss. No price for looking. . . . Indonesia very pretty."

"Except for the army." I couldn't resist a chance to gauge unrest among the student populace.

"Yes. Much army." But Datak was merely concurring happily, enumerating another sight, and these three words were all the dissent I ever heard.

"Bye-bye!" Iris picked up the pace.

"All right. Goodbye. I think you come from book I read. American book."

"What's that?"

"Yes. *Love Story*. All Americans know this book, yes? . . . 'Love, it is never having to not say you're sorry.' Okay?"

Once we saw the busses crisscrossing in the station as if they were part of an unrehearsed Keystone chase, we were the ones who were sorry we didn't have Datak. But Iris was determined that we find our own way to the right mechanized sardine can. Given the choice, she would have welcomed sincere companionship, but seeing none, she held more tightly to her Texan self-sufficiency. Iris, the excessively egalitarian feminist, the humble seeker of archetypes, the latent eccentric and renegade cracker, was reverting to Iris, the old-time frontier gal. Her denim skirt was fading, her sandals were getting flattened into leathery lily pads. Brown dust took up residence on her eyebrows. She was rising to any and all challenges, summoning up all her piss-and-vinegar pragmatism in the service of this least practical of continental crossings. But she could only do it because there was no gold, no land, no cattle at stake; the less she was after, the more she undid, and outdid, her ancestry.

"Prambanan!" she kept shouting to every wandering ticket-taker who could hear. "Where in hell is Prambanana, you-all?" I half-expected to hear. If Iris couldn't find it, then it wasn't meant to be. But after accosting several touts, she got us on what seemed the right line. We leaned out the open front door all the way and were nearly thrown off with each swerve. At least, we got a good look at the glut of lopsided yellow-green hillocks, the midget bursts of banana grove and the royal palms above them all snooty. This was a volcanic golf course, a landscape in perspiration. At the right stop, the driver initiated a wave of elbowing that ended with our being shoved out the door. We were the only ones on the dirt road to the temple.

Past the usual row of Coke stands, we found four blackened turrets rotting on a high platform of grass above more rice paddies. At first, it looked like Prambanan was worthless without a good sand-blasting, but as we got closer, the grime took on a formidable order. Turrets and ramparts were lined with rungs of writhing, gesticulating figures: peewee warriors and midget goddesses who were bit actors in the long-running soap opera of the Ramayana saga. Gods turned to deer, deer to seducers, but these chiseled good guys and bad took their place in one fluid, three-hundred-and-sixty-degree strip.

To our amazement, the untended grounds were equipped with benches. Iris and I found one under a banyan tree and contemplated. Like the native foliage, Prambanan was excessively ornate, striving to attain the overdone. The medieval Javanese designers could never have belonged to the Bauhaus. Their handiwork put curlicues around curlicues even when the statement was as simple as devotion to duty. Where daily life was pared down, the imaginative life could not help but grow terrifyingly complex. The aesthetic of purposeful spareness could only flourish in glutted societies that were attempting to unencumber themselves. Less was *not* more, not here. More was more, less was little. Less than that was nothing at all.

An incomparable stillness invaded us on our bench. Was this the first knocking of the nonrational bogeyman? Or were our usual preoccupations just wilting in the heat? Prambanan struck us as holy because it was the first destination of ours that appeared untouched by the sordid exigencies of underdevelopment. At last, we were getting a glimpse of Indonesia. It was provided by this testament of a time when Indonesians weren't Muslims, weren't even Indonesians, when they didn't wish to be anything but what they were. Suddenly, we didn't wish them to be anything else, either.

Iris and I were captivated, but she didn't want to talk. Quickly, she grabbed my wrist and coaxed me into a game of hide-and-seek around the redolent stupas. We didn't exactly take turns giving chase—it was too hot for anything that enterprising and we didn't want to appear irreverent—so we just circled the sculpted bases, climbed the sacrificial steps from opposite sides of the towers, shouted "Gotcha!" when we bumped heads in the shrines' mossy crawlspaces. We soon had a chance to play our game for real, when we spotted Datak, so cool in his Good Humor suit, breezing through the stubby portals of the sanctuary. Three Aussie lasses in sleeveless green dresses followed in tow, blond hair to their waists, camera straps shielding freckled, unviolated breasts. Obviously, he now had bigger foreign fish to fry, but the two of us did not want him to see that we'd lied to him and found this place without his aid. Escaping behind his back as he began an explication of the first Ramayana frieze, I wondered whether Datak could have told us anything more than what we'd intuited. What *World Book* facts could he have used to impress? Would he have brought forth more Erich Segal?

Buoyed by her first triumph, Iris insisted that we attend that night's performance of wayang kulit, the Javanese shadow play. "And let's do it without some fool guide who'll explain it all to bits." She shooed away offers from several more of those over dinner, asking only that they point the way. Each of them sent us toward the prince's candi. That seemed a logical enough setting for the venerated theatrical form, but we found no performance in progress there—only a lone guard who couldn't figure out what

we were after. Beyond, in the entrails of old Yogya, all was dis-
couragingly quiet. We wandered in a cobblestone maze, the high
walls on either side dotted with alert-orange lichen. An occasional
kerosene lamp twinkled, coaxing Iris on.

"Second time out, and you get us lost!"

"That's how I got kicked out of Girl Scouts."

"You've got an infallible sense of direction. You're like a Geiger
counter in reverse . . ."

"Does it matter?"

"We should head back to town. We've probably missed half
the show."

"But it goes on all night!"

"Well, I don't."

"Come on, crab. Look up there!"

Just before the next bend in the maze, a group of men had
gathered and was staring up at something mounted high on one
of their neighbor's stone balustrades. The attraction turned out to
be the communal television, which was showing a subtitled rerun
of "I Dream of Jeannie." Trying to follow the intrigue swirling
about a Formica High School PTA meeting, the men were trans-
fixed. None of them laughed at the situation comedy, and none
of them knew anything about where we might find the shadow
play.

"Just remember: the way back is always shorter than the way
there."

"Is that Iris' law?"

At our tenth dead end, three children pointed us three different ways. The last one led us to paydirt, where another inter-
necine alley opened onto an oval dirt lot, the kind where operators
back home might have staged a demolition derby. Thankfully,
there was nothing here to demolish and the tracks in the lot were
made by the thinner trade of a hundred or so vendors with their
wooden carts. Over each vat of frying shrimp, rice or dough,
wobbled a kerosene lamp or several candles. The aggregate effect
was a production number from *Peter Pan*: more fireflies, pure
candi-land. At the far end of this tremulous night market and
nymphs' convention was the one structure in Jogjakarta that made
a stab at indestructibility. Its style was congressional Greco-Roman.
Rounded steps took us inside an auditorium that might have belonged to any decent-sized American high school.

It wasn't so easy to tell if the shadow play had already begun. The house lights were on, children in baggy shorts romped everywhere. But a triumphant Iris led us toward two of the many empty folding seats. We had conquered the tropics, we had stumbled on culture—and, up ahead, at floor level, was the portable proscenium of the wayang kulit.

On the front side of the two side flaps of a rice paper screen hung the several dozen puppets used to cast the shadows. No attempt was made to hide this company in the wings or create some Punch 'n' Judy illusion. These solid forms, like ours, were deceptive. Reality was in the reflections, natch. These gods on folding skewers were representatives of the universe's controlling forces, and it didn't matter how fragile they looked. Local dramaturges had discovered long ago that what made the gods believable was the audience's belief. This theater was all the more epic because the viewers did most of the work. The concert-master remained unhidden and attempted no disguise of his manipulation. The puppets were hauled off the rack one at a time and held before a light bulb at center stage. They were thrust so close to the screen that hardly any shadows were cast at all, though the figures grew more spectral as the light shone through their gossamer hides. With their sneering, elongated chops, Jimmy Durante schnozzes, each of the characters in this eloquently deformed cast appeared to be flinging down curses upon their enemies, and us. Their headgear nearly crisped up with the flame of their righteousness. The puppets' attenuated grasshopper limbs brought to mind an eternal starvation—that permanent advantage known as lack of want—but the arms were their only moving parts. Needed to point, accuse and condemn. The man who controlled these few stilted gestures was also the principal singer. Kneeling beside the characters he animated, this impresario took all parts, muttering with an operatic cadence into a knee-high microphone. Again, artifice was shunned. Special effects were up to the viewer. The gods raged and were frighteningly well-defined, perhaps the most specifically imagined demons on earth, but their setting was minimal, their world static. Indeed, their mythical deeds took place right in our laps.

Was that why each performance took up to sixteen hours? It was hard to imagine that a single concert-master could last through the whole script, but this one had no trouble with speeches that droned on for half an hour, and we couldn't spot any understudies in the wings. But he got a break, as did the audience, at the end of each fierce tableau. An interlude was provided by a gamelan orchestra that separated stage from audience on the teak floor. No pit hid these musicians in their resplendent checkered sarongs and matching forehead wraps. Their instruments, too, were part of the spectacle, from gongs that could have been prized ceramic vases to sound-boxes that resembled sets of pachyderm ribs. Playing as one, the herky-jerk of this xylophonic ensemble resonated out of time and into our ears. Atonal modernists had prepared us to appreciate this most ancient attempt to give chaos a beat and magic precision. The men who sat on the floor before us, tapping their strikers and asserting the primacy of the bell, were making their music as stand-ins for the wind.

The Javanese did not tap their toes, or react overtly to lyrics or score. Yet this was clearly a big event for the town. The seats at the front were hogged by dignitaries, all male, who wore black felt caps shaped like the paper ones worn by managers at a McDonald's franchise. These bespoke a more enduring authority, as well as their Moslem faith. Throughout the performance, Jogjakarta's Chamber of Commerce kept their arms folded, most seriously, over bellies that were their most conspicuous show of wealth. They also did their best to ignore the noisy and irreverent peanut gallery behind them. Not only did the commoners chat away, but their pregnant women fidgeted and ambled about, their barefoot children played with string or leapfrogged the empty chairs. In this auditorium, there were few of the trappings that accompany Western "high art": no overzealous aficionados or determination to appreciate, no snobbery or diamond brooches or handy programs at the door. The shadow play was actually play, not some hallowed cultural expression to be endured. It was also historic, but since history's continuum was relatively unbroken in these parts, there was no reason the play had to be revered. It was an old friend that everyone took for granted.

There could have been little forced solemnity, since the audience was mostly children. It was a sight to which we'd soon become accustomed: always enough children to outnumber their elders, always more hands clutching at fewer resources. Just don't tell that to the kids of Jogjakarta. They were getting a full measure of entertainment from their "night out." Many were unaccompanied, and the rest were strikingly unleashed, joyfully tolerated. Darting and squirming around and over the folding seats, their black hair uniformly shaved, this local gang looked like monks who'd taken a vow of cuteness. The shape of their skulls seemed equally anti-Western. They came to no points, were not sharpened at the cerebrum, but remained unbiased toward the rational, rounded on top and bulging at the sides like squashed fruits. They all seemed stuck at that age where their heads were too big for their bodies. In turn, the heads could not contain their eyes: such perfect spoons of white pigment.

Many of those eyes were drawn to a rotund German who'd plunked down in their midst and was beckoning all the boys. When they weren't climbing all over his considerable terrain, or returning playful slaps, or bouncing on his ham hock knees, we could see he was dressed only in an orange sarong girdle around his middle. This son of Saxony had gone thoroughly Gauguin, though that only revealed how luridly pale and blue-veined he was beside all that *kinderfleisch*. The rest of the audience paid him no heed, didn't seem to notice the vague prurience in his beaming. Never had this man had an opportunity to so fully ooze with paternalism, to fondle so many pups. None of his changelings seemed to mind that he stroked their shaved domes as if trying to polish brass knobs: they didn't know that a pat on the head carried a price.

It was hard to keep our eyes on the concert-master's dexterity instead of the German's. But we had a train to catch in the morning and walked out on the third act, which was indistinguishable to our eyes from second and first. Was that why the Javanese went on gabbing throughout? Sneaking away and down the front steps of the auditorium, I was about to hail one of the hundred waiting rickshaws—no doubt, they, too, would be there until the play ended at dawn. But Iris flinched and tugged at my arm. Standing in the lot, front row center, before the aisles of shaky pushcarts and quivering candelabras, was our nemesis, the shadow we cast.

"Australian?" The approach began once again. But, no—this wasn't Datak, just another of his lanky cousins, who looked just as sporting, and as clownish, in pleated white pants.

"American."

"America! Long way to Jogjakarta!"

"Yes, long way."

"You see shadow play?"

We nodded. What else?

"You see Prambanan temple?"

We nodded again.

"You see my house?"

"Thank you, no." Was it one of the local treasures? "Catch train tomorrow."

"I know. You go Bali. . . . But first, you be friends?"

"Why?" Iris asked. It sounded like an awfully dumb question, but she was learning through imitation.

"Friendship good. Understanding. Then we take pictures. Then you buy batik."

Perhaps there was some friendship in such an interchange, but for us, it too resembled a kind of mutual bondage, the boys on the great white father's lap.

"No, we go to sleep now."

"All right. Very good. I see you wish to be alone. I see you are very much in love."

"We are?" Iris asked again.

"Yes, yes. In Indonesia, we call love 'the meeting of feeling.' " And our shadow said goodbye to us by illustrating the phrase with a clasping of nimble-jointed, tweezer-shaped, marionette fingers.

"You see," I told Iris, my arm around her in the becak, the recitatives of the real shadow play fading, "we're fooling the whole world!"

Later that night, we were most strenuously reminded of how much we were a part of the "whole world." An earthquake, brief but insistent as a cough, made Iris and me sit up in the dark. Blinded, we could hear new fissures being released in the loesman plaster, the teeth of tin roofs chattering, and the women who slept on blankets along the boardwalk raise up a wail. They did not seem to be baying so much from fear as out of nocturnal arousal. These ladies of Java couldn't be afraid, I reasoned, half-swallowed by the ground as they already were. They didn't have such a long way to fall.

BALI LOW

TICS OF LIGHTNING twitched from nervous clouds. They outlined a dark gorilla chest, matted with palms, that had to be Bali. "Morning of the world," Nehru called it, but this morning was having a difficult birth. It came in spasms of thunderclap further shaking a ferry that moved like a vibrator in a Vaseline sea. Still, there wasn't much discomfort involved, though considering Iris and I were in transit from Banjuwangi to paradise.

The troubled dawn enlarged to show other volcanic tips beyond, another atoll, another and another, beyond and beyond. Coming into view was the primordial, and also the paradoxical. For if one of these South Seas sanctuaries was truly "undiscovered," how would we ever find out about it? If we could get there, how would it stay pure? Only through its quest for unspoiled surroundings did our civilization admit how spoiled it was. So Iris and I were hardly expecting to be thrust into the pages of an anthropologist's fieldbook. Yet wasn't Bali the place where the Dutch governor's wife had once ordered the women to cover their breasts during an official procession only to have them comply by lifting their skirts? Bali had to be the last holdout of innocence, even if the first ladies we spotted fetching water along the highway

were well-covered, bottom and top. Bali was equally renowned as
the one remaining bastion of a frenzied, sensuous Hinduism amidst
the ostensibly more sedate Islamic archipelago. On our first bus
ride, we found confirmation of that in the statuettes of pygmy
deities sprouting from the jungle sop everywhere, blackened and
mossy, serving as curvaceous milestones along the narrow highways. This anachronistic isle was India made mirthful (hence the
Nehru laurel). One floating shrine: where the homes were all
temples, the temples homes. At first glance, it appeared that nothing, and nobody, could be defiled.

Yet Bali was still a little bit too large to be just Bali. One had
to have a more specific address, and ours, unfortunately, was Kuta
Beach. According to our guidebook, this was the place to be, and
the name we gave the hot-rodding becak drivers who met our bus.
They took us there through undulating groves of palm to a bungalow that came with a poster bed and two candles, several dozen
mosquitoes and a complimentary bunch of bananas we imagined
had fallen off nearby trees. Kuta! To sleep until evening and dream
you've found Xanadu; to wake and discover an Australian surfers'
convention in plenary session. Our first stroll down the dirt strip
lined with thatched-roof gift shops, open-air bars and guest houses,
revealed a paradise that was not so much lost as made too palatable.
Kuta could indeed have been Eden, had we loved ourselves and
our Western accoutrements as much as the Balinese apparently
thought we did. Iris and I had not been taken from our place,
we'd been put right back in it.

Still, this beachcombers' ghetto had certain advantages which
kept us pinned there. One could hop from hotel room to banana
fritters to fruit drinks to batik browsing to next ineffectual tube
of Bain du Soleil. The juice bars were all the rage, featuring shakes
that combined avocado and pineapple and the acrid, mucous rot
of the prickly durian. Fastidious sun worshippers who wouldn't
dare drink the local water lined up to gobble the ice made from
it. You only get sick from what you think is going to make you
sick.

Was it the corruption of Kuta that did us in? Iris and I couldn't
bear the imported night life. We eschewed the crush of Aussies
in floppy tropical shirts at the bars. They didn't care where they
were, just that they could do what they wanted. Drink the beer,
mate. Ride the wave, mate. Screw that pretty little native girl,

mate. Instead of watching the Balinese try their hand at imitating Grand Funk Railroad, we trudged with the stodgier set to the outdoor arena where the traditionally fervent dances, and much of the accompanying folklore of the interior, were presented nightly. Another convenience, with colorful signs posted everywhere to remind us of the endless repertory: Thursday night was the heated ketjak, where a kneeling chorus chanted and screeched until they'd metamorphosed into a brood of nattering monkeys, Saturday was the wistful legong. This time, the Christians were in the makeshift stands, and threw the heathens to their flashcubes. We had come so many thousands of miles to still be miles from seeing the dances in their proper setting.

Road's end, at Kuta, no matter which bottle-littered path you took, was one curve of sand that stretched as far as any shipwreck survivor could want. Fringed with lime marsh and more thickets of palm, the beach was wide enough to accommodate dune buggies, motorcycle relays and crisscrossing throws of the conspicuously plastic frisbee. The ocean beyond was a heated green pool, warm and salty like semen, but without the stick. What was the water's name here? Sea of Respite, Gulf of Honkies, Bay of the Batik Bikini. You could stay in it all day, without chill, and finally know what it felt like to be a seal. The Utamaro woodcut waves were high enough to thrill but not to threaten. Kuta, from beyond the breakers, looked to be the perfect combination of campground and resort.

The only item you couldn't buy here was privacy. Bali's own "l'il rascals" made certain you knew you were still on hungry Bali. They accosted anyone caught reclining on beach towels with sacks of puka shells and coconut oil and wood carvings and forged ancient scrolls, T-shirts silk-screened with unflinching demons. Your money could buy other goodies they didn't display. For every thirty seconds of sun, these subequatorial *luftmenschen* blocked fifteen seconds of the ultraviolet. A tenacious sales force with their very own company credo, they'd point to our beige skins crisping red. "That number one!" they'd remind us. "That number one!"

Could we really have looked as beautiful to them as they did to us? The boys' teardrop eyes, colts' manes, their brilliant white teeth exhibited without restraint, were the only proof we had that our own pockmarks and puffiness weren't contagious. Some of the "locals" who shared the Kuta scene did their best to imitate us. In the muck of the strip, the more enterprising spun their new Honda cycles and jerked the front ends up in wheelies. In their tacky Bali-Hai snack bars, lit by kerosene and candles, others played snooker on shiny new tables. More ravaged kids roamed the rutted alleys selling blocks of seats to the dance performances, insisting we buy tickets for a sweepstakes without discernible jackpot. Dogs and their mangy masters waited together for scraps at restaurant kitchens. Yet the pint-sized children matched the stump-legged statuary in animating Bali. This miniature world seemed to flame up, a spiritual brush fire raging in every direction we stamped. "Many children good for Bali," a pregnant shopkeeper told us. Whether Bali was good for them wasn't a concern. Children and parents seemed of a single generation, one copious litter. Planning for an overpopulated future was crowded out by a present that was all too vividly peopled.

Most of the foreigners seemed more than willing to brush the poor aside, or forget the world that perpetuated them. This was easily done by ordering a delicacy that appeared on Kuta menus as "special omelette"—meaning stuffed with psilocybin mushrooms. A Canadian in the bungalow next to ours said he spent his whole trip in the water. Ten hours of flux and flow in the amniotic sea. A line of dancing palms to choreograph his dizziness.

Iris wanted to try one, but I didn't need any more "escape." This place, by itself, had already put me in as heightened a state as I could handle. Too bad our first week on the road was no hallucination. However, Iris was a small-town girl raised amidst lulling trust, who'd always walked barefoot through the shrapnel of big cities and gotten away with it. She reacted to difficulties by denying them; she convinced herself she was safe by upping the levels of danger. We bickered over the omelette, over her persistence in sampling the most exotic and hazardous foods, over the cavalier morning swim she took, always going too far offshore. Finally, I was forced to join her, intent on being a lifeguard.

"You can't keep this up," I insisted, treading water. "You're not invulnerable, you know!"

"I *do* know. Only how can you travel without risks?" With her hair wet, Iris' stubborn prow of a forehead emerged. Her dimples were black streaks, permanent war paint.

"But why increase them?" I asked back, still over my head. "I won't let you blackmail me into heroism."

What I really feared was that I was inhibiting her, letting her down. Judging by my first week's caution, I'd convinced myself I wouldn't be able to fulfill my promise to escort her through the Himalayas. After all, Iris' idea of a good time might have been a pot of beans over a campfire, but I'd never had to pitch a tent in Central Park.

"I don't think I can be your mountain climber."

"Take your worries one at a time," Iris advised. Then we kissed and she wrapped her legs around me in the charged, boggy sea.

What fed my worries most of all was that no one else seemed to mind Kuta. One evening, we shared a table with a dashing photographer from *Paris Match* whose assignment was to capture *le vrai Balinesque* and got him to admit that he'd stumbled on it only by accident. We compared notes on the dances, agreeing they were modern a thousand years ago. The costumes might be cumbersome, crustacean, but the movements were all breathtakingly simple. Sometimes just the eyes shimmied back and forth. A hand turned itself inside out, the fingernails sharpened for destiny. Iris spoke for us, more skilled in French, but got rewarded with Gallic resignation. "Only banalities can pass between two languages," the photographer sighed. *Seulement des choses banales.*

At least, when all else failed, there was the beach at night. The surfers were replaced by furtive dealers who crept up and down the beach. Sneaking up on us through the always hot sand, they whispered offers of morphine and laced "Thai sticks." By now, even Iris preferred to dose herself with the overflow of stars, the rustle of palm leaves, the breeze that blew tepid as a living breath. Hidden by dunes from Kuta's cut-rate hedonism, we could end our days in reverie. Poor, trampled Bali! Where was its golden soul?

Still adapting to the climate, we had trouble locating the will or the horsepower to explore the island's terraced heart. We did take a mini-bus tour. Our companions were an Italian pair on the last stop of a two-week package deal. They'd started out in Fiji, gone straight to the beach and received third-degree burns. Their vacation had been spent blistering from neck to ankle. Our driver and guide was a peppery Balinese, bursting with patriotism and occasional information. We learned that Bali had a caste system, as in India, divided into four major groups. A man remained in his hierarchical station, though he didn't say whether a tourguide was high or low. His name was the same as his grandfather's, who'd lost his as soon as his grandson was born, so the names could be rotated into eternity. When the first stop on the program turned out to be his home, most of the family appeared to disown him. They were too busy, and too scattered, for greetings. The Balinese, he explained, had a house for cooking, a house for eating, a house for sleeping, a house for lovemaking. Each was pointed in a specific direction to placate different gods. Between the various structures was communal space, claimed by roosters and parrots in bamboo cages and rivulets of well water.

Bali also had a so-called aboriginal village where, we were told, the dead were not buried, but merely left on the ground where they'd croaked. It cost plenty extra to see that, the guide informed us. All we got on our cut-rate excursion was a volcano: unforested Mount Batur, cross-sectioned with clouds as dark as its lava slopes. At Kintimani, barefoot girls in lavender sarongs held white melons to the gray sky. Iris insisted on buying a bag of their remarkable "green oranges." They looked like some hybrid we'd never seen, but Iris learned her lesson. Even in Bali, a green orange was weeks from being edible. The charming maidens pocketed our change and ran.

We were deposited at several mossy jungle shrines, an extra charge collected at each one. We paid to step inside the "elephant caves" that housed old bones in a dark catacomb; but there were no elephants left on Bali. Were these really the human remains of the princely elite who'd committed mass suicide rather than be colonized by the Dutch? They had seen what was coming. At the stop entitled "holy springs," a priest pinned a white lotus blossom on Iris and collected again. Lily pads and swans floated near naked bathers who were completing sanctified rites. Blessed waters bubbled in turquoise currents as salmon-colored gravel spewed from Bali's effervescent core. Garuda birds with sharp beaks and terrifying scowls were carved all around the serenity. And above us, we spied a streamlined bunker that had been built by modern prince Sukarno. The only sight in Bali that was off-limits. We were whisked away through winding layers of paddies that made one green sunken living room. Next came the future Bali: a T-shirt factory where aisles of eight-year-olds dribbled patterns of maroon wax over cloth for as long as there was daylight. Cisterns filled with hot dye bubbled over, the runoff smoldering in gutters close to the children's exposed toes. And we still had to see silvermaking, weaving, and woodcarving. "Famous old Balinese craft," the guide explained. "Handed down many generations. Always cover statues with famous Kiwi shoe polish."

Denpasar, the capital, wasn't Bali, but a blight. Call it a tumor caused by exposure to twentieth-century radiation. The main street offered a constant jam-up of putt-putting becaks, soda shops and one movie house with a gaudy, hand-painted facade that clarioned the arrival of another Charles Bronson epic. Cockfights and fly-swathed markets and women crouching in the sun beside straw baskets filled with rotten fruit. Urban life was urban life everywhere; an invention of others, the Balinese couldn't make it their own, just surrender. The confused pinwheel of streets was broken by several mammoth and frankly martial greens. A parade of army units was forming in one: black boots prancing off to nowhere, keeping down a populace that showed no inclination of getting up.

The parade, it turned out, had been airlifted from Jakarta. Indonesia was playing host to a summit meeting of Asian leaders at the cottages that belonged to Pertamina, the nationalized oil cartel, which were just down the beach from Kuta. Suddenly, the army patrolled our stretch of surf in their full battle regalia. But these soldiers weren't too imposing, since most held hands and showed hair swaying in ponytails out of their helmets. The Kutans began frantically, poignantly decorating the strip. Their notion of politics, and a good one, was that it was one big birthday party. In the burning sun, trimmings of dried palm leaves looked like glittery confetti. The statues—more statues than people—were suddenly covered. A checked tablecloth went over every set of granite genitals. No pricks could be exposed but those of the visiting dictators! Word spread through the compound that the meeting had produced its first casualty: one of the innkeepers was electrocuted while stringing up the rare set of bulbs. Next morning, Iris and I watched the Balinese chomping on pineapple cores and shuffling barefoot behind the lucky man's corpse as it was borne on palm leaves toward cremation.

We decided to get out before the heads-of-state arrived, arranging the quickest bus back to Jakarta and a romantic deck passage on a steamer to Singapore. But after lunch on our last day, Iris vomited her crab and avocado. At first, all we had to

worry about was that everyone in our row of bungalows was privy
to her retching. She was convinced it had to be simple food poi-
soning, but fever set in, and a few hours later, as I stroked her
brow, I realized that my growing weakness was being induced by
more than sympathy. An uncontrollable force pinned both of us
to our poster bed; a strange burning tra-la-lad through us at will.
By evening, we couldn't even struggle out the door for tea. Our
world had been reduced to the straw confines of our hut. All we
could diagnose was that our disillusionment had made us suscep-
tible.

Neither of us could have imagined we'd catch the same thing
at the same time. In the morning, we counted ourselves lucky to
find a German couple next door who had the same disorder. They
would serve as our harbingers, and we were reassured that they'd
nearly recovered after four days of siege. But why was it they,
too, lay prone in their room all day or hobbled to chairs set out
in the common garden? After two years on the road, both were
beggar skinny. They could savor the irony of catching their first
real disease just a few days before they were flying home. That
did little for us. How would we be able to cross the globe when
we couldn't even manage the few yards to the Mandara Guest
House dining room?

Days merged with days; our inner vapor rose to meet the
tropical pall. The only salvation was a trough of standing water
and the pail provided, with which we sluiced ourselves and flushed
down our sizzling wastes. At night, we got vicarious showers as
the first monsoon storms washed over us. Enough humidity seeped
through our slanted roof to dampen our already damp sheets.
Strapped to our stiff, elevated bed, the bungalow's romantic centerpiece, we could do little more than contemplate the rungs of
our bamboo cell. We counted each leaf and nexus of thatching.
Somewhere in there, just before dark each day, a gecko lizard
joined us. We could never see him, but we sure could hear him.
He was an amplified crooning frog, crying for love (or perhaps
tetracycline) with a human rasp. His moan wound down like a
talking doll's soliloquy.

At last, Iris, prone Iris, and I were in tune with the dark,
animist Bali. The Bali of tradewinds and churlish demons and the
perpetual sweat too much life breeds. In the morning, to celebrate

having remained whole through a dozen breaks and rises of the fever, I could peek out our rented hospital's torn opening toward the next compound and watch a rotund grandmother with breasts flattened like falling bombs shower herself by overturning a huge clay cask of rainwater. Her graceful lack of shame was my joy, her sloshing cooled me. Equivalent soothing was provided nightly by the wafting of the gamelan orchestra from the nearby dance shows. How could we have asked for a better soundtrack to delirium? The chimes pinged like raindrops on our puddled brows; the gongs rung inside our gourds; the fainter the reverberation of bell, the less we could tell where we left off and our visions began. Now we knew who those midget carvings were: figments of a world in which everything was fevered. One god fulminated from the fever of streams, one from the fever of insects, one from the surefire fever of volcanoes. In Bali, the temperature was always too dangerous to be measured in Fahrenheit; and life was but a triumphant virus. Best to placate the force that gripped you! Feel it utterly! Revel in your weakness! Pray in rhythm with the storms that swept the island clean each night and the killing sun that followed. The gecko was a god, too, scaly as he might be, invested with the power to toll sunsets.

In our bungalow, Iris and I were Dorothy Lamour and Bob Hope, on the road to oblivion. But what did we have? All the guidebooks warned us off Indonesian doctors, but our reflex was to consult one. The boys who ran the guest house, who brought bananas and porridge to our sick bay, who never wore more than swim trunks and thongs, who gave us the feeling they'd seen many others in our condition, told us of an M.D. who had an office right along Kuta's strip. By day five, we managed to stagger over to his outhouse-sized office. He wore a purple shirt stamped with yellow sailboats and the crooked silver eye over his forehead, just so we knew he was really a doctor. His examination consisted of a peek down our throats with a flashlight. He didn't take our temperatures, pound our chests, or ask our names. He'd been to the States, but obviously hadn't made it into the AMA. We hoped, at least, for some herbal cure. "Bad air on the trains," was his diagnosis. "Too much motion." And should we keep taking penicillin? He answered, "Why not?" But the prescription he put more stock in was a swab of Tiger Balm, the all-purpose, all-knowing liniment,

applied to our brows. Our worst tourists' nightmare was now confirmed. We were on our own. It was either get well or send off
the penultimate postcard.

In the meantime, in our sugar shack, Iris and I remained bliss-
fully stoic. Made equal by the emergency, no one tested anyone.
Who had the strength? We argued only over whose turn it was to
retrieve the porridge from our doorstep. Together, we played
childhood games like "Ghost"—but, please, no "Geography"—
and recited every poem we ever knew, and sang the remembered
hits of a faraway top forty in wavering duets. "Company" meant
one another, plus gecko and bathing lady and when the reception
was right, the "Yangtze" shortwave bought in Hong Kong. At
sunset, the world was briefly bent toward us. My Maoist device
did not decode, discriminate or make corrections. The Voice of
America brought us word, via Washington, of the summit meeting
that was now issuing communiqués from just down the beach. In
a place called New Hampshire, where they had something called
snow, the primary election had just been won by some hayseed
called Carter. The Bicentennial had begun—and we tried to calculate how many such anniversaries the Balinese could have marked,
had they bothered to count. We were more glad than ever to miss
the forced hoopla, the piety merging with public relations. Then
jazz faded in and out on the Yangtze, and America was forgiven.
We heard Fats Waller lilting, "I'm gonna sit right down and write
myself a letter . . ." The blues' bittersweet call mixed curiously
with the malarial stop-and-go of the gamelan. Two listless sets of
feet began tapping. This was our jazz, our clear and unexplainable
corridor to the spirit, and nobody else could jazz it better. The
Balinese had to feel the same way about their bells. There was no
way around one's upbringing, or uplifting. O, how America beckoned with its panoply of peoples, gadgets, diversions! How America tinkles and resonates when you are far from it!

Lost in strange lusts for late-night movies and ice cream sundaes and stoplights and plenty of things we didn't even like, Iris
and I figured we could hardly get much farther away. But our
homesickness hurt good; it was a salve that worked better than
Tiger Balm. A week after our first attack of the dread Bali bug,
we managed to struggle into town. We had to suffer the ultimate
indignity of pleading for visa extensions so that we could stay
unwell in the country which had made us that way. We also began

writing letters that weren't just to ourselves. In them, we could be brave, almost smug. We could, in fact, boast of this standard obstacle we were now hurdling. After all, nobody was immune to new microbes or new ways of being. We were having the natural, the healthy response.

What if Bali had not made us sick? What if we actually found what we were looking for at Kuta Beach? Or in "the real Asia"? Then we would have really been feeling woozy. We would have been in the most grave condition, which was the condition of having to start our lives anew. What if there'd been no opportunity for self-contented disappointment? What if the signs had not all read "English Spoken Here"? What if the earth had turned out to be square? What if there was such a thing as a journey without return? And what if we could have managed to keep from going around the world in a bad mood? What if?

Each night, when the fever clamped back down, I would heap curses on Asia and all things Asian. Without telling Iris, I cursed Suharto and Siam and Prince Souvanna Phouma. Curse Tokyo Rose, curse Keye Luke, curse Akira Kurosawa and all those Samurai flicks. Curse Satyajit Ray and Maharishi and Mukhtananda and curse the Beatles, too. A curse on Lin Piao and people's war, on crafty Chou, on the Chairman himself. A pox on won tons and tandoori, on nasi goreng and gado gado! To hell with the Vietnam War and all its vampire newsmen! They were the ones who'd first got me curious to investigate these parts by the light of peacetime! They were the ones who'd ordered me out on this search-and-destroy! Curse the soil and its humus, curse defoliation! Curse Uncle Ho's prison poems and his tunnel-dwelling armies, curse Buddha and anyone else who could sit still, who was willing to wait, who could accept boredom and not be bored with acceptance. Curse the monks and the concubines and the opium runners. Curse Gandhi and Genghis Khan alike! Curse curried anything, curse rice and tranquility. The price was too high. Curse all the know-it-alls who'd come before us, everyone who lived to tell the tale. Curses, many curses, on the day I left my true home bed.

KEEP SINGAPORE CLEAN

THE jet we'd sought to spurn became our ambulance. How many times had we cussed at the take-offs that jolted our defenseless beach hut? Resistance weakened, we crawled back inside the unsettling machinery, rejoined the race that trumpeted its dominion with sonic booms. Throughout Asia, and in Bali particularly, the airplane was the farthest leap in what seemed an idle, technological hopscotch. From the sweltering hovel to the pressurized cabin, from contaminated water to the Thai stewardesses' "coffee, tea or me" made one absurd illustration in what Chairman Mao termed "the skipping of stages." But our sickness exposed the greater disease of our dependence on all-inclusive, all-intrusive convenience. With a roar only behemoths could have found soothing, Iris and I were rescued from the South Seas—and reminded that, for those who could afford it, the world was of a piece.

Once aboard, we knew we were going to be well, or, at least, given our general malaise, cured. Landing in Singapore, the "economic miracle" sucked us up like so much dust in a high-powered vacuum. No two tropical isles could have been less alike than languorous Bali and this driven city-state. At the Singapore Airport, the welcome was mechanized, a foretaste of a nation ruled by government notices. Was anything more modern, or more repressive, than the standard, uncompromising sign? From "have passport ready" to "no longhairs admitted," the gods of this place spoke with a uniform, disembodied firmness. I was grateful to Mack Schreiber for having made me clip my hair to far less than the Berkeley norm. I wouldn't have done it to get into Disneyland, but Singapore, I was sure, would have better rides. The first was through customs, down rubberized paths, past the inspection of my grooming and a gauntlet of police who wielded free brochures instead of nightsticks.

"This cleanest city in Asia," our cab driver was the first of many to boast. We didn't mind one bit when he was proven right. Our Chinese hotel could have doubled as a Chinese laundry: the sheets were clean as old-fashioned barbershop toweling and the showers were communal but gleaming and gecko-less. The bamboo blinds clicked shut and the ceilings fans actually rotated at more than three revolutions per hour. Downstairs, beneath covered sidewalks, the peddlers and noodle vendors made their usual, listless rounds. But the goods here were a little newer, the woks more briskly scoured—responding to competition from the many-tiered shopping malls that made logical, high-tech extensions of the old bazaars. An astounding range of peoples browsed the outdoor and indoor stalls: the whole gamut from "Indo" to "Chinese," illustrating how ancient the linkage of roots in that word. Singapore's races did not so much mix as homogenize. Seemingly, they did so with little rancor. That may have been because their crowded pen's dairylike hygiene was enforced by more edicts, no other bills posted. No littering, loitering, spitting or smoking, with fines of a hundred dollars and more for each transgression. No laughing or lounging, no griping, *defense de* politics. The stiffest penalties were the unwritten ones for speaking out against Lee Kuan Yew and his ruling Chinese mafia. The dominant ideology here was a rampant anality, justified as "creating a proper climate for foreign investment." But who were we to complain? Singapore had to serve as our sanitarium, and a spot of fascism kept the wards spiffy.

First morning in ours, we had to see the doctor. This time, we made sure he'd have more diagnostic tools than a flashlight by phoning for a recommendation from the American Embassy. They directed us to the old administrative center, where the imposing bureaus left by the British curved with the sweep of the main wharf just as they did around Piccadilly. On the fourth floor of one of these monuments, we found a living monument, stolid as the gray stone facades. Leaning back in his armchair, a view of the anchored sampans' swaying masts in the harbor beyond, he was the perfect specimen of empire's true and tireless servant, distinguished enough to have retired long ago to some cottage in Kent, but staying on out of sheer pluck. He might have been a stock character out of all those films based on Dickens, as played by Finlay Currie. His eyebrows were bushy, his manner belonged to a trusted family retainer, all the stints at exotic stations had not killed off a tolerant Scottish lilt to his voice. Thumbs in his vest pockets, he listened to our symptoms and announced, "Ah, me, children, it's not so uncommon. It's nothing but a spot of dengue fever, you see."

That sounded scary, until he went off on a scholarly discourse. "The Dutch called it the 'five day fever,' most aptly. A cousin of the malaria, but it does this vanishing act. Lucky for you. Smitten by rest and vitamins. . . . Spread by the mosquito, you should know. Haven't had a case here in town since the authorities started powdering the swamps. But there's nothing to be done when the whole archipelago's a breeding ground." He leaned forward to ask, "Have you started the itching?"

We hadn't, and didn't particularly want to, but the Scottish doctor assured us that the palms of our hands and the soles of our feet would soon be wildly irritated. That was the dengue's last stand. It was, in fact, the only reliable way to confirm his findings. But he had no doubts; for him, the disease was ordinary as sniffles.

Iris and I nearly felt that we'd let the doc down. But we left his examination room elated. Now we could pin a name on our trial; we knew what to engrave on our first medals! It didn't seem to matter that we were still staggering about like vampires, or that the blue sky was a horror, its pale field of view disintegrating into gyrating molecules of blackness each time we looked up. Along the Singapore River docks, wooden dentures of barges knocked against one another chattering with the tides; but we'd reached safe harbor. In the Chinese quarters, rows of undertakers, anticipating business, tapped at the lids of new coffins; but they weren't for us. We gripped each other gleefully across single beds—like we'd received a singing telegram—in the middle of the night, that night, when the itching arrived. We could only marvel at such ingenious excruciation, while we twitched and did Al Jolson hot-cha-chas with our burning pads.

All we could do was wait for the inevitable recovery, the way Singapore's recovery awaited new businesses to set up their low wage shops. Luckily, the place did not spur reckless tourist expeditions. Singapore was trying hard to sell the spectacle of Singapore learning to look at itself, but was that really anything to look at? Most available amusements were Sunday school sedate: the parks, the aquarium, the botanical gardens. Not much pruning was needed to encourage equatorial growth, a choking of fronds or day-glo bougainvillaea. One lovely pond stocked with swans fooled us into thinking we were on the grounds of Blenheim Castle, until we noticed that even the hedges were a sign, trimmed to spell out, "Keep Singapore Clean."

Five days more recuperation from the five-day fever: we were bracing ourselves for a series of train rides through Malaysia and Southern Thailand that would take us to our planned rendezvous in Bangkok with Mack Schreiber. But the distances no longer seemed so imposing, now that we'd completed nature's most grueling excursion. When our initiation into the tropical fraternity was nearly complete, Iris and I stumbled on the perfect spot to celebrate: the Raffles Hotel. Dwarfed by Hiltons and Hyatts, its stucco propriety chipped, the Raffles still "kept face" as the archetypal colonial roost, still displayed the hand-quilled tributes from Kipling and maintained its elegant courtyard bar. Sheltered amidst the hotel's potted jungle, we had no hesitations about what to order. Two Singapore Slings, please. We pretended to be old hands, and fit right in with the other white ladies and gents who were wasting away so demurely. We shared their secret now, which was that conquerors were merely perennial convalescents.

"To the Scottish!" I toasted.

"To the itching!"

"To the longhairs!"

"To the bougainvillaea!"

"To the mosquito!"

"To the hundred-dollar fine!"

THE PLUNDER
OF PAPPA DIN

S HE GOT OFF the bus we were waiting to get on: a full-blown
Mary Pickford, too tall to be anything but Australian, with
blond curls cascading from under a straw hat, in a universal peasant
dress that was cleaner than any peasant we'd seen on the island
of Penang. The bouquet of long-stemmed calla lillies she clutched
were her match: so white and ostentatiously serene. Surrounded
by the usual crush of attentive "guides," she nonetheless radiated
a tranquility bordering on sedation. Gliding past our ill-defined
line, more like a rugby scrimmage, she twinkled at every foreigner,
suggesting that we shared her secret. But she was hardly disoriented, and must have been working the crowd with an acute
eye. She zeroed right in on Iris.

"When you get to Batu Ferringhi," she sighed, letting the tips
of her flowers ordain the communicant, "be sure to ask for Pappa
Din."

"Really? Thanks a bunch," Iris gushed back, inadvertently pun-
ning. "But what is he? A holy man?"

"Perhaps. But there's more." The breathiness nearly disguised her outback accent. "He's a master of real Malay cooking. So difficult to find."

I was relieved. We weren't receiving knowledge, just a recommendation for lunch.

"But how do we get there?" No shyness fettered Iris' quest for the genuine.

"The whole town knows him, anyone can point the way. It's a trifle off the path, mind you, but so worth it. A treasure."

"Thanks again." But the girl did not want to leave, or let go of the fervent light in her blue eyes.

"When you get there, say Deirdre sent you!" She was being tugged off by her Malaysian beaus. "These flowers . . . they're a remembrance of him!"

The line surged forward, shoving Iris into me. Despite the combat for seats, she'd been left exhilarated by the previous encounter. At last, the two of us had been party to that blather-of-mouth which was the traveler's best guide. We'd been given the boost that would lift us out of our programmed rounds and into adventure.

At last, it seemed, we were doing everything right. We'd chosen to escape the fetid confines of Georgetown, the island's main city and former trading outpost, now crawling with beach bums and moneychangers. We'd even boarded the battered silver bullet in time to land two prime spaces, just behind the driver. It wasn't until the bus had gone through its first rumba of gears that we discovered the hump of the exhaust system just under us. Our toes, exposed in their ten-yen rubber thongs, crisped like cookies on a sheet. The engine was soon at a boil, and we had no room to withdraw from the scald. What was the opposite of frostbite? On this Asian steeplechase, there were new obstacles each time around the track; one was always on some hump, never quite over it. Being able to watch the man at the wheel was no added comfort. Our Chinese driver took the curves of the island's outer edges like a gleeful runaway. With each squeal of his swampy tires, he chortled posthumous apology.

Still, where the curves broke right, I could peer down mossy cliffs at a simmering sea the color of a rusted penny. The jungle fell almost to the water, the banana plants bulging with gawdy yellow trim, marzipan fruit. The beaches that came into view along our route's centrifugal warp were shell white. They were spotlights

of sand waiting for the principals to enter stage-right and solilo-
quize. A few of the tiny littorals were welcome mats for rocky
caves whose front doors were a chain of drippings off the island's
ferny flank. Each gully was a Fernando's Hideaway. Disney could
not have done them better.

Fighting a whiff of motion sickness, I glimpsed the incarnate
character of Penang, whose name was Bahasa for "island of the
betelnut palm." O eternal silted passivity! Here came Hindu,
Chinaman, Englishman, Sultanate, Potentate. Here came Long John
Silver, no mere tourist he, marking his plunderer's stash with an
"X." Pirates pirated, traders traded, conquerors conquered (the
local one bore the fortuitous name of Sir Francis Light), accidentally making a city, in the accidental country of Malaysia, which
travel agents were now trying most purposely to turn into Asia's
quaintest beach resort. But I wasn't washed up on one of those
luscious coves, living on mangoes, hoisting my personal flag, or
manning a clandestine ship outfitted to my peculiarities. I was
toasting my tootsies in a 1946 Leyland bus with a leaky radiator
and a homicidal driver and three passengers for every seat. It was
one of travel's cruelest lessons: even while moving through countries as fast as you could, you could still only be in one place at a
time. The pictures on the posters that had lured you were always
on some distant wall, images without dimensionality and therefore
uninhabitable.

At least, in time, we came to our stop. Batu Ferringhi, which
looked to be a single Coke stand beside two palm trees growing
from one trunk to form a braided peace sign. Through the big
"V" was a well-trod path to the beach. Its sand scorched us worse
than the exhaust vent, but here we had the quick remedy of the
sea. It was indeed cooling, though the Straits of Malacca were a
murky medium, a kind of turquoise lotion in which we did not
swim, but were suspended. From off shore, the lanky palms seemed
to follow the sweep of narrow beach so precisely they looked like
a line-up of Rockettes showing off their insteps. A few anchored
junks, sails down, divided the swimming area. There were no
umbrellas or lifeguards. This stretch of beach was supervised by
a boy in shorts who strolled past with a basket of fried curry pies.
But we didn't buy them; we were off to find Pappa Din.

Back on the highway, we saw no signs of our tropical Toots
Shore, just a shack that sold souvenir shirts made from the broad

woven sacks of the Malaysia Flour Mills. If there was a town around here, it had run to the jungle for cover. A little girl showed up eventually from behind the shirt racks, but shrugged at the mention of the fabled Pops. Around the next bend we did find a roadhouse. It was just another lo mein joint, where mounds of raw noodles waited to be devoured, melting on the counter in direct sun. This couldn't be Malay food. The proprietress spoke a proprietress' English.

"Ah, Bamboo Den! Bamboo Den! Farther on you go? Why you not stop here?"

I decided to let Iris try and answer this one.

"Is Bamboo Den the same as Pappa Din?" But her stubborn exactness was met with mystification.

"Do you really think we have a choice?" I asked her back, as we continued down the steamy Rural Route No. 2. From what we'd seen so far, this place was too poor to afford dirt.

But Iris had already spotted another barefoot child up ahead and picked up our pace, shouting, "Pappa Din? Pappa Din?"

She nearly frightened him away, but at last got him to point and squeak, "Bamboo Din's!"

"Bamboo or pappa?" The boy shrugged. "Din or den?"

"What's the difference?" Iris was no longer asking directions, she was testing the populace with a random series of Rorschachs. "I want to be sure it's the real thing!"

I didn't dare suggest that our lady of the calla lillies might not have been the best judge of that, or that we would hardly find anything more "real" than the terrain through which we were tramping. No need to worry about stumbling on McDonald's in this semi-Borneo. Around a bend our bus driver would have used to bring soprano voices from Goodyear rubber, we found the overgrown hillside hacked away, crosshatched with mud lanes and crowded with lean-tos. This had to be central Batu Ferringhi, or so we hoped. The driveways bore signs that Iris insisted were family names.

"But what if they say, 'Beware the tiger'?"

I stayed several paces behind my Livingston, retreating farther when she asked for more guidance from a bare-breasted matron hanging out a wash of brown sarong streamers. She was friendly enough. Was she a Malay? As far as I could count, we hadn't seen one yet in our four days in Malaysia. The train from Kuala Lumpur had been filled with Sikhs and Singaporans whose only lineage was businessman. Georgetown's street signs and street talk were all Chinese, its restaurants nearly all Indian. In the historical museum, we'd seen exhibits of Sir Francis Light's letters, ex-Prime Minister Tun Abdul Razak's medals and medallions, a typical bedchamber of the seventeenth-century nobility, even the underwater tribes of the prehistoric coral reef. But no Malays in this patchwork land. What was a Malay anyway? And who did you have to know to get to be one?

I was beginning to think fondly of those moldering noodles a half-mile back. Before the last house at the top of the heap, near the edge of a clearing that looked like the setting of some fiendish work-camp out of a B. Traven novel, Iris gloated, triumphant as a climber at the peak. By her knees was a crooked board leaned against a rock, bearing psychedelic lettering in primary colors, which spelled out, "Pappa Din's. Real Malay Food." There was no arguing with that.

I followed Iris around a fence of corrugated tin to a shack whose front end was a patio covered with a bamboo trellis. Through a row of dim, mud-walled rooms, we could see an open-air kitchen, protected from the sliding mud by more sheets of tin. We had our choice of tables, since there were three folding card tables and no one else was here. On the center table, there was a bunch of calla lillies like Deirdre's, drying out in a vase made from an old can of evaporated milk. We sat there, and waited.

"Let's get out of here. It's obviously closed."

"Nothing's obviously anything," Iris whispered. "You should know that by now."

I knew, too, that Iris' zeal for native gastronomy stopped at nothing. She was determined to ignore all the guidebook warnings and cautions of the World Health Organization. She would probably have tried cannibalism if it was what passed for the indigenous.

I also found food to be one of the more telling cultural cross-references. Food was the only way to get through the 1970's. Still, I preferred to admire the primitive from afar, rather than ingest it. My appetite required the priming of "atmosphere." Casting about for some, I notice some glossy photos pinned against the beams of the trellis. They showed a golden-colored man with taut bags under his eyes and two tufts of black hair, like deep holes, behind each ear. In every snapshot, some visitor with flowing beard or beaded choker embraced him. At the back of the patio, there was a battered little desk that looked stolen from a kindergarten. There were menus on it. Inside the room behind the desk, on a stone slab, we saw the feet of an old man. Then we heard his snores.

"We don't want to wake him," Iris whispered again, her fear of being even the most inadvertent sort of plunderer getting the best of her.

"Great. Let's hit the wind."

Rising to leave, we were snared by an excessively pregnant woman who'd emerged from the kitchen. She did not speak, but registered surprise, then motioned forcefully for us to sit. She brought menus and went to wake the restaurateur.

"Please don't bother!" Iris called, knowing she could not be understood.

The menu had been typed in English, no doubt by one of the satisfied clientele in the photos. I had the feeling that some loosely communal, perhaps telepathic, effort was keeping this gourmet raft afloat. The food, I figured, had to be divine. There were a dozen curries offered, several soups, and all varieties of fried rice. No magic mushroom omelettes.

Pappa Din was ready to give us an audience. He stumbled forth, frail and thin as pictured, his uncombed tufts like horns. He was barefoot, in gray pants and a collarless Mandarin-style shirt, also gray. His eyes didn't have any Mandarin-style slant, just drowsiness. He spoke softly, and hoarsely, in a language neither Iris nor I had yet heard. That didn't appear to deter him. He made a joke and laughed at it. He pointed to items on the menu, to the flowers, and explained everything to himself in his arcane tongue. He made some reference to Iris' radiant beauty, or so Iris hoped, and they laughed together. I was getting hungry.

I ordered, by pointing. A chicken curry, vegetable fried rice and tea. None of the items seemed particularly Malaysian. Pappa Din nodded, then went on mumbling. Between more solicitous smiles, and the blushes that followed when she realized neither of them knew what they were smiling about, Iris did her best to order too. She tried to ask about several of the dishes, but Pappa Din's replies were just as incomprehensible as her queries. He continued chatting, coaxing, stroking the air above our heads. Yet he was not being suppliant. I got the feeling that it was not so much an honor for him to have us as it was an honor for us to have him. We had shown good judgment in seeking him out; we were welcomed as seekers; his welcome made his speech plain. He was not casting off his sleepwalking air, this Pappa Din. (At least, I presumed he was Pappa Din.) I hoped the cook was more awake. Yet I didn't hear any water boiling or clatter of dishes behind the partition. Our order hadn't even been placed.

He just hovered there: grinning, mumbling, then savoring whatever he'd imparted to himself. Iris would shrug her shoulders and he would laugh again. She looked at him to say, "Well?" He only found that more amusing. He seemed content to carry on this encounter session all day. Luckily, the pregnant waitress brought out a mottled tray bearing our lunch. Pappa Din took the saucer-sized entrées from her and proudly laid them out. None of the dishes resembled anything we'd ordered, which was not surprising, since there was no reason they should. We attempted to appreciate, and identified with some sign-language, two gnarled chunks of spice-humiliated fish, mostly a thick bone at the center of a tail section, which had been sitting so long in a lurid orange curry sauce that the bone had turned to sludge; two rounds of canned (could it be?) pineapple preserved in the same syrup; two dishes of baby food, presumed to be tapioca pudding, which Iris knew to be the product of the locally grown manioc root; and two spoonfuls of white rice. All of it was cold, amazingly colder than the air or the water or Pappa Din's eyes. Last came two glasses of lukewarm sugar cane juice with black ice floating in it.

Still Pappa Din supervised, nodding to encourage us, though he may have merely been palsied. He kept on beaming, as if to announce, "Aha, you've arrived! You, too, will be initiated!" The curried fish was days old and disintegrated when my fork jabbed at it. I did not think it would be polite to dig in while he loomed so close, and now I wished he would stay. Iris gobbled hers heartily. Interminable minutes later, our host retreated ten paces to his seat behind the tiny desk. Just above his place of honor, a flat horizontal beam, painted in the same lurid spectrum as the sign outside, seemed to crown his beatitude. On the beam were emblazoned two words: "AWAS! AWAS!"

Was this the password we lacked? The key to the unpaved highway? The opening salvo of some Indochinese Hammurabian code? Would it beckon the prophet Mohammed or the Galloping

Gourmet? It was just one more factor in the Pappa Din mystique. He was watching us so lovingly. We were his covey, his transubstantiants. I forced down the pineapple, a bit of rice, and gave up.

"Come on, worry-wart. Try the pudding!"

"I'm not hungry suddenly. It must be the heat . . ."

"But when will you ever get to try real Malay food?"

"How do you know that's what this is?"

"At least try to be polite. . . ."

I looked up from my plate and nodded toward Pappa Din. He smiled like a cat.

"I don't *have* to eat it." This was a free country. Or was it a military dictatorship?

"But it's his offering, can't you see? Food is love, right? And he's giving all he's got."

I could see that very well. If there was anything more unappetizing than a subjugated people, it was their diet: an *haute cuisine* garnished with scarcity. But if it wasn't much of a spread, at least it was theirs. What the foreign devils and traders took from them and their land hardly ever belonged to them, they could not even assess the booty for what it was worth. What use did Pappa Din have for tungsten? All he knew was tapioca.

When Iris finished everything on her side of the table, Pappa Din sprang toward us. He motioned inquisitively at my leftovers. I waved my hand in front of my closed mouth, then smiled like a debutante. Just to make sure he got the idea, I rubbed my belly to show it was full. He looked at Iris, shaking his head. Strange fellow, he seemed to mumble. He and Iris shared a good laugh. Then I was laughing, too. I was a strange fellow all right; in Malaysia, anywhere.

But Pappa Din did not clear the table. Instead of reaching for the dishes, he raised his hand significantly, pointed one finger toward a patch of open sky ("AWAS! AWAS!") and strode off. From the one drawer of the desk, he removed a bulky, loose-hinged leatherette notebook, an oversized version of the kind signature hunters used to corner their favorite celebs. He laid the book open before us, on top of our plates. Then he disappeared impishly. This was a moment for privacy: now we were part of the cult.

"I don't understand," Iris confessed, for the first time today. The contents of this holy book required not so much a leap in consciousness as a leap of faith. The flower-bearing Deirdre commanded an angelic infantry beating its way through the bush to Pappa Din's door. Each page was bordered with floral patterns, peace signs, yin-yang emblems, cartoons, and maps tracing who had gotten here from where. The centerpiece was always the same: glowing praise, in poetry and prose.

"This voyager for one has found a marvelous haven of peace. If only every man could keep his house like Pappa Din's!" Was he suggesting Pops open a chain of franchises?

Or: "The food was extraterrestrial. Ambrosia! The vibes, extraordinary. Pappa Din is a man of the heart. This place is spiritually exalted."

Or, simply: "The best food on the continent. *Il Pappa* is a stone genius!"

This had to be a mirage, like all those dappled pirate coves. But there was buried treasure here somewhere. Was the pineapple laced with some native herb that had not yet taken effect? Or were our fellow travelers just astoundingly hard-up? And if they were, what did they say for what lay ahead? More than likely, they'd just learned what we were coming to grasp, which was that the local glories were often glories because they were all the "locals" had.

Further research in the guest register turned up a few spoilsports. I didn't know much German, but from a few root words I could make out a reference to a horse's behind. One Englishman scrawled lightly, "The pudding made my spleen curdle." An American added, "Trader Vic can't hold a teriyaki candle to Pappa Din! Personally, I prefer cow patties." Feeling vindicated, I showed that last one to Iris.

"Is it all a giant put-on?" she asked.

I hadn't considered that possibility, but when I saw Pappa Din return so he could dig in the drawer for his one functional ballpoint pen, saw him hand it so cordially to Iris, saw her struggling to come up with some high-minded response to our banquet, I had to wonder if it was some kind of gag. The travelers winked at Pappa Din; Pappa Din winked back at them. Through this catalogue of hyperbole, the travelers winked at each other. The wisdom of the East was apparently nothing more than a tropical dementia, spawned through mutual, cooperative delusion.

Iris passed the blank page to me. "You're the writer!"

"No, it's all yours. I don't do Hallmark cards, or restaurant reviews."

Iris weighed the various advantages of forthrightness and tact.

"Do you think he can read it?"

"I don't see how, unless Deirdre drops by to translate."

Iris strained herself to be tactful, scribbling, "We learned something in coming here."

I refined it, down to, "We came, we ate, we were conquered." That had a better rhythm than "George Washington Slept Here."

Iris closed the book and rose to pay. Even in countries with coin shortages, she always seemed to have small change. It was all Pappa Din required, no piracy of overpricing here. Following him to the desk, Iris bumped her head against the painted beam. It was a good jolt to the noggin, but not enough to simulate nirvana. Pappa Din was quick to warn her, but he was too late. He reached for her, trying to press her down, to make her as small as he was.

"*Awas!*" he cried out, a genie leaping from his bottle at the utterance of the magic word. "*Awas! Awas!*"

I will, Pappa Din. I will.

Music:

❖

BUDDHA'S FEET

ENTER the Emerald Buddha's lair: interlocking patterns of spun glass, mosaic and gold, that mesh like low gears climbing the hill to eternal clarity. Sculpted sentries, taller than the gates they protect, glitter in chain-mail leotards, are dancers in curled slippers, forever stilled. Stalwarts rising above shimmering ramparts, their helmets cracked by Bangkok's smog, they cradle jeweled axes and seem ever about to swing them, ever about to shatter and stomp. In this courtyard nursery, the flowers that grow are fat fluted stupas that attest to the prophet's erectness before the world's quivering disorder. The earth's grubby mortality punctured with stone dildos in magenta and puce.

One skeletal fern flutters like a fan across the temple. The facade is an architectural lily that's gilded, but I don't care. Thai design is purposely hither-and-yon. The peaked roofs are sloped like the wings of great predator birds, batting to get off the ground. The sensation of flight is increased by the fluted carvings that give aerodynamic lift to the red tiles. Buildings dotted with tracers of wind, or are they the straining necks of migrating geese? Real pigeons perch, one to a flourish, confounding all allegory.

Under the corners where eaves droop, can't alight, there are curious pillars bearing brass umbrellas, half-open in hinged plates. They provide little shade from monsoon rains or subsequent sun, yet the pilgrims are having their likenesses snapped under them. These umbrellas epitomize the Buddha's wisdom-in-the-round, an awning that is the breadth and depth of all. Is this the message sought, or attested to, by single files of supplicants, mendicants, no-you-can'ts? Also priests of the Buddha, attendants of the Buddha, groupies of the Buddha, janitors of the Buddha's four-baht pay toilet? So many squatters call this national shrine a home that they overwhelm with daily chores the tiny jade relic which is supposed to be the center of all reverence. This is my first look at the rice-boiling, tea-brewing entourage of women and dependents who form the religious flotsam of Asia, seen washing up and tending to business at each holy site—but what business exactly? I know nothing of the life of these spiritual moochers, these vagrants who prefer a blessing to a park bench.

In one corridor, a lone temple-dweller takes up residence among the idols. She's a delicate young woman in brown blouse and white sarong, oval face with lost eyes. She tenderly combs her waist-length black hair, a calico cat in her lap. The bronze Buddhas on either side stare ahead, ignoring her beauty and its upkeep, which can hardly defile them. How many figurines, all in a classroom row, will make a believer out of me? How do I "get religion" when there seems to be so little to get? Must I renounce my worldly goods, my knapsack full of rash-preventing boxer shorts and my vial of Lomotil, when the Thais are obviously hanging on to whatever they've got, including their raw silk and their duck in brown sauce, their lapus lazuli and their four-eyed king? What should I make of "the city of angels," or Krung Thep in Thai, original name for Bangkok, that put-puts, motorcycle mad and mufflerless, beyond this enclave? I do not know what to call this war town without a war, frontier town without frontier, ant-heap with pretensions of karmic order; this pluralist scramble supervised by generals, this cat-house overseen by conscripted Bodhisattvas, who chain-smoke and read Hollywood fan magazines while sporting shaved frontal lobes and uniforms of draped saffron.

Best thing to do is see every Buddha. Iris and I got the Buddha blues, oh Lordy, the lowdown tourguide fixin'-to-genuflect Buddha blues. We can hardly pass up that one in the corner that's touted as pure gold all the way through. This ten-foot bracelet charm had been encased in lead for centuries, until it was accidentally cracked open. How did they drop a five-ton Buddha? Who dreamed this one up in the first place? And why is the ever-on-his-duff sage so satisfied, so appeased by the offerings that surround his pose on the teak floor like a mantle's worth of old bowling trophies? Elephant tusks, wilted geraniums, formal family portraits on stands, even photos of the very same Buddha are laid before it in mixed media tribute. Somehow black-and-white film robs the totem of its shiny sway. Would the graven image approve of its image engraved?

In the shade of covered passageways, claiming all sides, sit less valuable but equally unnamed godheads, production-line polished anonymity. Every plump, scheming deity has been chiseled with a suspect's circumspect smirk. This is a beatific police line-up, though the criminals are on pedestals. An artist on salary to the homicide squad has sculpted these types. It's God according to eyewitness reports. Will the real Gautama please rise? One is a leprechaun, one tight-lipped, one contrite. All are impassive, devoid of plea-bargaining. They confess nothing, challenging their interrogators to reveal their own truths.

Where the walls behind them are dabbed with frescoes, we get more variations on the Buddha, sitting under a favorite meditative tree. A disciple in white linen hands him a persimmon. But the gold leaf is flaking away, imparting a modern statement on the mystery inherent in mistakes. Here, a remaining smear of gold blots out the prophet's eyes, as if shielding his identity; over there, the ground he walks on is metal-flecked.

And have you seen Buddha's feet? I have. They are weightless, leave no outline, do not meet the ground. Otherwise, how could I have seen them? The feet are at the foot of a Buddha who's reclining next door, in the Wat Po, Temple of the Reclining Buddha (where else?), since even a Buddha, captured spirit, trapped light, caged emptiness, must follow humanity's predictable blueprint. This Buddha to end all Buddhas relaxes lengthwise on mindfulness' divan. He lounges in a dim coffin, built just to his dimensions of sprawl. The recliner fills all but a narrow walkway of the sepulcher. Instead of a few Catholic relics, the presumed femur bone of San Ignacio, Buddhists reconstruct their saint in his entirety, the bigger the better. He stuffs the shrine to the rafters. It's the opposite of Chartres: God is not airy, but solid. He does not ascend in "Hallelujahs!" but sinks, accepts, is a trifle bored. He slouches on one elbow, head propped by a hand that strokes his lupine, pear-shaped ear. He is not edging forward to hear the cries of hucksters outside, who sell carbon-copy rubbings from the temple walls on wrinkle-free rice paper. Buddha's eyes are dewy and clogged with mascara, a Hollywood starlet's. His hair is a brittle Rastafarian conk. His chest is smooth and unpocked; the pleats of his robes are more lustful, more animated. The Buddha's feet are unshod but by darkness.

When we can see them, we see they've been planed even by all the preacher's traipsings. "Flat-Foot Floogie with the Floy-Floy . . ." The soles are curved to bear the toes, squared-off on the bottom, resembling the shape of Moses' Sinai tablets. But they bear no strict edicts, only a representation of Buddha's ten thousand reincarnations. These are diagrammed in cartoons, etched in the jet stone by diaphanous mother-of-pearl. All that's missing from the comic strips are balloons bearing expletives. This Buddha won't even offer a "Gadzooks!"

The bottoms of his feet may be storytelling slabs, but each toe is delicately newborn and distinctly rounded. They wait to twitch and grasp and curl, to seek their proper ground with a Babinski reflex. And every black toe is again inlaid with mother-of-pearl, sister-of-pearl, son-of-pearl. They glisten in whorls cascading toward an infinite center. This is a daring touch of specificity. Our suspect has finally been foot-printed. Are these really his paws? Can any others have walked so far? Who else has been sparrow, rainbow, leaf, hound, cobra with diamond head? And did you glance upward as he passed? On which spoke of the forever slowing wheel? In what color cloak? Whose dharma dream chamber? Were you, too, in Krung Thep once?

Snapshot:

❖

THE INCURABLE STRAIN

NAKED, shivering, irresolute. Mack Schreiber can't figure out how he's gotten into such a state. He's far more adept at reconstructing catastrophes that aren't his own. And he's tried all he could to avoid this one. But Bangkok is one place where there's no point in trying. Bangkok is a town for catastrophes. They sell them, second-hand, in the doorways of Patpong Road, along with fake passports and morphine, Shan mercenaries for one's private use and slightly less private performances of "pussy blow out candle."

Mack hasn't come here to buy anything, not even contamination. He's flown in to cover his very first coup. What will it be like? Do the names of the boulevards change overnight? Is there a run on the brothels instead of the banks? Will his traveler's checks be confiscated? And can the seizure of power, the forcible rape of government, be transpiring at this moment, as he sits in a sexual holding tank with one scratchy towel draped across his groin? Sits naked, shivering, irresolute—with massage girl number seventeen on her way.

Maybe this was the way his colleagues did their "background-ing," but not Mack. Since his arrival the night before, he'd been so very conscientious. He'd checked into the Maya Guest House, a rat trap on stilts that had once catered to Vietnam troops on "r. and r." There was no such thing as "r. and r." for Mack, not even in his sleep. He had kept his short-wave radio going all night beside his pillow. He'd actually begun to dream in bulletins. There were moments as he tossed when he wasn't at all certain who was bringing him the latest from where, when he became his own "well-informed source."

But no scoops came to him from inside or outside concerning the coup, so Mack braced to seek them out. At first light, he sprang into action. He slipped his People's Republic "happi coat" over a back that looked like the ninth moon of Jupiter, the result of acne brought on by his "nervous condition." But that condition was the primary tool of his work, enabling him to keep up with a nervous world. The Chinese script on Mack's robe read, "Be tranquil," but the motto he muttered, borrowed from a seasoned Asia hand, was "Keep showering, keep shitting!" Mack trotted through the bamboo divider to the toilet, where he tried to comply with both commands. The more seasoned he'd gotten, the more wary he'd become of "bugs." He ushered them through his system quick as he could. Afterward, he swabbed himself with Wash 'n' Dri's. He brushed his teeth with bottled water. He methodically swallowed the contents of an American corner drugstore that he lugged about: antibiotics, antihistamines, antiseptics and especially antacids, in anticipation.

Then Mack reached for the telephone. Next to Gelusil, the most critical item in Mack's luggage was his address book. What good was a journalist without his "contacts"? Mack had learned, without much effort, how to harvest such people for free guidance, free rumors, free meals, free beds, free women—no, he'd still not accepted the latter. In an hour, Mack filled up his week, setting up many more appointments than he could keep, even landing an invitation to the foreign correspondents' club buffet at the Hilton. Best of all, Mack's very own coup, was that he'd reached a leftist reporter named Thanam, one contact he'd kept in his book since the antiwar days, who he'd cash in for the real dope. They would meet in the afternoon. Mack figured that anyone he wasn't able to reach would probably be downstairs, in the Rama's open-air coffee shop.

Sure enough, there was Raffson, a junior BBC man, with

thinning orange hair and the perpetually crumpled look of a lost public school boy; Nyls, his puppyish and usually stoned cameraman; and Hal Nations, rumored to be a CIA agent and much too purposely looking the part in sunglasses and ascot, contributing editor to some obscure economics journal, a magazine no less prestigious than he was besotted. These were the jaded Bangkok regulars, and Mack knew they viewed him as green and far too enterprising. But he couldn't avoid joining them for scrambled eggs and slabs of fresh papaya. Over breakfast, they assured him he'd arrived on schedule. "The duly elected government doesn't last three days," said Nations. "You can bet your next bush jacket on it."

Nyls and Raffson wanted to wager something else: one live "LBFM." Mack soon learned that this new bit of colonialist lingo stood for "Little Brown Fucking Machine." It was more convenient to abbreviate, especially when sending telexes on company money. "Six LBFM's await your arrival," they'd cabled friends, and Mack didn't doubt it, considering how hard they'd tried to set him up with one. Last visit, they'd taken him on the complete whoring tour, from the Mississippi Mermaid, where a locally infamous set of twins—who could be rented out ensemble—danced on the bar in nothing but go-go boots to the Grace Hotel, once a stodgy retirement home that now boasted a lobby so crammed with saleable bodies of indeterminate gender that its population density rivaled the walled city of Lahore. "Let's go right now!" Nyls proposed, "Before the generals spoil our fun!" But Hal Nations gave Mack more grounds to beg off.

"It's a miracle that these boys haven't caught the incurable strain." This was a formidable new bug, resistant to all Mack's pills. "One dose of that, and they put you on a slow boat up the Irawaddy River."

It occurred to Mack, at breakfast, that there were other reasons why he didn't want to become one of the boys—though he would have "lost face" to speak them. Losing face was something he was more and more concerned about, the longer he stayed in Asia. Mack knew he was different from most of those prowling this hedonist beat. He was no self-proclaimed exile or malcontent. He hadn't fled to tropical climes because of defeatism or self-disgust; he was pursuing a sincere passion that had begun when he started taking private Chinese lessons in the ninth grade. Being in Asia, for Mack, was an extension of being a good Jewish success story, the obedient son of respected academics. He wasn't straying so far as it seemed, and had little desire to wander with the callous and pillaging army of "men with Yen." He wanted a woman, yes, but one woman would do. Besides, he'd supported the feminist cause since college days, and seen little in the Orient to make him transfer sympathies. He prayed that he would never see women as "brown fucking machines," see the local populace as "low Mexicans, universal peasants"—which Raffson called them in his best Etonian drawl. He wasn't itching for more My Lai massacres to cover, for the excitement of "another juicy war." He was like the others around the table only in that he had no one to sleep with that night.

Mack was relieved to escape the coffee shop panderers. He was pleased that he could excuse himself for an afternoon of checking the wire services. He didn't tell them about his date with Thanam; he wanted this source all to himself. Hitting the streets at last, Mack didn't mind that those streets were hazy with monoxide and the fumes of burnt rice. He hailed a wobbly samlor, the motorized tricycle with covered bench in back, that was Bangkok's version of a cab. The driver steadied the bike with both legs, preparing to haggle for the fare. Mack was prepared, too.

"Four baht," he offered, asking to be dropped near the network bureau.

"Eight baht," came the reply.

"Five baht!"

"Seven baht!"

"Six baht!"

"Okay!" The joys of the East!

Too bad the wire services gave no hint of a coup, no matter how many hours Mack scanned. And Thanam, waiting in the slow tropical dusk at the entrance to a university cafeteria, turned out to be a tame-looking contact. He looked to Mack like an Asian Peter Lorre. His English was impeccable and so was his grooming. Only the man's unsquelched impishness gave some hint that he might be a link to the radical Thai underground. Also his driving. After the obligatory pot of tea, Thanam proved determined as Raffson to careen through the night, to cruise Bangkok's sinuous arteries. "Cruise" was Thanam's favorite word.

That was sure easy to do, in this "city of angels" so like its

California counterpart. The same convenient Los Angeleno tags applied: sprawling, sooty, impersonal, unrestrained by good taste or the past. Bangkok was one of the few capitals of the East that was Americanized rather than Anglicized. It flattered with imitation the coffee shop, the western wear round-up, the supermarket, the shopping mall, the plastic shrub, the billboard, the eight lanes of asphalt. Endless traffic turned in gears of huge rotaries; boulevards fed one another in grandiose interchanges, where hovering clouds of exhaust twisted loosely to form smoggy knots. But many of the most modern avenues were still divided by klongs—excremental ditches, oily canals—where unidentified corpses floated up with the sewage. Mack was dizzy. There were too many rotaries, radiating too many alleys that reeked with cilantro and fish sauce and shit. Too much darkness, too much for sale. Bangkok, from the passenger seat, was slithery and portentous, all entrails. It was a battleground, too, but this evening a truce was in effect.

Mack wanted to learn more about the politics that dictated such a truce, but his guide steered him to an outdoor arena for the nightly card of Thai boxing. Was there a story for Mack in these rickety bleachers? Placing immediate bets, fans bobbed up and down like stock exchange runners, nearly oblivious to the parade of peasant boys below. Entering the ring, they bowed before Lord Buddha, then proceeded to kick each others' kidneys out. At dinner afterward, Mack hoped for an entrée to some student leader in hiding, but the only entrée Thanam gave him was a bowl of prawn soup chock with peppers. While Mack gagged, Thanam chortled, "The revenge of the oppressed!"

Would this be Thanam's only stab at analysis? Cruising again, Mack kept at him until Thanam mused, "Thailand's pageant marches through many dynasties, and the worst horrors come as no surprise." He hung a reggie. "The deadline for the removal of the last U.S. bases is just a pretext, the bell ringing for round one. Whichever general emerges must save face by getting the Americans to go, but, as you see, the Americans will remain." He hung a louie. "In the meantime, the left and the right will bow formally and slit each other's throats. The right will do a better job because rightists always suffer from deficiencies in conscience. It's their great advantage." He burnt rubber. "The coup will happen between lunch and brunch and shuffleboard, as arranged by the social director of a Hawaiian cruise." Stop light. "Yes, the government in the middle is bound to fall. What is a government anyway but a working arrangement by which some men take orders from other men?"

Thanam was awfully philosophical for someone who might lose his job and be forced to flee for the hills. Journalistic obligations met, he asked Mack, "You wanna banana split?"

Mack was getting worn down with surprises, and considered that Thanam might be testing him, trying to sucker him into some act of Yankee chauvinism. But it was Thanam who declared, "Mmmmm. I go for it!"

No wonder the left was in trouble! Thanam took Mack to a reasonable facsimile of an Indiana luncheonette, complete with red leatherette booths and waitresses in paper tiaras. The piped-in banjo music was authentically rinky-tink and so were the sundaes, which they wolfed down with authentic speed.

That was when Thanam proposed "one more treat for tonight." Mack acted like he didn't know what that meant, though he knew how all nights in Bangkok ended. Mack gave in because, with Thanam, he didn't have to feel like he was yielding to a white man's privilege. And because he was curious.

Thanam drove on, slowing only when he could point across stalled traffic at a concrete cube that rose six stories and occupied a full block. There were no windows in the front of this huge vault. It looked like a Southern California Savings and Loan. The entrance was around the back, discreet as a hospital emergency ramp. The driveway's welcome for the ailing was a wide fountain, set in a pink-lit marble dish, that sprayed with monotonous suggestion. Thanam gave his car to the waiting valet and Mack followed. There were no solid portals to pass through, just tiers of short steps leading from one overhang to the next. A sign in Thai script flashed the name of the establishment, but to Mack it was just a purple neon doodle. "Fragrant Rose Club," Thanam read.

The levels of stairs became levels of lobby. They were now walking on soft carpeting, past rows of flower arrangements lit with crouching spots, interrupted by alcoves displaying plaster Buddhas. Where there were paintings, they did not depict voluptuous majas, but the stages of the coconut harvest, sentimentalized in honey colors. In each new foyer, the moods and textures were of one piece—everything modern and carpeted. This was no parlor, it was a think tank; not sin, but industry. What had happened to the shabby, rickety whorehouses of Somerset Maugham stories? There were no ceiling fans, bamboo curtains, crippled attendants. Instead, a fastidious maître d' who attached himself to Thanam. They chatted like two old friends, perhaps because they were. Mack wondered which political faction the "Fragrant Rose" endorsed.

Their host led them to the first and final door, a point of no return that was solid teak. It opened onto an l-shaped terrace, a long indoor café with a bar against one wall, yellow parasols above the round tables. Mack hadn't seen any females yet, but guessed they were getting closer by the frantic tone of the café chatter. The men here were boldly Teutonic, plenty drunk and ruddy and raucous, and no doubt shipped over from Frankfurt on "sex tours." Were they flushed because they'd just finished their "massages," or because they were getting tanked up enough to start? They didn't look in any hurry, so comfy and pink. Was the vagina itself but one sodden *bierstube*? When the host suggested refreshments, Mack wanted no part of them. But neither did he want to choose a girl.

It was a Herculean task, since the staff was on display through a one-way mirror that faced the whole length of the bar. On a staggered platform long as a bowling alley, they sat in identical sky-blue gowns. These women were fish set in an aquarium tank— no more think tank—and Mack wondered how often they were fed. There were at least a hundred in this school, scaled in imitation satin, so many it was hard to differentiate between catches. There may have been all varieties here, but the enforced anonymity of this efficient set-up robbed them of the eccentricities required for sexual appeal. Worst of all, each lady had a number pinned to the strap of her dress. These prisoners all faced one corner of the room, staring at a television, chatting listlessly, waiting for the warden to bark out their number.

Mack wasn't sure he could go through with it. How could he appraise these beings so coldly? And how would he explain to his choice about the incurable strain? He asked for one who spoke English, and the host assured him they all did. Well then, he could just get a massage. He could play it safe while not "losing face." Or so he told himself. Mack and Thanam leaned too eagerly against the glass, little boys before a candy store window. Mack had to admit, he liked what he saw. Thai women were fabled through the Orient, and their appeal to Americans seemed particularly clear. With their high waists and higher cheekbones, autumn moon skin, fairy tale princesses' black manes, they were the absolute antonyms of the Saxon brownie-bakers back home. They gave the word "lithe" a devastating new meaning.

The maître d' kept reeling off numbers, but Mack couldn't find them. He didn't want to have a girl foisted on him, when all of this had already been foisted on him. He noticed a very dainty, very thin one, with cropped hair, a nose with colt's flared nostrils and a dress already off one shoulder. "What about number seventeen?" When he was complimented on his choice, Mack worried all the more. If she was popular, she was more likely to be diseased. But he wasn't going to do anything. He wasn't!

"Does she give a good massage?" Mack asked. Thanam and the manager chuckled.

"All girls give Thai-style massage. Very relaxing."

When Mack asked how much it would cost, Thanam chuckled again. "Please do not worry. I keep a running tab."

Still, Mack assured him he would only need a half-hour, the minimum.

"Don't watch the clock," Thanam told him, understanding nothing. "You Americans must learn to take your time."

Number seventeen had stood up and was coming through the door near where Mack stood. He could not look at her, but felt her grab his left hand. With the right, he waved goodbye, playing the condemned man. Now he was purposely provoking the other men's laughter: it washed over Mack like forgiveness.

Number seventeen led him down a narrow, pinkish chute. *Très* fallopian, with doors on both sides. She deposited him in the second room on the left. She showed him the rack of clean towels, motioned for him to undress, giggled at his hesitancy and was gone. She took off so suddenly that Mack was certain he'd been ditched, until he remembered that no one had taken his money. He still wished he'd been dumped, that the poor girl would spare both of them an awkward scene by never returning. But he was stuck with her, stuck with all this time to review how he'd got here.

What is number seventeen doing anyway? Making a last-minute inspection for chancres, Mack hopes. And what is he doing, except sitting pockmarked and cold? The couch where he waits is hard, one cushion upholstered in a Thai highlands tartan, set on a concrete platform built into one wall of the narrow cubicle. The lighting here is also dim and pinkish, slightly engorged, but pulsating off tiled floors and walls. Mack feels sealed-in, chink by chink, the way he did when he'd been taken, as a kid, to see the full-sized replica of a Pharaoh's burial chamber at the Metropolitan Museum. At least, this tomb is more hygienic. At the back, separated from the bed by a low divider of more tile, there's a massive tub. Beside it, on the floor, sits a navy blue air mattress, much like the ones Mack used to ride Cape Cod's tame surf. He shudders to think what sort of rides are given on this float. But the room smells just like a Howard Johnson's and the bath appeals to Mack. There's no social disease he can catch from hot water.

He trusts that number seventeen's English will be good enough for her to understand that he only wants a bath. When she returns, unobtrusive as a fragrance slipping through the door, she does not appear to understand Mack's "Hello, I'm Mack. . . . I've never done this before."

"Macka? . . . What you want do? Please English slow."

So this girl's talents are not entirely as advertised: Mack keeps his fingers crossed that the rest of her is also a come-on.

"What's your name?" he tries, working on his radio delivery.

"Udorn," she answers. "Udorn in North."

The name will do, even if it is not who she is, but where she is from. And Mack is from America, that much gets through. The rest may have to remain mystery, a literal and trans-literal groping.

The girl stands just a few inches from where Mack sits, the belt of her gown at kiss level and already partly undone. She finishes the job, letting the slinky stuff run off her like rainwater, revealing a body more lean and unblemished than he imagined. She stands on one foot, scratches her neck, and lets Mack look for as long as he likes. She has the body of an animal, he thinks, which is not the way he thinks of his own. It is the body of anyone you don't know, only better. Mack likes her hair, trimmed short and, at the back, to a peak that's the shape of a split diamond. Her collarbone nearly pierces the skin, a symmetrical necklace above faintly pigmented nipples. There's little pubic fur, conjuring up images of kiddie porn. It is like a large mole down there. Mack has to admit that he wants to examine it. He assumes this costs extra, and holds himself back. Besides, he doesn't want number seventeen to get the wrong idea. Is there any room for right ones inside this hot oblong box?

"Macka?" She is getting tired of exhibiting herself, so he feels obliged to put his arms around her. Her waist is so small they could go around twice. Touching brings her alert. Udorn shakes her hair, shaking out demons, and her penciled eyes flash messages up, down and around the tiles—finally at Mack.

"Very nice boy."

"I bet you say that to all of them. . . ."

"What? What say?"

"Nevermind."

"You touris'?"

"No, I'm a journalist." Mack can't see why he should be proud of that here, but he is. He would show her his press pass, if he had it, or anything, on him.

"Good! Fragrant Rose special for journalists." Did she really say "flagrant"? "Udorn good friend for journalists. You need friend for whole visit?"

"I don't need friend."

"No? I think journalists need friend. Far away from wife, yes?"

"I have no wife."

"I see, young boy." But not as young as her. "You come for coup?"

"Yes. How did you know?"

"I know journalists. Always come for big stories only." Now she imitates one, trying to look serious. "*Exclusive!*"

The laughter makes Mack hold her tighter.

"Who taught you to say that?"

Udorn answers with the name of a highly regarded newspaperman, one of Mack's early idols.

"Listen," she continues. "Journalists always quick, fly in and out. Journalists expert at in and out, no?"

"And who taught you that?"

What follows is a who's-who of the foreign press. Suddenly, this girl is more than a body. She's an information source, a comrade of the front lines! And she's so comfortable with herself, so unashamed. White slavery with a human face! Mack is beginning to see why Raffson and the others stationed here can hardly keep their attention on anything else. Still, Mack can't believe that all Bangkok's prostitutes are this genial. Perhaps she's just here to run his bath. The proper term for Udorn may be "courtesan," exemplar of an ancient tradition, trained in numerous variants of hospitality. Mack now recalls that Udorn is near an American air base, one of those about to be closed, and that the whores there have recently been taking to the streets in protest of the closing, carrying placards that read, "We Love You, GI Joe," and, "Americans, Please Stay and Keep Us Warm." Mack has been told that the bond between Thai women and American men is not strictly economic, that many of the girls actually prefer the puritan and often deferential rednecks to their own preening, haughty and offhandedly brutal men. He has always dismissed such talk as yet another racist justification. Until now.

Number seventeen laughs ingenuously, and pecks at Mack's cheek without the least prodding. Slouching back onto the seat beside him, she slips one leg across his thigh. She plays no tricks, she neither rushes nor teases him. She waits calmly to do Mack's bidding, but Mack no longer knows what that bidding will be.

"You like Bangkok?" They are two naked people, having a conversation on a bus.

"Yes. Very much."

"You stay in Rama Hyatt?"

"No, no. The Maya Guest House."

"Maya Guest? No good. I find you nice house."

"No time for nice house."

"If you like, I come stay with you in nice house. Cook and clean. Go for weekend to Phuket Beach. Very nice swim. Very good dancing. I be your Thai wife. Even send Christmas card."

Once more, Mack is confounded. He's refused, for so long, to become a typical Asian whoremonger because he's believed, steadfastly, that the girls were not merely to be bought and sold, couldn't just be "LBFM's," but were individuals, too. Now that Udorn's showing him just how individual, his logic's been tossed upside-down. Then, too, there's still the matter of microbes.

He doesn't want to hurt her feelings, but he has to ask, "Udorn. Are you clean?"

She laughs again, to put him at his ease. She's been asked this question many times.

"I'm very clean girl. Always taking baths!"

Not very helpful, but the reply's buttressed with a guileless stare and besides, she can't be a carrier. She's slept with nearly every network's Bureau Chief.

"You want bath now? You better, you get cold."

"All right."

"Jus' all right?" She strokes his chin, shrugs her creamy shoulders and hops the few steps toward the tub. She stoops to adjust the water and Mack counts every vertebrae. He follows her to the wide edge of the tub where they stand awkwardly, outer thighs touching in the rising steam. Mack's body and hers are remarkably similar, both wiry and dark, though her complexion hasn't been ravaged by antibiotics and stress. Still, they might have been Eve and Adam in an Eden with faucets.

Mack can't wait for the tub to fill, so he'll be able to keep himself from an embrace. He steps in while it's too hot, but bears it, leaning on Udorn's shoulder. She coaxes him further down, with light finger pressure on his hips. He sinks back, scalded to the chin, and lets the bath do its job. Water is water everywhere, and with the temptation of Udorn temporarily removed, he nearly forgets where he is. Soon enough, she is sitting on the square rim and starts rubbing Mack with a hard black sponge she wears like a glove. It's not in her training or her nature to leave him alone— he's not come here to be alone, has he?—and when Mack opens his eyes to see her leaning over him, working away so diligently, he can't help blubbering, "Your breasts are sad eyes." Udorn doesn't understand. Mack laughs, sinking back below the water line. She is turning him this way and that, scrubbing every rutted square inch of Mack. He's not catching the incurable strain, he is getting rid of the one he carries with him all the time.

Mack doesn't want to get out, ever. Just when he's convinced that he's had the full treatment, Udorn climbs in. Without solicitation, she lies back with her head against the tub's opposite end, raising the bath level until they are both nearly drowned. Beneath the swell, number seventeen twines knees, presses her matted crotch to his. Mack pretends that the heat keeps him from noticing the underwater clasp. He is thoroughly muddled. What's a whore if not someone who goes along unwillingly and ungraciously? The customer pays for coldness, he's always figured, pays to be reminded that he has to pay. That's why Mack has been resisting. The girl moves up and down mechanically, and mechanically, Mack's soggy penis responds. Udorn is content.

"In and out, right? . . . If you like, I bring phone. You call in story from bath. Very nice. No need for interruption. . . ." And she tells him about the time she did just that for yet another distinguished correspondent. Mack doesn't know whether to be jealous or reassured. Everyone does it; he already knew that. Everyone needs it, he is being reminded. Especially the successes who fly in and out.

When Udorn feels he's properly stimulated, or tires of waiting for some signal which Mack is still unwilling to give, she stands delicately and gets out. She touches Mack's shoulder to see if the bath has yet pared skin from muscle. She does not dry herself, but first brings a gigantic towel meant for Mack.

He lets her dry him, hold him through terry cloth. O, what sordid cleanliness! But the bathing isn't over. Next comes his first lesson in the use of the air mattress. Mack is shoved playfully down onto it. He lies on his chest while Udorn sloshes water out of the tub and onto the tiles. She scoops with the methodical fervor of a washerwoman, causing her nakedness to look momentarily absurd. Why is labor equated with clothes? Mack can feel himself rising on the shallow cove she's made for him. He floats. Fresh steaming water and a perfumed lather are applied to his back. Udorn knows how to make suds. Mack is on a liferaft of love, cushioned by air, enveloped in bubbles. The point of all this sloppy mirth soon becomes clear. Udorn climbs atop him and grinds herself into the suds and Mack. So this is the advertised "Thai-style" treatment! Udorn is a human wash cloth, practitioner *extraordinaire* of the full-body technique, rotating her breasts against his shoulder blades, using her toes and kneecaps to scrape Mack's dangling nerves raw. She yanks him from back to front, then climbs astride and rubs anew, matching every possible combination of anatomical friction. She does this in a purposeful silence, punctuated by their skin squeaks. Mack feels too pampered. It doesn't seem right that paper money, with a king's picture on it, can buy all this.

There's nothing left but a collapse on the plaid loveseat for complete meltdown. Shouldn't such activity have come first? Mack's resolve is being flushed away in stages, and he can only hope now that he'll be saved by the timekeeper's bell. This hasn't all happened in a half hour, has it? While he sits upright, staring down at his belly to spy the new openings in his pores, Udorn lays across his knees, laying all the way down, and writhing a trifle.

"Macka!"

"Macka no . . . Mack no fuck." That word sounds awful. It sounds worse than "imperialism." Number seventeen does not appear to understand either.

He points to his penis. It's gotten too damp this time, too flooded for an erection. As he points, the dampness wears off. If only they could just continue talking!

"Udorn. You like Americans?" He will do an interview. Yes, he can get a story out of this. "Thai Politics—The View from the Massage Parlor." This is one angle the wire services have clearly overlooked.

"Sure. Nice guys."

"Do you want the Americans to leave?"

"What you think?" Her hand is on his penis. "Journalists, they ask only about what they already know."

She's right, about that and so many things. Mack is tempted to ask, "Udorn, when is there going to be a coup?"

"Very soon. Any day!"

"How do you know?"

"Boys like you tell me. Generals and policemen, not just journalists. . . . All come to Fragrant Rose massage. And Fragrant Rose must know! Must satisfy customers!"

Which includes pumping his penis, which includes reclining and opening her legs. Udorn makes a sign for him to lie down there, between her. Mack begins to comply, when she makes another sign: the open palm.

So she does want something extra! Mack is happy again, given a last means to be spared. He shakes his head firmly, the way he's learned to shake it when bargaining with the samlor drivers. He waits for Udorn to play her end of the game. Instead, she lies back, ever more compliant. She laughs a laugh that does not need translation, that says, "Do it anyway!" Her attempt to get a tip had been *pro forma*. Now that he knows, Mack inadvertently baits her by reaching for his pants. He doesn't want to seem cheap; he finds several bills.

"Okay!" Udorn spreads further.

"Not for that," Mack tries to go stern. "For you!"

"For information?" she teases. She is, Mack concedes, a sharp cookie.

And now, as he plays with her shaving brush's worth of mons, he can't help showing more appreciation, and he lays over her, but without touching, as though doing push-ups.

"Come on, Macka. I won't tell!"

He is aching to mount her, but his hypochondria—and something else, something more trustworthy, more ingrained—further forestalls his instincts. He sees a headline, "Promising Correspondent Succumbs to Fatal Clap!" And another, "Good Jewish Boy Goes Bad!" And a third, "Mack Schreiber Grows Up!"

He can't decide which of them is worse, or best. He is straining to keep from entering Udorn, humping her instead by using her underfed belly as slack. Udorn's giggling tells Mack she suspects that he does not know how the act is properly done. She starts pushing on his buttocks, pushing him further down. Then mistakenly, miraculously, he is in. He risks everything.

For what? Udorn isn't giggling anymore and her eyes are shut, very tight. She is a birthday girl trying hard to make a wish. Mack studies the face of number seventeen in submission, under his shadow. She looks properly flattered and fearful, and very very foreign. He doesn't entirely like what he sees, so he buries himself in the nape of her neck. Both Mack's hands cradle her diadem of locks. He rubs flesh against flesh: Caucasian against Asian, shockingly the same. He meets membrane with membrane: another white man using a faintly brown, a tad yellow woman. He is doing as history commands, and in following that command, he escapes. He is one of the boys. He is finished.

"I won't tell, Macka," number seventeen murmurs. "I won't tell. *Exclusive!*"

ELEPHANTS AT PLAY

Could Chiang Mai have looked so wondrous as I imagined it? My vision of Thailand's "Rose of the North" was a city with petals for cobblestones, wind chimes for sirens, perambulating Buddhas for cops. But the tremulous lanes and filigreed ramparts of my revery were ground to gravel by all-too-real Pepsi emblems, dust storms and unmuffled taxis and shabby, leftover GI clubs like the "Buffalo Bill." There were temples, too—their grounds caked with chipped mosaic and cow dung—but these were outnumbered by the usual hangouts for "Occidentals," unromantic outdoor cafés featuring fried rice and papaya frappes, that lined the city's rectangular and stagnant moat. Along the strip, one-man companies offering excursions into the nearby hill country hung out their shingles. Promising a weekend of guaranteed primitive experience with a guaranteed unspoilt tribe, one outfit bore the telltale name of "B.S. Coach Tours." Another sold rides to the teak forests for a one-hour performance of "Elephants at Work." Next door was the big daddy: "Mister Moo's Tribal Tours."

Through Mack Schreiber, we'd found our own Mister Moo. He was called Kittaporn, a rather common Thai name. What wasn't so common was that his name was the only fact about him of which

Mack was sure. Accompanying us to the north in hopes of unearthing a sixty-second's spot worth of objective truth on the fellow, Mack took half the night's train ride to enumerate the difficulties of such an assignment. Over a bottle of stinging Mekhong whiskey, in hushed tones that kept his speculation from becoming known to a pair of soused generals at the next table in the dining car, Mack reviewed, and relished, his subject's aptitude for intrigue. Was Kittaporn a former CIA agent caught smuggling drugs, or had he really been a former drug smuggler caught working for the CIA? And what was he now, given what he may have been then? What about the other Thai arrested with him, who'd committed suicide in the States? Kittaporn's trial in a Midwestern city had made quite a splash. He'd eventually been released and deported to save the Agency further bad press. Now the hometown papers were hungry for a "follow-up." So was Mack, who phoned the ex-spy right from the Chiang Mai train station. Kittaporn's willingness to be interviewed the following day, along with an offer to take Mack for a ride through one corner of the infamous "Golden Triangle," raised a whole set of new questions.

By the next afternoon, Mack was worked up into his best foreign correspondent's frenzy, already writing leads and popping Gelusils. A long taxi ride toward Chiang Mai's sparse and swampy version of suburbia gave him time to explain once again—still whispering, as if the cabbie might be in on the plot—why he wanted Iris and me along as witnesses, as "insurance" against being penalized for his curiosity. We were thrilled to comply.

The secret agent's lair looked new enough to be a Thai condo, but the materials were time-honored, lots of bamboo. The design was also suited to the tropics: a first floor that was open to fresh breezes and neighbors, a second-story loft for strawed-in privacy. Approaching this house with front wall removed felt like stepping into a stage set for Maugham's *Rain*.

"The traditional form of construction," Mack buzzed, as if that were another bit of intelligence. "We've got to leave our shoes by the gate."

We did so, and waited for someone to appear on the proscenium. In the meantime, we studied the set: a modern Danish couch, desk and bookshelves. Ever intrepid, Mack called out the two Thai words he knew. Neither meant hello. Still, a tall woman wrapped in a single piece of cloth glided down from the loft. In the crook of one arm, she balanced a baby. From what Mack had told us about Kittaporn, we were ready to believe that both madonna and child might be part of the spy's well-constructed cover. But this young wife certainly looked genuine; her offspring was nursing. She blushed, beckoning us to step inside the play.

"Please be at home, thank you!"

That had to be Kittaporn, shouting from upstairs with barely a trace of accent. We looked up and saw the head of a tennis racket and one incongruous leg in sneakers and white shorts dangling through the trap door. "My wife speaks no English, thank you. . . . I've just come from teaching tennis lessons. Must change. I'll be a moment, please."

This Kittaporn was clearly a man of varied skills. While we tried out his couch, the wife brought us tea in thimble cups. Mack nudged me in the ribs so I'd take note of Kittaporn's library. It was a spy's collection all right, full of Eric Ambler and Simenon thrillers, exposés of "the Company," lots of E. Howard Hunt and Watergatiana. But would a real spy keep such reading so plainly in view?

Kittaporn descended. He was diminutive, his face compact, with high cheekbones and skin like recycled newsprint. Thai men tended to be slight and feline, but their effeminacy was the effeminacy of the gunfighter. These delicate Zen dandies were known to carry hip pistols, beat their wives and swig that potent Mekhong malt.

It was hard to imagine Kittaporn playing Asian *bandito*. It was even harder to envision how such a gentlemanly specimen could have survived six months in a U.S. County jail. Nattily dressed in tailored gray slacks, native silk shirt and country club loafers without socks, he made a thoroughly credible tennis pro. He greeted us with a worldly, dignified warmth that made us feel he'd been anticipating our visit for years, not days or minutes.

"Your journey was not too wearing, I trust?"

"It was terrific," Mack spoke, without asking for a consensus. "Lots of high army brass on the train. Any idea why?"

"So you're starting in on your story already, friend!" He teased Mack, shaking all our hands in turn. "I'm afraid you won't find one here."

"You can speak freely around us," Mack assured him, with no particular logic.

"No, no, my friend, life is very sedate now. I play tennis for my keep, as you see. I've been hired also as a guide by a group of horticulturists from New Zealand. United Nations types. That's how I support my poor wife and child. As I speak many of the tribal tongues, Lahu, Meo, and such, I still have some skill to offer the foreigners."

"As you did during the war?"

Kittaporn laughed. "Yes, thank you."

"You are Lahu yourself, correct?" Mack surprised him.

"Yes. By birth only. . . . You have been reading your newspaper clippings!"

"I try."

"Sometimes it helps to come from a tribe. Just this morning I met with an Australian economic minister. You see, I've been chosen by the government to be a representative for the displaced mountain peoples," he told us, erecting the shield of such status. "I must tell them what the mountain peoples say to their investment schemes, thank you. The King himself has called such a meeting. . . . These officials are a gang of damned fools."

He went on, illustrating the point. "Chiang Mai is ruled by suspicion. I am no longer trusted by my own people to hold down a job."

"Except by the King?"

Kittaporn let Mack's prod pass.

"Anyway, there are advantages. The New Zealanders have left me their Land Rover. See it parked across the way there? We'd might as well make use of it, don't you think?"

"We'll go anywhere you'd like to take us," Mack's enthusiasm echoed strangely.

"Very splendid. He's a good reporter, isn't he?"

"The best," Iris answered with a wink.

"And you? Are you the best travelers?"

"Just average."

"Could we see an opium-growing village?" Mack asked. "Or are they off-limits these days?"

"Oh, no. They are for tourists and innocents." Did he mean us? "I am currently involved with one such place, thank you. As a sort of lawyer for the community." Kittaporn added another profession to his list. "You see, the Thai police, from the narcotics control division, as it's called, had come to make their yearly pickup of the raw opium. They were 'on the take,' as I learned to say in your country. They had an agreement with the Meos, an arrangement rather, very regular. But on this occasion they decided to act like the police, if you see what I mean, and confiscated the goods. They simply didn't pay for the delivery."

"What happened?"

"What do you suppose happened? You are a reporter. Three of them were shot and killed on the spot, thank you. Half the village was arrested and charged with murder, though they've all been released since. I must do my best to defend them."

"And why did they choose you to do it?"

"Well, I'm an old friend. My client knows the quality of my services," Kittaporn smiled faintly. "Shall we visit this place?"

"If it's not too much trouble."

But trouble, like the hills, was home for Kittaporn. We left his wife breastfeeding the child. He didn't say a word to her. Mack got in the front seat of the jeep while Iris and I rode the metal benches in the covered back bed. Kittaporn drove Thai-style, passing recklessly on blind curves and hitting the horn instead of the brakes when obstacles slowed his progress. Iris and I studied the slower traffic powered by water buffalo. We skittered remarkably close to a pack of elephants: veritable armored vehicles. They tramped calmly down the recently laid highway's emergency lane, just like Barnum & Bailey's best, with their trunks wound affectionately around the tails of the ones ahead of them. Big schoolkids holding hands at the safety crossing. Depicted so often in souvenir shop hangings, folk drawings, and silk pillowcases that they'd become purely decorative motifs to us, we were pleased by this confirmation of the models' existence. On fabric, or in the landscape, they were such patient friends. Overtaking them, we picked up the elephants' scent: no sawdust or peanuts, just the faint perspiration of their labored march.

"The elephants at work!" Iris reminded me.

These had to be the elephants on coffee break. The elephants in transit. What was their per diem? Maybe they were the elephants on vacation, like us. Tourists who didn't need to take snapshots, just consult their fabled memories. They looked like the elephants at peace. I wanted to see the elephants at play.

Kittaporn wrenched us off the main road and we began climbing.

Where these hills began, so did all stripes of insurgency. Here Asia's tribes, as numerous and tenacious as Africa's, if less celebrated, put the concept of nationhood to the challenge of indifference and the test of automatic weapons. Each country we'd visited had its nomadic fringe, but none was so alluring as Thailand's. Proud Siam, unconquered for so long by the Europeans, was still unable to form its own boundaries. A hundred hands clutched at this disputed bit of geometry formed with drowsily militant Laos and xenophobic Burma, a hundred bribes offered to procure the triangle, a hundred gangs sought to muscle its illicit trade, a hundred ideologies wrestled to tame it.

Iris and I bucked on the ribbed benches, which resembled tool chests but may have been rifle cases. Now the back wheels spun up the topsoil of winding back roads, covering us with a rich brown flour that blew through the flaps. We were heading through an unclaimed buffer zone toward a country within a country. The valleys were modest, a murky mint color, only recently hewn from the coming mountains. The foliage was too sparse to support camouflage.

"And who is the client we're going to see?" Mack has been trying once more to get his man to talk.

"Why, the chieftain, of course," Kittaporn half-smirked. "I have known him for many years. . . ."

"Since you were in the CIA?" Kittaporn wasn't hungry for that kind of bait.

"Since the war," he conceded. "These tribes were greatly coveted, you know. Laos is not very far off. . . . When I could be of use to them, I was."

"To the Americans?"

"And why them only?"

"To the Russians, perhaps?"

"If you wish to write about me," Kittaporn lectured, "you must see all there is to see. I am translator. I am a guide, I play tennis. I speak to the King on behalf of the poor. I have wife and baby to worry about."

But what did any of that have to do with where he was taking us? Mack couldn't ask that, so he went back to journalism. "You've been back from the States for two years?"

"Almost three. I liked the States very much. I worked at a

country club while on probation. . . ." Kittaporn knew how to suffer.

"You were released without a final verdict. Did the Company obtain your release?"

"Under your system, it is difficult to keep an innocent man in prison for long."

"You don't expect me to believe that."

"Ah, then you're not the 'ugly American,' I see."

"We all fought against the war." Mack could still cite his own history when it served him. "All of us here marched and were gassed."

"You did right then," Kittaporn told us, though he couldn't help adding, "It is just that sometimes I wish there was still a war. It seems there's so little to do now. . . ."

"The opium trade never ends."

"That is behind me," Kittaporn replied, nearly admitting something. "You must write about what is now."

"But aren't you still a marked man?"

"Thailand is full of spies."

"And drug smugglers?"

"And many who are both." Kittaporn shifted gears. "You are a clever young man. You will go far, thank you. You are surely aware of how the great powers take people and make garbage of them, throw them away. I was thrown away, but I am lucky. I know how to play tennis."

Mack knew Kittaporn was not merely being philosophical. He'd followed the story about the suicide of the other young Thai arrested with Kittaporn. Now Mack mentioned the dead man's name.

"Not a word about this!" Kittaporn was too sneaky to be very stern. "This you must not write about. It is over. But I will say this, in confidence. I made inquiries when I was released. I talked to detectives, I did my own investigation, if you will. He was my friend, thank you. I had to know how he died. I was about to find out when I was forcibly returned to my current circumstances. I was close to the truth, if such a thing matters."

"Then it wasn't a suicide?"

"Look, we are coming to my village!"

We saw nothing. But around the next curve, a new hollow revealed a scattering of low, oblong huts climbing both sides of the canyon. The hills were cleared beyond the tumbledown encampment. But the ground was charred and blackened, burned away, as the Thais did when rotating crops.

The inhabitants of this village weren't Thais, they were Meos. Iris had already bought a parcel's worth of their traditional clothing and purses in Bangkok. They dressed in black, with severe patterns of primary color at the borders. It was a strikingly abstract costume, funeral garb as it might have been designed by Vasarely.

Kittaporn stopped the jeep on the bluff overlooking the settlement. It was here the policemen had been killed, and Mack couldn't resist hopping out, then clicking away furiously with his Leica. He got some priceless shots of the bushes where the bodies had been tossed. The road wound farther down into the hollow. There appeared to be a large parking lot for the village, but there was a "T" marked out with white powder so that helicopters could land in the center.

"But whose helicopter? The chief's? The police?"

"The King's," Kittaporn answered nonchalantly.

"This is a loyal village?"

"Oh yes. The King has given a vow to all the tribal peoples. They are his special ones. They are his . . . his charge? Is that what you would say?" In Thailand, the King, army, and government often moved unilaterally. "He guarantees them their independence to carry on with the old ways."

"With the growing of opium?"

"Yes, if you like. Of course, there's always much talk about crop substitution."

Kittaporn led us up the side of a ravaged hill. The soil, the huts and the trees were all parched and vaguely uprooted. Meo women worked a crude loom at the side of their narrow lean-tos. The women wore as much jewelry as two arms and a neck could hold, as did the children who scampered about them. The children also came with raggedy hair, bare feet and their basic black getup. To my eyes, they looked like little devil's helpers. We passed a ten-foot slingshot with two movable rock parts, which I could only guess was for grinding millet. Surprisingly hefty pigs were on the loose everywhere, though many chose to slumber in the shaded mud around the shacks' foundations.

Looking at the Meos only made me look at myself. My blue jeans and T-shirt reflected the whole of my culture as surely as

each silver trinket glinted with theirs. But I was much more interested in the Meos than they seemed to be in me. We were in
one of the villages closest to the flatlands, and it appeared that
people here had reached the disquieting stage where what they'd
seen of the modern world had left them sincerely bored with both
who they were and what was being offered to them. It was said
that the Meos had difficulty breathing at the lower altitudes. Perhaps this explained the stupor in which I found them.

Kittaporn was taking us to the top of the heap. A small man,
standing casually, arms akimbo, bowed gently from the opening
of his hut. We got closer and he welcomed Kittaporn in his tribal
tongue. The language was full of squeals and held notes, nearly
universal enough in their inference for us to follow. The man's
tone was subdued. He was barefoot, but wore light green drip-
dry, sta-prest slacks beneath the customary felt tunic. The man,
who we presumed to be the chief, made no acknowledgment of
us whatsoever. He seemed always to be peering directly into the
sun. His features were far more Mongolian than the average Thai's;
jaw rounder, skin duskier, eyes more deeply set. Though he was
tiny, the chief carried himself with deliberation and authority. He
looked to be figuring, always figuring his way out of some terrible
squeeze.

Kittaporn gave us permission to enter the chief's home. We
had to stoop to get through the opening. Once inside, we knew
we'd been invited to lounge in prehistory. The dimensions of the
hut were grand, oblong again, but the floors were packed mud
and the walls were unevenly fashioned from gnarled planks, so
that plenty of light and air got through. At one end of the hut was
the kitchen, a cannibals' pot straddling a bonfire. Children and a
wife hovered around the ever-boiling, oversized kettle. On the
far side, built into the corner, was a platform of wood planks
supported by posts. Benches came out from either side of this
bed, and we sat around it. Kittaporn and the chief chatted about
business matters or the upcoming trial. Our guide translated, or
made up the dialogue, when it pleased him. The Meo still had not
looked directly at any of us. I knew this because I couldn't keep
my eyes off of him. His motives and values fascinated me, yet I
hardly had a hint of them. His expression was wary as an old dog's.

Not even Mack could crack him. We were offered jars of
bitter tea that the three of us gulped down to stay in the chieftain's

good graces. When Mack asked, most quietly, if Kittaporn would pass along a few journalistic inquiries, Kittaporn readily agreed to interpret. But they only brought forth the chief's ancient rendition of "No comment."

Without fanfare, an old Chinese hobbled through the doorway, carrying an armload of stacked bamboo steamers full of buns stuffed with sweet bean paste. Each one was stamped on top with candied dye just as it would have been in any Chinatown pastry shop. Strangely, I felt relieved: the man and his cakes were nearly as out of place as we were. Chinese, it seemed, were everywhere on earth, and always unassimilated, always devastatingly Chinese. This one was followed by a pack of Meo kids; he was obviously a sort of Good Humor man who went from village to village. He was also the first person in sight who managed a smile.

And Mack Schreiber could converse with him! His college Mandarin was now put to uses his professors could not have imagined. Once more, Mack was at his best in a foreign tongue: worldly in the most practical sense, charming and deferential, professional because his profession so expressed his compulsion to burrow and to know. The old man was delighted, and finally, the chief looked impressed. I had the feeling he had considered it impolite to gaze at us until he found something about us to respect.

From Mack's running account, we gathered that the bun vendor had once been a private in Chiang Kai-shek's army. There were thousands of Nationalists like him who'd been driven down from China, all of them waiting, like their Taiwanese counterparts, for a repatriation they knew would never come. He had made a life here; he was happy. History lived in the Good Humor Man's eyes. His face told of unreported skirmishes and surreptitious raids. Were his bean cakes just another cover? Everyone in these parts seemed to have one. Over and over, the old man's tongue rolled lingeringly at the word, "Kuomintang."

Though the brewing cauldron was far from us, the atmosphere had warmed. Kittaporn now thickened his own plot.

"Would you like to try a little opium? Shall I ask the chief?" His tone was professional, but he grinned involuntarily when he was through.

"We don't want to displease anyone. We wish to be proper guests." Mack was our self-appointed spokesman. He was also unprepared for this unusual enhancement of the interview. And what would this do to his stomach? Mack looked nearly ready to reach for an antacid.

"It will be no trouble, thank you. For the Meos, that is the one and best way to be . . . what was it? . . . 'proper guests.' "

Mack was trapped and turned to us. "What do you think?"

"Oh, let's!" Iris was primed for another whiff of the real. I shrugged, ready to be swept along.

"All right then," Mack told Kittaporn. "Perhaps we'll give it a try."

"For your newspaper?"

"And will you smoke?" Mack countered.

"Yes, thank you. But I'm no addict." Kittaporn added this assertion so nonchalantly that I was forced to doubt him.

He spoke to the chief, who stole a glance to check what mettle of men—or women—we were. He did not show any pleasure. We did not hear him issue any commands. But it became clear we were waiting for the delivery of the goods.

"They, too, must hide their supply," Kittaporn explained. "These are bad times. Last year's crop, what they couldn't sell, is kept in the forest."

So why was he telling us? Either Kittaporn volunteered his information to keep Mack from getting what he really wanted to know, or he trusted us far more than we did him. In this terrain of caution and double-caution, we appeared to be dealing with immoderate men. If the chief needed to hide his stash, he wasn't trying very hard. If Kittaporn was out to prove he hadn't been a drug-runner, he wasn't going about it too logically. It was possible our guide really wanted Mack to "see all there is to see." Or maybe he was just "being of use," as he put it, and cared little about who used him. Though Kittaporn was at home with supersonic jets and covert operations, he was, at heart, still a man of his tribe and his word. With our kit-bag of contingencies, it was Mack, and I, who were the cautious ones, refusing to accept that the only plot these various conspirators were brewing was a good time.

A shriveled Meo slipped through the doorless doorway bearing a gauze-wrapped bundle. He was clearly an addict, looking just like one of those wan caricatures reaching continually for the pipestem in old engravings of Shanghai's smoky dens. He treated the drug and its implements with holy, ritualistic care. We all peered unabashedly over his shoulder while he unraveled the packet.

Inside was a soft brown ball that reminded me of chewing gum left too long under my seat at school. The addict heated it on a squashed bronze coin, rolling it carefully until a match's flame had condensed it to smokable form. Then it went into his foot-long pipe. He lay flat on his side across the platform and sucked hard, eyes shut and head easing backward into eternity. The opium in the bowl glowed. Each of us lay on the platform and snaked over to take a turn. Kittaporn was last. The chief just watched.

Mack had once warned us, back in Hong Kong, that smoking opium for the first time could make you vomit. In deference to that, I did not inhale as deeply as I might have wished. I could see Mack didn't either, and Iris was also more tentative than usual. Besides, we had to keep our wits to deal with the secret agent. Luckily, the process moved slowly. We were called back in turn until the resinous lump had given off the smell of a thousand meadows and been extinguished. When we'd had all of what we were after, or what Kittaporn thought we were after, or what we thought Kittaporn was after, he began urging us toward the door. The three of us were relieved to emerge from the hut's permanent darkness.

At the entranceway, we thanked the chief, and the addict, and the old Kuomintang baker. We imitated their semi-bows and clasped hands held to the forehead. We waited for the opium to carry us inside its dense universe, to cover us with the dreamy cloak that the others wore all the time.

Stumbling down the hill, none of us were surefooted. The day seemed brighter. Our vision rippled at the edges; the setting waffled and was rent apart. The women at their looms turned to wax statuettes. Once inside the jeep, the rhythm of the bumpy road worked to mesmerize us. We shared a few moments of special silence, but soon realized we hadn't smoked enough to feel the drug's full effect.

Mack, the persistent one, took up his interrogation where it had left off. Perhaps Kittaporn's ploy had paid off, because Mack's insinuations had grown fuzzier. Kittaporn finally threw one arm around his adversary as he drove. Now we were all "friends," Kittaporn declared. It seemed, by my Western standards, that the word had been used too lightly, too blithely.

Still, our instant pal had given us something few travelers obtained: authenticity. We held our breath waiting for the bill.

Something for the wife and baby. Or to avenge his past treatment by the Americans. When the Land Rover suddenly swerved off the route, Iris and I gripped each other, feeling some terrible denouement might be upon us. Kittaporn must have sensed the tension, announcing, "I want to show you something beautiful." Again, his word was good. Again, he did it for nothing. "Something beautiful" turned out to be a local waterfall that boasting guidebooks called "the most spectacular in Thailand." We posed for pictures before its soft, formal descent. My memory has it that Mack's Leica changed hands many times, that we recorded each other in all possible combinations, documenting our adventure and leaving the hard questions behind. When the snapshots were developed, our friend Kittaporn wasn't in any of them.

THE SNAKE PIT

"THERE ARE MORE poisonous snakes in Taiwan than anywhere else in the world," Mack Schreiber intoned, trying
out his deepest and most authoritative radio voice. "But Thailand
must rank second. . . . Obviously, snakes thrive on certain political
ecosystems. They do well in military dictatorships."

Mack was all a-twinkle in the back of our samlor. He was
taking us to the Snake Farm, which was the one and only stop on
his tour of Bangkok. Our journalist friend had shown no interest
in the city's shimmering, spired wats, the solid gold Buddha or its
fewer karated replicas, the floating market clogged with bargeloads
of green mangoes and red chrysanthemums. His job was to keep
tabs on what little was current; he couldn't be bothered with the
time-honored sights unless some "contact" insisted on showing
them. But Mack didn't have to think of himself as a tourist at the
Snake Farm. He was merely doing research, checking up on the
latest estimates of Thai cobra population. He was getting as close
as he could to the front line of yet another Asian war of attrition,
and an under-reported one at that. It may have been a battle
between peasants and pythons, but it certainly resembled politics.
There were components of the Thai campaign to eradicate fatal

snake wounds that were like the Vietnam assignment he'd missed: daring raids in the rice paddies, reptilian counterinsurgency, a mounting death toll.

Besides, we had an hour or so to waste before the rally and march against the continuing operation of American military bases in Thailand.

"With the coup coming, this has to be left's last gasp," Mack assured us. "After today, it's into the hills . . . with the snakes!"

He paid the driver, without tip, and led us through a lawn vibrant enough to camouflage its own killers.

"Don't worry. Bangkok specializes in the human variety. The Red Cross takes care of the rest."

Indeed, we could see from the signs that we were entering a Red Cross hospital. But Mack knew which wing of the peeling, ocher compound housed the combination immunology center and circus sideshow. He led us through two dusty rooms that had been emptied of beds and replaced with charts and specimens and faded dioramas. Hung around the four walls, they told "The Snakebite Story." It had a predictable ending.

Excitement was lent to the place by the hourly venom-milking, and we were just in time for another performance. Mack became just another gawker as two handlers in surgical gowns climbed into a deep oval pit behind the hospital. Their job was to lure a variety of hissing things from under the built-in concrete igloos, perfect mock rocks. The snakes that emerged were teased and baited with long, leather crops, then nabbed at the height of their irritation, and stretched like so much electrical cable. Pert and hood-aroused, split tongues engorged, they coughed up into a jar—but by this point, neither we nor the rest of the Colonel Blimps in the gallery, could have cared that a life-saving serum was being produced. Here monsters were turned into housepets, and the temptation was to start naming them: Blackie, Spot, Lon Nol and Lon Non. Somehow, despite the white coats and grim deliberation of the procedure, the influence of the bazaar crept back in. The technicians were modern charmers; their expressions were far haughtier than science required, and they stamped their feet like matadors once the serpents were flung off. They also held their rigid donors to all sides so everyone could get a snapshot. It made a good show, except when some of the actors refused to uncoil, remaining dark, scaly donuts. They had apparently been through these sessions a few times too often. Like surrogates in a sex lab, their instincts had been abused and exhausted. If there were results, they were results of pure reflex.

Attack and retreat: every struggle, viewed by those who did not share the interests of the participants, was doomed to appear mechanical. Retreat and attack: it was so easy to get cynical.

But Mack wasn't cynical in the cab on the way to Thamassat University.

"This is the first story I've covered that's felt really personal since the Red Guards quit running around," he confessed. "You'll see, it's just like the old days."

"Why's that?"

"We're so close to Vietnam and its consequences. Out here, the war's never ended, and so the antiwar war hasn't either."

That was the great thing about American power: it extended so far that one could never escape the opportunity to fight it. Mack wanted to show the two of us that he still could, just by bearing witness. His usual agitation was approaching a nail-biting giddiness, but I, too, was feeling that tightening in the upper gut that had always accompanied a mobilization, another parade into the tear gas.

"Can we chant, 'Hey, hey, L.B.J., How many gooks did you kill today?"

Of course, we couldn't; but Mack was eager to record the Thai equivalent. Traffic stalled, and he leapt from the cab. "Come on, we'll walk! This means it's already started."

Our view of the boulevard was blocked by an immense monument, set in the center of one more futile Bangkok rotary. Mack explained that the smooth granite blade, ten stories high, commemorated the site of another student uprising. "The first, and most successful. It forced the start of the so-called democratic era."

Half-sprinting around its base, I was reminded of an oversized sundial, which was fitting, since the riots that took place here marked a zero hour, Modern Standard Time, when Thailand had been forced to adopt representative rule, with all its ensuing and crazed parliamentarianism. If only students in the United States could have been so crucial, so heeded! But there were too many of them. The truth was that the college education we used to lambast for being "elitist" had been too damn egalitarian. In a place like Thailand, where college was only a vague rumor to most of the rice-tending populace, students became an instant elite, a government in training, and therefore held appropriate influence. The factions within university enrollment acted out the entire drama of twentieth-century politics; they *were* the body politic. Here "student power" wasn't just an idle boast, but reached tantalizingly close to the state.

We had come to the great park that ran for several miles along the riverfront. At the far end of this threadbare green mat, stood the glories of the past: the golden spikes of the royal palace, distorted into curlicues by the heat. At the near end, camped the conflicts of the day: the university, with its foreboding gates and great halls. In between, the "silent majority" played their games. Children zigzagged across the dry fields on tricycles; band shells offered the competing din of Thai rock groups; inside a nest of wooden bleachers, fans bet on volleyball and cockfights; dozens of kites strafed the neutral sky with bands of color.

On the sidewalks that ringed the park, old women peddled sliced coconut and Parisian-style bookstalls sold and re-sold Irving Wallaces and Mickey Spillanes. This noontime, the expanse was also dotted with agit-prop. Lurid posters, twice the size of the wispy trees they leaned against, offered explicit imagery: a red-white-and-blue meat grinder with the limbs and skulls of yellow people going in one end and a stream of greenbacks coming out the other; a haughty tank, its bazooka raised, that trampled a road of Thai flags and bore the license plate "CIA." All writing, where it was necessary, was in English, suggesting that students here, as elsewhere, were posturing largely for themselves. Or that they were trying to make the message clearly legible for journalists like Mack. He jotted down, "U.S.-Thai As Equals, Not Puppets," and "Yes to the American People, No to Kissinger's Militarism!"

Iris and I realized from our time here, and Mack knew it more conclusively from the ladies of Patpong Road, that such a distinction was strictly maintained. We felt entirely at ease joining the back fringes of a mob in white shirts, perhaps ten thousand, facing a speakers' platform at the main entrance to the university. We didn't feel that we had to show credentials, or remind the Yankee-haters next to us that we'd put in our time at such events. I wasn't even made to confess that Mack and I had once driven a Dow Chemical recruiter off campus by brandishing water-pistols. I hoped these compatriots of ours were better armed, and more willing to live out the full implications of their indignation. Craning my neck, I could see that the canvas backdrop to the rally was decorated with peace signs, raised fists, and a white dove fluttering against stars 'n' stripes. Which country were we in? The fiery orators taking their turn at the microphone wore work shirts and overalls. The college choir sang a repertoire of early Joan Baez. "La Paloma," "Bread and Roses," "He who rides with the Klan is a devil and not a man. . . ." This movement, down to its nonviolence and guitar strumming, was a passable imitation of the very influences it sought to expunge.

"They're like us even when they don't like us," Mack shouted over applause. "Maybe I could tape a piece on that. . . . No, they'd never run it."

And what would they run? Nothing Mack really believed. But he didn't seem to mind, and went on jotting notes furiously, up-holding his end of a one-sided bargain. There was no other choice if he was going to be a foreign correspondent—the only employers with the power to send him where he wanted to go did not want to hear what he wanted to say once he got there. How many other eager young cubs were letting their compulsion to join the clamor of the world get the better of them? Did they also tell themselves, as Mack did, that they'd get in their "politics" later, in twenty years, when they were on top? But what would twenty years of expense accounts and ah mahs, of hotel lobbies and palace cocktails and enforced foreignness, do to those politics? And what good were politics anyway when you were covering a plane crash?

I never could bring myself to ask Mack these questions because I was a good enough friend to already know the answers. Instead, I tried to follow a nervous coed, with the warbling delivery of a classical Chinese singer, who'd been designated to read, in choppy English, the leadership's statement of principles. I got the drift by deciphering the hatchmarks Mack made in his notebook: "Thai must not be U.S. radar station. Gov'ts must honor deadlines. Pro-tect our sovereignness." Mack was more versed in the rhetorical code. It was too bad that the students had to use it, since all they were really demanding was the right to feel that this was their own piece of the planet, the right, above all, to make their own mis-takes. It was a shame that when Mack filed his report he'd have to couch it in the usual jargon, too.

The rally ended and formed into a march. We stood aside with Mack while he jotted down some more slogans and recorded scraps of raw sound. Then we fell into step for the eight-mile parade to the official residence of the currently unofficial Prime Minister. We didn't see the rest of the press corps—prompting Mack to bubble over with visions of an "exclusive"—until the heat caught up with us. Filtering back toward the march's trail, we were soon beside the other Westerners. Mack chatted with Raffson, the BBC man in his dirty safari outfit, and Nyls, the strapping and long-haired cameraman who might have been mistaken for a rock 'n' roll drummer were it not for the Arriflex on his shoulder. We were surrounded by an honor guard of "people's medics." Identified with white arm bands made from bedsheets, they were also strikingly similar to their New Left counterparts. They carried kits for every calamity, stirring another familiar reaction in Iris and me. We were touched by their absurd preparedness: it always seemed that the presence of these volunteer do-gooders backfired, became a dare. Where there were so many bandages, there really ought to be wounded. Yet nothing ever happened at marches like these because the marchers did not want anything to happen. At least, nothing happened in the States.

Mack must have been thinking the same thing, because he rejoined us to ask, "How would you like the best flapjacks in Asia?"

"Mmmm," Iris surprised me.

"We're going to be passing right by Smitty's Pancake House."

That wasn't surprising, since the march was already streaming through Yankee turf. Hiltons and Sheratons and Holiday Inns rose on all sides like credit cards balanced on their edges. In one of the shopping malls that connected hotels, there was a curious coffee shop called the "Puberty Restaurant." What could be on their menu? Just past it was what beckoned Mack: a facade of false logs and pegs, a thick knotted door that bore the signature "Smitty's," in rope lettering made to look like a lariat.

"Shall we make a discreet exit?"

"It's your story."

"We can catch up with it later."

"Anything you say, correspondent Sugar Daddy!"

Out of the heat and through the cabin door, we had to squeeze our way into the line for a table. Momentarily blinded by our jump from the overexposed tropics to this Dalton gang dark, we could sniff coffee brewing, Virginia ham frying, even the plastic lamination of the counters, the Lysol in the kitchen. It was the Lysol in Smitty's bathroom that Mack valued most, and he began jostling his way toward it. Coming from the rally, we half-expected Mack to start chanting his favorite slogan, "Keep showering, keep shitting!"

Iris and I ordered strawberry waffles and bacon, a tall stack of buttermilk silver dollars for Mack. The Thai waiters hadn't learned to simulate a drawl, but the rest of the place was disconcertingly authentic. With its wood paneling, mounted wagon wheels and checked tablecloths, Smitty's was the Bar-Double-X-Ranch, the one where all true Americans were presumed to have been sired and raised. Mack rejoined us and immediately began gossiping with a genuine, down home Aussie.

"Hear the latest on Olshansky?"

Mack explained that he was the *Chicago Tribune* man.

"Seems he went bonko. Tore up his Telex, took his Master Charge and headed for Goa. Last seen with two lovelies from the Darling Massage under his wing. . . ."

"Too many deadlines," Mack reasoned, acting like he'd heard it all before.

"Too many LBFM's . . . ."

Just then, there was an explosion. Mack ducked, and we ducked, and everyone in Smitty's ducked, bowing to the supreme authority of gunpowder. The blast wasn't near enough to signal danger, clearly outside. A second charge followed, farther off. As if answering a roll call, all the journalists, including Mack, rose instinctively—dabbing maple syrup from their lips as they went to join the fray. Smitty's solid door became a bellows, expelling the reporters, sucking in an equal number of whooping, whimpering demonstrators.

We tried our best to keep up with Mack. At moments like this, he did not hesitate. He forgot all about his various bugs, he risked a fate worse than gastroenteritis, he threw himself, terminal acne and all, into history. Barely out the door, he already had his recorder switched on and was blabbering impressions into it. But his live track would not include the actual bombing, and was soon interrupted by Raffson, who was retreating from the explosives' range. Nyls came with him, but aimed his camera the other way. The camera was having conniptions.

"Cisco Kid! I thought you'd bit it!"

"Are you all right?"

"People like me are never all right, old boy. But look at them . . ."

At first, all we saw were several dark gashes in the pavement, halfway up the block. Around the gashes, students lay flattened. A kindergarten class obediently taking their naps. Their pillows were hard: something red seeped through their dark pajamas. Many of those prone had covered their eyes with both hands. It was hard to tell if they were trying to keep from seeing or being seen. Mack scanned the rooftops for signs of a raiding party. As it turned out, two or three grenades had done the job. The right had struck, or perhaps the CIA, clearing the road—literally—for the generals to roll in.

Creeping up that road toward the nearest hotel awning, we were now close enough to see torsos writhing with shock. Plenty of medics were already swarming about, checking for vital signs— so Mack didn't have to choose between helping the wounded or yakking into his machine. Then we realized that most of the victims were medics. They were the ones who'd been marching right alongside us.

As Mack continued his charge toward the blacktop partisans, he must have seen himself lying there, seen Iris and me. Moving out into the boulevard's shooting gallery, he kept peering back at us on the Hilton steps where we clung. The three of us had been saved by his sweet tooth! Saved by Smitty's being right where it was, saved by our craving for anything from home and the ease with which we were allowed to find it. Saved by a false sense of our safety, and the safety of free ideas. Mack, for one, should have known better. Like us, he'd had Asia play another trick on him: this Asia that was so vivid, so unrelentingly real, it made you feel you were its intimate so long before you really were. It was certainly real around Mack at the moment. But he had his job to do. He scurried ahead, through the panic, toward the ambulances, to assess the full damages. He was after his story and kept waving for us to follow. Iris and I stayed where we were. We watched him descend farther into the pit.

NEAR NIRVANA

NEAR NIRVANA

Music:

❖

CALCUTTA IS FOREVER

W HAT MAKES a city a city when all benefits are gone? What purpose in swarming when the honey's been licked clean, siphoned off to officials, exported, or bartered for lapidary work meant to invoke the presence of honey past? When all that beckons now are reports of black market goo, traces of stick, the maddening twitch of antennae up ahead, beyond reach, which indicates the fleeting appearance of sweet? And where the sustenance in gathering with so many other pilgrims of the stomach, when what most have in common is a dwindling of the stamina required to console? Kindness is one commodity that cannot be hoarded. Progress, when it just means centralization, an enlargement of the undernourished hive, is nothing more than proof that misery loves company.

In Calcutta, one cannot lack for company. Each night, you're invited to the world's least exclusive, no-host pajama party. Moment the heat falters, charpoys, those hammocks on stubby legs, are pulled from some communal closet, materialize out of a snake charmer's bottomless basket, to redecorate the sidewalks. A civic scramble for bedtime turf, with no ideals motivating, no services provided beyond pumps for washing and drinking and laundering.

This outdoor show is no longer mere housing overflow; the claims staked here are for permanent quarters in the flux. The only item in Calcutta of which there's no shortage are these portable hospital cots and bodies to fill the ward. An evening stroll here is but a bedcheck, an obstacle course through the prone.

The electricity in Victorian streetlamps is tentative, giving a silent-movie flicker to the proceedings. The sleepers' only blanket is a murky fog that clings to the pavement—suggesting the old Limehouse, and reminding us that this place rests on a swamp, reclaimed by the British East India Trading Company in order to create this other swamp. What's being played out is Dickens in brown skins. But these characters aren't scheming to stay out of debtors' prison, they're already in it. The colonialists have played Indian-givers to the Indians, taking away all the goodies and leaving behind an aborted industrialism's dislocations. Stodgy and imperturbable government buildings also remain, blood red armories the pillows for bled people with one bowl and ten kids' belongings wrapped in single indigo-colored cloth square. Picnics laid across sewer lines, there's a curious intimacy to the subsistence rituals on view, and no intimacy to what comes after. No goodnight whispers, campers' pranks, no fondling after lights out. Absolutely no undressing, for modesty's sake and so folds of dhoti can serve as sheets, best sandals can't be stolen off the feet. Just nutshell bodies with itches all over and no compunction about scratching them.

Or is this a slaughterhouse haze through which swoop the crows immortalized by Kipling? Smirking black tyrants, so privileged to be winged. Occasional baboons waltz by, or tarry on ledges overhead, pondering suicidal leaps, goaded senselessly to the city, driven from their natural habitat like the rest, except that they know when to screech and go berserko. To run from the gradual kill. On makeshift platforms, agitators harangue their captive audience, albino devils all in white with white beards before lecterns strewn with white petals. Bare bulbs sway hypnotically over them; the amplification is too great and fanatic waftings carry for blocks around, swabbing the tear-stained sidewalks with promises. These demagogues sell ideologies like elixirs. The solution, one zealot claims, is mass immigration to Bangladesh. The land of opportunity! Where the only consensus is malnutrition, political acts are consigned to the agenda of the surreal. On each lamppost above the dormitory, the placards of Mrs. Gandhi's "emergency"—like, "Punctuality for the Railways? No, For You Also!"—exhort further sacrifice from those who've already given everything.

"Emergency?" goes the folk wisdom. "There is always an emergency in Calcutta!" Here, waking hours are the bad dream and sleep's the only time for realism, really. The best city to live in is the one that's made and unmade as public snores mingle. It's a pointless exercise to plumb the actual when there's no possibility of control, and once the morning traffic of bullock-carts serves as their alarm, this snoozing citizenry relinquishes all to duty lack of options and the marching orders of appetite. Change is a business unsuited to these avenues of exhaustion where sleepers turn and turn trying to find buoyancy in their netting, a soft spot in the concrete. One more turn and they may slip into purgatory. Is that what makes them do it so gingerly, what constricts their restlessness? Or is it the sheer quantity of snoozers and groomers and mothers crouching to protect handfuls of rice or half moons of silver nose rings that every other woman hoards as well? What schemes circulate in all these districts turned indoors-out? Is there at least lust for affection, approval, status, birthday parties, new underwear, an afternoon at the picture show, a front door, something to do? How about an urge to escape?

I'd like to know the secret of such obtuse contentment. Or would I? I cope with this place by turning clinician. I observe the fiendish experiment in hopes of reporting my findings to someone, anyone. I have to think these subjects' travail must lead to discoveries. I feel a curious lack of personal despair. I sleep long, rich hours, uninterrupted by nightmare. The day's thick broth of images never boils over, just bubbles away and gives off reassuring steam. At formal dining services in our colonial relic of a boarding house, I eat as much as the uniformed bearers will allow, even though I can look down from my room on their barracks where, stripped of white gloves, braided turbans and epaulets, they reveal apalling skinniness, drift into between-meals myopia. I take second helpings of Yorkshire pies and starchy curries, I nurse the contents of my cozy at high tea. My pulse is regular as the climate allows. And I feel this sahib's itch to catalogue. I have no illusions about rescuing people with words, only hopes that the rescue of words will keep leading me back to these people. After all, the streets are so dirty and my notebook is so clean. My fingers burn from the pen as a throat burns from crying.

I have to know: Do human beings have a center of gravity? Could they lose it without noticing? Can they be toppled over, cast down, just when they think they're most steady, upstanding and confidently striding forward? There is deceptive activity here, in the morning markets, steeplechase jockeying between taxis and oxen-drivers. Plenty of rickshawers, runners, cobblers, bobblers, chattel and rattle. Is this commerce or just the proliferation of cancer cells? Witnessing it makes the corners of the retina singe and curl up like burnt paper. And rooftops likewise shrivel in. At least, a town turning shanty makes for a fix-it-man's heaven. Plenty of trickling leaks needing new washers, lots of opportunity for unsupervised tinkering. In Calcutta, big changes would be wrought by a dozen nails. In Calcutta, no one can find a hammer.

In Calcutta, the most genial stroll is always uphill, the surest ventures impossible, the flattest and broadest boulevards logjammed with vertigo. Also, despite appearances, loneliness: not just the ordinary tragic variety, since tragedy too requires privacy, but a generalized furtiveness that turns each day into one great scalding hot sigh. It's those who've lost their way longing for the old ways, the present hankering after the past. Whether it's the command and costumes of caste, or the more mundane dreck of Victoriana, clogging the rusted shopwindows with sets of wooden false teeth beside duck blinds beside mustache wax beside shuttlecocks beside howdahs beside shaving brushes beside "Try Once Our Betel Nut!," the past is so much more vivid than the present.

Like that mausoleum of the raj called the Victoria Memorial, where portraits of viceroys have a crispness that's startling beside Calcutta's frayed condition; like the zoo, where the elephant Sambari and Sawazdi look so much better fed than their keepers; like a steam-powered steamroller with rusted wheels that's probably an original Fulton design but is still a new-fangled wonderment used for Calcutta street repair; like goatherds leading their braying charges across Dalhousie Square, oblivious to the traffic and packed trolleys; like the leftover English commons, the maidan, that forms Calcutta's civic apron, gripping the heat to its greens; like the park's plotters who huddle in closed circles (no women allowed), underneath soccer stadium bleachers, on abandoned cricket pitches, their work not mere sedition but seeds of sinister vigilantism, religious seething spread across Etonian fields turned fiery at sunset. Poor lonesome suitors! Which past do they court? Under what flag? Day's end is rope's end, and like everyone else, we find ourselves unraveling in the direction of Howrah Bridge. Just slide with the shift in mass weight toward Calcutta's only way out, a squat piece of crochetwork in metal that's nonetheless the singular bit of past that still supports and exemplifies the crossing to the future. Along the embankments nearby, massages *en plein air* are offered by healers; swamis attempt to out-dissolve the lozenge sun; acrobats cartwheel in celebration of open space; beggars are so plentiful they seek hazard pay; makeshift villages form, stage feuds, disperse. Aboriginal kids roam in khakis tattered to loincloths, eyes puffed with hunger, pausing to shit out the pure luminescent green of chronic dysentery anyplace on the stone expanse. Following Iris and me, they stage games of barefoot chase, but when I dare to photograph them, we become their playthings. They skip along, taunting us by imitating a camera with circles of fingers, then empty cans picked from the garbage and held to their eyes. I'm Mister Specs to them, and the kids get full entertainment value from it. Though they may not know exactly what I'm up to, they sense something's inherently wrong, that documentation is a denial of life, which consists of feces and river and tag in the twilight.

We climb the utilitarian girders of this gangplank for six million. Off either end, the sharks wait, a city with fangs. This one funnel for all human traffic is Calcutta's roost, agora, exercise yard, hatch. The scramble does not exactly end here, on sagging truncated black-as-Blackfriars causeway, but at least is forced to move in definite tos and fros. A few cars climb up, too, all of them the rolling bowler hats called Ambassadors, made-in-India and consequently the only kind available. They're instant antiques, brand-new 1947 models, churned out on assembly lines that haven't been retooled since the British left. Such improvements are irrelevant where time is suspended, as on this suspension. Once on it, stray cars and the two of us must fight the waves of commuters who come twenty across, a stampede in both directions. From afar, this mass had been indiscernible from the bridge's underpinnings, a current of living buttress no less unbroken than the arms of iron. At what points does a crowd become a multitude? It is enough to say that people hold up Howrah Bridge as much as they burden it.

Leaning over the railings, we're surprised at the lack of jagged skyline in either direction. Just a neon sign for "GWALIOR SUITING" on the far side, outlines of the railway station, and Calcutta a Zuni pueblo out of control, a worn-to-smoothness jumble in the deepening haze. The crows are all that's distinct against brown banks meeting brown water. Docks fall in staircases chiseled with erosion. The Hooghly, sluggish tributary of the Ganges, turns deep wheat then rouge then a blue without iciness. Barges powered by bony oarsmen ply the shallows. While a dash of coriander falls from the pitiless sky, half-sunken cradles push off from the ghats in one century and return to shore millennia later.

The human flow on the bridge is the one that bears us off. Don't call it a rush hour, though. No one's rushing their salute to the cast-off sun, this funeral for another dirty day. In the barrage of brown wiry legs in ten-thousand fabric folds, starched but going amber in the dusk, of cheap, sticky plastic shoes that come to Sultanic points at the end, of wrapped homespun and amulets and holy man body paint, what colors exude, what strata of evocation! The resulting spectrum's as constant as from any perfect crystal. Each man who passes is a duplicate, triplicate exemplar. Every crease of dhoti reflects in a series of invisible mirrors, cascading back through generations, as though someone's always been there to take up each pedestrian's exact space and form. And someone always will be. The names don't matter: Gopal and Krishna, Chatterjee and Narayan. They may not be terribly pleased about it, but they're all one.

These trampers comprise the fortunate set, with portmanteaus to grip and hovel homes awaiting, but all are punished by a hovering spirituality that won't go away. Where life's but a passing annoyance with flies circling 'round, no man can be at peace, yet all go in peace. The pack is kept moving by wandering dazed shepherds who prod their flock with piercing stares. The sulk, the scowl, the glare, the glower: there's no site in Hindustan to compare with the sight of one's own self reflected in saddhu eyes deep as wells of the soul.

Meeting those eyes, we're invited inside a trance state that tells us we're of this place, not just at it. Having come westward, westward with the discovering sun, we're finally East as we can get—and don't mind if that restless sun abandons us here. The here-ness is all around, a here-ness of which we've heard so much. Iris and I must hold hands, shameful public display, so we won't be swept off into the parade and become separated amidst the earth's largest lost and found. Where lost is found. We also grab tight so we can share Howrah Bridge's momentary lack-of-present that is present, lack-of-change that is change, lack-of-wisdom that is wisdom. "Calcutta Is Forever," the Tourist Bureau billboards dare to boast, and a claim like that has no way of being proved false.

GODDESSES, SAINTS
AND JANITORS

HOW COULD WE wake one of the cabbies napping along Chowringee Road and ask him to take us to the dying destitute, please? Fortunately, Mother Teresa's Home for the same stood beside the Kalighat Temple, from which the East India Trading Company got the name Calcutta somehow, so we were prepared to offer as our destination this city's beginning, and not just its lurid end result. Luckily, if such a word could be applied to this grimmest of touristic missions, we got someone else to give the instructions for us. A passerby saw our hesitant weave between drivers snoring over their wheels and swooped to our rescue. "Please, don't be afraid! They are cur! Let me show you how it must be done!"

Our dashing Gunga Din turned out to be a member of the local gentry, clearly educated in the West, with Etonian inflection and tweed jacket even in such heat—also a black beard perfectly trimmed, green eyes practiced at exasperation, and bristling officiousness. "Please, seat yourselves!" Not only did he half-throttle the cabbie, but he joined him in the front for the ride. "I am your personal bondsman. I guarantee that you'll finish up where you wish to be going. And where is that, please? Out with it! Of course, of course. Don't be chagrined, friends. . . . Where else could you view such an enterprise. Yes, yes. Where else?"

He gave the address of the Home for the Dying Destitute to the cabbie, adding some gratuitous Hindi beratement. Of course, after such an aristocratic cracking of the whip, the motor wouldn't turn over. The cabbie lumbered out and opened the hood, which he peered into at length, perhaps hoping to clean the carburetor through telecommunication. "Look at him!" our rescuer scoffed. "It's not that he doesn't have some notion of how to maintain his machinery, just that he doesn't care a whit. Oh, come on now, chaps!" A whole turbaned team had gathered around the engine, chatting calmly and continuing to stare it down. "They seem harmless as sucklings, don't they? But I assure you, this one would have overcharged by ten rupees and perhaps attempted something more devilish. The way these people carry on is a blot upon me personally." Yet somehow, they got the car to start. "Good show! Miracle of Kali! . . . And what do you make of India?"

This was the first of two questions we were getting used to being asked. We were still groping for an answer when the next one stumped us further.

"And what are your qualifications?"

By that, we presumed they meant educational degrees, professional status, but it seemed pointless for Iris to spout forth, "B.A., psychology, University of California," or for me to joke, "Ph.D., college of hard knocks, school of failed revolutions." Such labels revealed little enough about us back home, but here, they were futile. So instead we tried to ingratiate ourselves by replying, "Curiosity."

Our chaperone was too polite for a show of disappointment, but rushed on to list his training instead. Unfortunately, the finest universities hadn't helped him out of his bind. Feeling responsible for his nation's disrepair, he nonetheless went on trying to disassociate himself from it. "I often wonder why it is I've come back to the Black Hole," he confessed, "to a place where one cannot feel at home, where no man feels at home . . . not even this surly bloke, I'd imagine." Glancing at our driver reminded him to bargain for the proper fare and have us pay it while he witnessed the transaction. The man at the wheel groused at this last bit of interference, then let our saviour off on the next corner. "This is my station. Carry on, friends!" Our conflicted prince gave us a regal bow, one hand clutching his waist.

Relieved to be rid of our overprotective escort, we soon wished he'd stayed close at hand. From the far end of a cobblestone oval crowded with tour busses, we could see the Kali temple's sandstone turrets, permanently tanned and curved like some very large, very primal woman's outer thighs—overstated proof of the axiom that where the people are puritan, the gods will be horny. Inviting enough, but there was a noisome buzzing that kept me from springing out of the taxi's safety. There were gnats all around, who happened to be people. Once again, we were lucky, since it was nearly noon and many of them were clinging to the shade of the temple facade. Underneath the busses were endless matched sets of ankles, tarred pairs of feet modeling sandal irregulars. Could a hundred mechanics be working under the chassis? The beggars had formed a huge centipede in search of cool. But once we'd slammed the cab door, we were surrounded by a convoy of professional tramps, mothers ever with child and open palm, taunting gypsy girls who danced frenzied circles about us, whining street urchins who climbed, primate-like, up our arms, shoulders, necks. For the first time, we heard the call of "*Baksheesh!*," that all purpose Third World word—the world's third word, after "yes" and "no"— meaning bribe, gift or sop. A payment for services rendered or unrendered or just payment: everyone expected, few received. Was this the just punishment for our morbid sightseeing impulses? The kids were hounding us so nastily that I couldn't believe they really wanted anything more than a ride. The rabble was undoing itself, something it knew very well how to do. These people were making sure they couldn't have what they wanted by making it impossible for us to reach into our pockets. If we had, we'd have been devoured, pulled under. It was refuse or join them, so Iris and I locked arms and made a goal-line plunge for Kalighat. The yard markers were our tormentors' immobile counterparts: deaf and dumbs, paraplegics, all manner of *mutilés*, even fake fakirs who'd painted bandages green to simulate terminal infection.

Inside the eroded gates, we hoped for sanctuary, a stern Presbyterian minister in his frock, but instead we found more swarming, more chambers where the gnats hid. The kiddies started to drop off only when they were slapped aside by a short yet powerful man in gray kurta. He identified himself as a priest and guide, but he appeared a trifle crazed: so wall-eyed the circle of ash on his forehead seemed to wander. He spit wetly with each memorized English phrase of his tour, but he was our second rescuer of the day, so we stuck by him—even if he assumed we were idiots who'd taken a wrong turn at Fiji and wound up in India by accident.

"This Hindu temple. Indian people like Hindu religion." Really? Our guide then listed a panoply of deities, as if we didn't know Vishnu from Adam. But what we really wanted to know was left untold. Like why people were touching hands to smears of tar on rounded cysts of altars inside brick cubicles that looked like outhouses. Or why there was fresh blood coagulating on shrines that doubled as slaughtering posts. Or why I couldn't tell worshipper from worshipped, priest from beggar, devotee from temple janitor sweeping up. Or what that huge cafeteria was doing in the midst of this swirling other-worldliness, these cubbyholes of fetish. But once I saw bedraggled madonnas lining up for alms, I recognized this last bit of bafflement as the local version of a Salvation Army soup kitchen. At the hive's center, there was a main altar protected by brass doors laden with strings of bells, another crush to cram into. I was grateful when our guide warned us that non-Hindus weren't permitted to enter.

I couldn't help but label what I saw as chaos, and sympathize for the first time with olden missionaries' cringing horror at "paganism." Shiva's many arms were moving in too many directions. This was religion turned drunk and disorderly, with each man inventing his own benefactor, soothsayer, nemesis. It was not a game that rationalists could learn to play because the rules were constantly being revised and nobody seemed to win or lose. Never sinning, always sinning, never knowing, always certain—aside from dogma concerning sacred cows and such, the rest was subjective as any passion. Didn't these anti-utilitarians ever keep score? Fix blame? Turn on their favorite gods? It looked like they wouldn't know where to find them if they did. But Iris had already gotten into the swing by choosing her favorite: Ganesh, the archetypal elephant at play, depicted blowing off steam through his trunk, always cavorting on a bed of rats (his natural complement). Merry

Ganesh couldn't really be a god, a moral persuader. Surely, he came rumbling out of the forests once a year, on a binge, buying drinks for everyone! Aside from pointing out each elephant on each bas relief, I did not know how to order this clutter of vestibules, to chart the bustle of a stock exchange where only hope rose and fell.

As in Macao, religion wasn't separated from life's madcap flow. Our priest, if he was one, certainly wasn't above using the tactics of the street to gain a larger tip. He greeted our first, unsolicited "donation" with a glare and more forceful spit, this one at our feet. He raised up a howl that drew a dozen famished ladies from the kitchen to serve as enforcers. We left the sacrifice that was required by Kali's handmaidens.

Still, neither of us dared ask directions for Mother Teresa's. The temple had provided enough ghoulish surprises for one day and we had no idea if we'd be led to inspect the work of a saint or to watch our very own "snuff show." Death turned the living into voyeurs. It was far less of a participatory act than fertility worship. So we made a dash to the left of the temple, toward a stucco women's auxiliary sort of building, a miniature YMCA, just two stories, and no windows—that was promising—which had recently been done up with a coat of that umbral paint found only in India, a yellow with lots of mustard but no sunshine in it. Past the busses, at the corner, we got close enough to read the sign over the door. It told us we'd found the place we were both seeking and dreading. At least, there was no barker outside.

This time, I was the one yanking Iris inside, though she'd once given me a fancy speech about how death was a natural process that should not be sequestered. She wasn't held back by squeamishness, just the fear of showing disrespect. I wasn't held back at all because guilt was the emotion I handled best. We entered a bare anteroom, no reception desk or potted palms or muzak, no appointments necessary, just more welcome shade and the prospect of dankness. A nun in starched white, from her habit to her surgical mask, appeared under an arch at the back. Her fawn eyes beckoned without words, her marble fingers offered two fresh masks for us. With just a few steps, we were lead past a modest brick divider and into the female, then the male wards. The smell of ammonia overpowered whatever else was there. Floor to ceiling, it was all hygienic tile, in a faintly Victorian crockery pink. The floors were crammed with cots that were less adequately filled with the dying. These cots, which were easier to study than the people, were on sliding frames that could be easily moved (or removed) and sat but two or three inches above the oft-swabbed floor. Was it to keep the patients from falling and hurting themselves more than they already had? Or to recreate the curbsides from which most had been swept? As the scale of suffering in the streets was colossal, so the solution was typically Indian in its meagerness. For all the fundraising and international acclaim, what had the good Mother wrought? Two dingy locker rooms for the quick change from life to afterlife.

Did it matter to any of these people? "They're too weak to cry out," the nun whispered. Obviously, she'd given this tour before. Undoubtedly, we would have to tip her for her services as we'd tipped the priest. But there was really so much less for her to explain, and this was hardly the spot to raise questions about the efficacy of troubling with specimens so far gone when there were so many others who could still be cured. Clearly, the yogic Catholic who'd founded this enterprise wasn't so much interested in extending lifespans as in eternity. Even here, where they were of so little use, these martyrs were being exploited by someone else's idea of salvation. Where there was too much opportunity for it, charity had run amok. Charity is always help that is offered too late, just as revolution is help offered too soon.

Faced with such fatalist reasoning, the dying destitute offered only a "No comment." With labored, open-mouthed gulps, these carcasses on slabs hyperventilated toward a final breath. Each shriveled in stages toward a fetal curl, bony knees drawn up against ribs. But where being born made for a splashy Moulin Rouge review, dying tended to be a one-man show done with lights dimmed. Just as Calcutta's "poverty" was relative, a step above savagery, implying its citizenry had the right to expect something better, so death, too, was a matter of comparison. It didn't look so bad with no life beside it.

If these fellow beings could still offer us anything, it was the relief of disappointment. Comparing notes over a dinner of steak and kidney pies, Iris and I found that we had not been titillated, not enthralled not even, for once, made guilty—because the condition on display was one we would someday share. Coasting toward death on sleighs down slopes greased with disinfectant. On our very own "Flexible Flyers!" That was the only real travel, a journey that could be set out upon without the diminution of return; there was the surest way to cast aside nationalities, biases, "qualifications." Soon enough, we would all have the chance to become so uninteresting.

SPECIAL CAKE

OUT OF THIS WORLD, yet already too much of it. Having flown above the Gangetic plain's dusty rodeo ring and straight toward the icy flank of Everest and his pals, we found signs everywhere of the others who'd already befouled Kathmandu. The first wave of exploration had broken, leaving haggard surfers strewn all about. There were the aging Peace Corps volunteers, who'd come to vanquish tuberculosis and stayed to run pie shops with quaint names like "Aunt Jane's" that catered to the sweet tooths of hash heads; there were the primitivists who'd become so much a part of the confused tribe that they, too, sat in basement clubs papered with posters of flower children and Jimi Hendrix; there were the shivering junkies of "Freak Street," waiting, just as they might have done in New York, to make furtive scores in pissy doorsteps. The old publicity calendars hung everywhere: "R. Bhavan & Sons, Purveyors of High Quality Hashish, Ganja, By-Products, Etc." They were uncannily like the type main street hardware stores hand out at New Year's, except that the accompanying illustrations weren't snow scenes of Vermont, but lurid portraits of Shiva and Krishna with kewpie doll eyes. These, too, were holdovers from a flourishing period just ended. A tacit ban on drugs was one of the dues Nepal had just paid for admission to that smug country club known as the community of nations.

Still, on our first afternoon in Oz, we knew it would be easy to find the local specialty. We were tempted to sample it, not so much as an homage to the single-minded hordes who'd come before us but in order to find some reasonable purpose for having come to this most remote of our destinations. Besides, such a chore might even be fun. "When in Kathmandu, we should do as the 'duans," Iris argued, and I went along.

How did she choose amongst the dingy holdovers of Kathmandu's short-lived psychedelic boom? This time only, Iris trusted our guidebook when she recognized one restaurant—it was "Jumping Jack Flash's," or something equally suggestive—mentioned as a source for "knockout hash cookies." The name was painted on a shingle that wobbled alongside wind chimes, hung from a second story whose walls and shutters were one brown, whittled filigree. This dinette's facade crawled with a gleeful maggotry of carvings. Its menu, tacked to a portal through which we had to stoop, was hand-lettered, in broken English. "Rice fry . . . like home sweets . . . pot tea." And, at the very bottom, "special cake." But how special could one measly chunk of cake be? Special as the omelettes in Bali? Was this appellation another attempt at false advertising or just the proverbial Asian humility? Only ingestion would tell us.

Through one of the zillion atriums where the life of Kathmandu went on, wisely cloistered from the ragged streets, then up a creaky ladder, we stooped all the way toward what was, in every sense, a den. This narrow, low-ceilinged galley would have been Shangrila to the world's "head shop" operators: divided in beams that were aflame with the hallucinatory colors of a Tibetan paint job, draped with prayer flags and thankas, the floor laid with faded carpets and ottoman-sized pillows. Cloying scented candles melted into stumps of lacquered tables, and the prolonged twilight found in the mountains, completed the delirium-inducing ambience. Iris and I plopped on the first semi-sofas, and sat cross-legged, like those other Indians did at a pow-wow. We awaited Jack Flash, who did not jump to serve us. In the meantime, we got acquainted with the rest of the clientele. Sprawled on their cushions, leaning back into them so that only beady eyes and veils of hair emerged from the softness, were two couples well-dosed by something. Looking up long enough to nod a knowing welcome, one blond waif soon returned to his concentrated research on the patterns in a grimy rug. Set before the rest of the gang in hand-painted pots, the tea was ceremonial. No one was eating in this restaurant.

But could a single little Alice B. Toklas job have done them all in? We were too near the others to ask one another, and didn't see the point in trying for an answer from them. Now our Nepalese host was upon us, looking cocky and obsequious at the same time, in tight black Levis and a grandmotherly shawl over his bare, scrawny chest. His eyes, too, were glazed by a stupor that was exceptional for the East; he grinned and picked at his teeth while watching Iris point to the item on the bill of fare at which everyone pointed. "One . . . for two?" Iris leaned toward him, still unaccustomed to a drug scene that was so casual and open. "Is it enough?" Jack Flash answered by trying to laugh, but his face was too tired. He shuttled off to the kitchen, leaving us with the happy corpses and a Pink Floyd record that kept hitting scratches. Dotted on each wall was the all-seeing-eye of Buddha, the only narc in town.

Several dozen guitar solos later, our ghostly waiter got up the strength to present one massive, crumbling brownie on a chipped plate. He didn't bother to say, "Enjoy your meal"; the other diners didn't look our way. We began picking at the thing. It couldn't be that deadly, could it? The "cake" tasted like a slice of carob-flavored pizza. It was densely glutinous, perfumed dirt, and was thickened, rather than washed down, by the bilious tea. Of course, we could not know, for some time, how many nibbles would be "enough." So we kept nibbling. We spread our late-afternoon snacking over a half-hour, waited another half-hour to get change from our bill. Iris and I felt nothing but bored.

We headed for our hotel. The Snug! What wishful thinking went into the choice of such a sobriquet for that three-story shell through which Himalayan winds whistled. No rugs to warm the concrete floors, but plenty of bugs, thriving somehow in the demi-thaw. Toilets that flushed were no longer what we were after, but shower spigots were more appreciated if they gave forth water. This was one place that could not meet our ever-lowering standards. We returned there only because we'd made a date with an Australian couple who'd sat across the aisle on the flight from

Calcutta. They were a friendly pair, unabashedly Anglophile and a bit crusty, whom we'd found appealing because they were so willing to whine about Asian conditions and Asian pretensions. But seeing them now, shivering in the unappointed lobby, I noticed how caught up they were in their own teeth-gritting.

"There t' ey are! Ready for tonight's ptomaine?" The throaty wife, whom I could readily envision as a straw boss for aborigine ranch hands, was getting downright ill-humored. She seemed always to be "putting up with it." And the "it" was immutable, a collection of given circumstances for which she felt so little responsibility that she made no attempt to mitigate them. She asked Iris, "Where've you been, then?"

That seemed an irrelevant question, with the "where" of Kathmandu just beyond the napping desk clerk. Iris didn't tell her about the special cake, which now seemed an embarrassing scam, but recounted our earlier walk from town to Swayambanuth, the "monkey temple" built atop an immense rock toward the other end of the valley. She described, with unusual fluency, the bald white temple stupa, a bell-shaped mound of plaster, surrounded by bronze bells, prayer wheels and hundreds of smaller plaster buds. Little acorn stupas, dropped everywhere. At the center of this hodgepodge was a pointed golden spire on which was painted a pair of unflinching Buddha eyes, the corporate logo of Nepal, and a far more effective one than the CBS single cyclops scanner. The eyes were snaky, seductive, but also gravely fatigued: worn out by having seen so much truth, having broadcast so much resoluteness. The eyebrows, Iris told them, were blue question marks.

While the Australians fidgeted, she let them in on more than they'd wanted to know about the prayer hall, a dark Buddhist altar consumed in enough patterns of fiery red to warm the most chilling mountain desolation, and about the ritual we'd stumbled on there. In a back antechamber, monks in shaved heads and half-ton scarlet robes sat on mats before long benches and chanted mantras. The event seemed far more musical than theological, since the whole order wore hand-cymbals they clicked in rhythm to the chief priest's drone. Three or four novitiates at the far end of the table were assigned the task of syncopating the mumbles with periodic blasts from great horns that were twice as long as the arms that lifted them. The drawn-out notes produced by these extended drain-

pipe clarions seemed to harken every snow leopard and Bengal
tiger and living thing to come to them. "But," as Iris said, "we
were the only ones who did!"
I had never seen her so enraptured, not on our trip, not back
home with her favorite plants and pie tins and volumes of Jung.
She just had to tell the impatient couple about the view from
Swayambanuth's stone railings. Hindered by Nepal's summer haze
and the occasional scampering of redheaded chimpanzees, this
lookout revealed the high country capital crouched in upon itself
for warmth, a wooden jumble of rooftowers and pagoda balancing
acts, a part-maze, part-circus tent that reminded Iris of a compen-
dium of illustrations from childhood fairy stories. "It's like something out of the Brothers Grimm, isn't it?" she asked. "It's the
way I imagine Hamlin. I keep looking for the pied piper."
"It's grim, all right," the wife cracked. "We didn't have no fairy
story, did we?" And out came her tale of unpleasant wrangles with
carpet vendors and insistent hashish salesmen. So far, she confided,
everything Nepalese was "shithouse."
She and her subdued, steel-jawed mate did enjoy playing social
directors. They tried to form convoys that might escort them safely
across Asia and on to relatives in Wales. We were flattered to have
been invited along, even if we were merely being offered body-
guard assignments. We were especially pleased that they'd met
another American couple, who would join up with us for dinner
at a place called Utep's. The Australians knew the way there,
through the red-brown labyrinth; past the lofty, mounted towers
and writhing "terror demon" bas reliefs in Durbar Square; all the
way across the Lilliputian world of Kathmandu. Staggered vistas
of pagodas, ascending in cantilevered awnings, led our eyes and
feet foward. The piles of woodworking around every door window
frames turned the facing rows of shops into architectural Medusa
heads, squirming with intensity. We shared the midget lanes with
soldiers of a dozen stripes, traders of a dozen tribes, thugs and
prophets of innumerable castes. Packs of short-panted porters,
with skin whose tone our guidebook accurately called "bronze,"
snoozed on each others' shoulders, between jobs, in the beds of
ox-carts. Women in layers of hand-dyed wrapping laid bunches of
chive on the mat of main streets without expectation of a sale.
Loitering would not be a proper word for much of what we saw,

because nobody was in anybody's way. No one had anything to do, yet our heads could not turn fast enough to take in all this nonaction. Something was always sneaking up on us. The cobblestones jutted unevenly to meet my tentative strides. The four of us were walking, like everyone else, down the middle of the ferment, trying to avoid the bicyclists who moved on either side, a traffic regulated by the insistent clanging of handlebar bells that echoed a more general tinkle, waffle, throb. There were no sidewalks to stay on either, just shallow gutters that formed one continuous urinal.

"We'll all have the K'du cough soon enough," the wife groused. She was obviously not yet attuned to the local concept of hygiene, which would have driven any epidemiologist batty. She was right, though: everyone we passed was hacking away, and we soon would. Breathing the world's least polluted air, the Nepalese nonetheless managed to play host to every known respiratory ailment. The ancient, unswept rock pathways were coated with spittle, snot, the upbrought phlegm of many generation's chest-clearing heaves. Where man was, there was filth: perpetuated by cigarettes and sewage and bare feet and a simple unwillingness to clean up.

But Iris observed, "It's the price you pay for all this life!" She could be obnoxious, especially when she was right. "Life needs muck to grow, needs this chaos, doesn't it?" And she wasn't afraid of it, bless her. She wouldn't take a bottle of Lysol to any of it.

"So does death, as these poor folk can attest," the husband shot back. He wasn't hostile, just enjoying the prospect of a juicy debate.

But he got none, because some internal command was turning Iris' words, and mine, into gulps. The hash brownie was taking its delayed revenge. The cake ate us now, it digested us in turn. Iris gripped my arm and I gripped her back. We were afire, akindled, abuzzed. We'd been wrong; this was strong shit.

Now we had to explain, just when explanations were beginning to strike us as pointless. "Oh, by the way, we took, that is, we ate, this special cake . . . y'know, special . . . not too swift a move . . . but y'know, I think we're starting to feel it." Think! We were turning to jello. We blinked our emergency lights at the Aussies, but they saw only a flicker.

"Sounds nice. A little appetite stimulation, eh." Drug taking was one aspect of Asia that the couple could condone because it had been expropriated and made part of the customs in Melbourne.

"But I'm so thirsty suddenly," I had to admit. Walking was effortless, but intensified the dryness at the back of my throat until I felt my glands could no longer produce saliva.

"Got the old cotton mouth, eh, mate?" The metaphor was adroit. "Got those hash cookie clicks?"

"The clicks, that's it. My lips are made of wood."

"Be there in a moment, friend. Buy you a Coca-Cola." He'd heard all of this before.

Iris glanced at me. Moments were no longer moments for us, but eternities crowded with sensation.

"This was some brownie. . . . I hope you don't mind. We, we may be a bit . . . incapacitated."

"Oh, come on now, it can't be that choice, can it? . . . Though I have heard they put pure hashish oil in those pastries. The pressing from the resins. Quite potent, I'll bet."

"Quite potent." So that explained the stunned cows on Jack Flash's pillows! Now it explained us.

"Don't fret, mate. We'll talk you through it."

But who wanted to talk? Under ordinary circumstances, if such a state ever existed here, Kathmandu was a carnival. Now it looked like a whirling humpbacked bacchanal. A frenzied picaresque, as captured by Breughel the Elder. No, he wasn't elder enough. The hash helped me race toward generalization. The Middle Ages! That was it! The tough plastic shield between us and what we saw went deeper than differences in skin tone, religion, race or values. It was the barrier of development and time. If the Nepalese spoke Lancashire English and wore Robin Hood outfits, we would have had the same trouble comprehending them. Looking around, really seeing for the first time, each man was in his precious niche and showed no need to stir from it. We passed the town blacksmith, the town cobbler, the town balloon man, the town wench.

It was a static, contented hierarchy reaching straight to the King. The Nepalese paid fealty to him as it must have been paid to Charlemagne. Only this ruler's name was Birendra, son of Mahendra. We would catch sight of him later in our visit, emerging from his palace in a Mercedes-Benz; it had to be him because we were the only ones who didn't bow as the limousine sped past. Birendra had declared his people unprepared for democracy, and no one put up the least argument. The King was the father, and in these hills, the sons were not yet ganging up on him. History, with all its ensuing strife, was a concept that had not yet taken hold. So little "happened" here. (And yet, it was happening all around me: birth, work, defecation, barter, soothing, glee, decay.) The local English-language paper, printed in broken hand-set type and called "The Rising Nepal," bore such urgent headlines as "Queen Mother Distributes Sweets to Children!"

This medieval fiefdom, then, had been open to the rest of the planet for less than twenty years. Was it any surprise that the inhabitants prayed to a "living goddess," one lucky ingenue who was tabbed to be sequestered in a palace, then cast out at puberty? This was better than any tale in Iris' Brothers Grimm! Later, we would see the poor girl's kohl-smeared eyes sending out fright while she was borne beneath a red canopy by a procession of black-vested, black-capped Newars. While she was trotted around the block, a band tooted discordantly on clarinets. Who knew what it all meant? The pillars of the most sacrosanct temples bore explicit erotic carvings. Was it really because the goddess of lightning was thought to be a virgin who would be repelled from striking such images? Or was that just what the Nepalese wanted us to believe? When it came to power, they might be at our mercy; when it came to the truth, we were at theirs.

Iris pulled me out of my speculation by dropping back, out of the Aussies' range, and whispering, "I love this place because nothing is clear!"

I was too stunned and disquieted to offer argument. It was true that everything in sight seemed subject to whim and mystery. The mountains set the rules here, and man tried to accept and play along. The beings who stared us down were silent, stoic types who judged others by deeds, not words. Their wisdoms were inarticulate, like those in Iris' constant, protective smile.

Then why did she have to keep reminding me that we ought to shed our biases, which favored the sharp image over the blurred, the result over the experience, the answer over the riddle? Was she claiming that sickness might be a more enlightened state than health? Who could sort it all out? All I knew for certain was that I was viewing another way to be on the earth.

And where I had automatically consigned the people I was

watching to the role of "relics," I now felt, down in my queasy gut, how little right I had to claim ownership of the present. We—me and the Kathmanduans—were on this earth coterminously. We took up the same space, depleted the same amount of dioxide, and our efforts came to a similar end.

If anything, this place was more surely what it was than I was who I was! And the effects of being blasted out of my gourd were almost redundant, just one notch more dizzying than being trapped inside this time-machine. The sights of our route pulsed and glimmered: we had to be sinking toward the deepest, most arcane chamber of this trembling city-heart. But no, we were going to dinner, to a restaurant. Neither of us were the least bit hungry, or even slightly interested in conversation. The best that could be said about the place we were being led was that it would shield us temporarily from Kathmandu's baffling overload of stimuli.

We tried to locate Utep's afterward, but never did. The place had a vaguely exclusive air, dark and surprisingly sumptuous, with a Western-style bar at the front. Alcohol was hardly a featured item in Kathmandu—it was available mainly in the form of Russian vodka and the German-sponsored Star Beer, "brewed with pure Himalayan spring waters"—and restaurants themselves were a rather experimental deal. Aside from the preposterous meringues at the sweets shops and Peace Corps spin-offs, all the cuisine offered was a potpourri of Chinese, Tibetan, Indian and mainly what the Nepalese imagined to be Western. What came on the plate was a kind of sketch in food, an approximation of what the local merchants thought might be required by these strangers who actually seemed to enjoy eating in the presence of other strangers. Utep's was no exception.

At a booth in the back, the other couple waited. They were two stocky, curly haired specimens with lusciously evocative Brooklyn accents. I felt kindly toward them for that, but not for the words that filtered through. Iris and I tried our best to get through the ritual of letting them know where we'd been and where we were hoping to go from here. They told us their itinerary in reply, but I instantly forgot it. The hashish occupied all my powers of recollection. One look at Iris told me she was in the same state. She was trying so hard to concentrate on the task of listening that the skin on her face appeared to be wrinkling up from a hot bath. The two of us were no less detached from our companions than we'd been from the sideshow outside. They, too, would now come under our giddy scrutiny.

Iris kept glancing down at her hands, and soon, so was I. They were fascinating because they looked so pale and raw and pulsing with unknown organisms. This sensation was another recognizable measure of the strength of our psychedelic dose: our hands, old pals, no longer felt like a part of ourselves. They barely functioned well enough to hold the menus. Iris and I had been reduced to toddlers on an Easter Sunday outing to Howard Johnson's. Though we weren't sitting in high chairs, the table seemed overly grand and up to our chins. The pink saucers of a Mad Hatter place setting looked enlarged also, as if underwater. The tea cups were monstrous, mutated and rubbery enough to expand on their own. Lifting them to our faces and swallowing their brackish contents was like trying to drain a lake. Iris and I were virtually helpless. The other couples seemed to understand, and kept deflecting our apologies, but their looks were perplexed, their manner condescending.

"Shall we cut up your meat for you, old boy?" the husband asked, and repeated the refrain, "It can't be *that* strong, can it?"

But it was, it was! This hashish made searchlights of our eyes, so that we could not avoid capturing the moves and dodges of these fellow travelers—such different "fellow travelers" than we'd known in our activist days! Iris and I had already learned to avoid political talk with the Australians. All the ones we'd encountered had bemoaned the American loss in Vietnam because it made them the dinosaurs of the Pacific, because it increased the weight of their white man's burden. We, the innocents that we were, instinctively came out on the side of the people, for the bands in the hills. Let them rise up, let them rise! Let the boys who had to be waiters in Utep's chuck us out in the name of sovereignty. We could always find some other place to vacation. (Or to feel disoriented.) Now, courtesy of our special cake, Iris and I observed the encounter between East and West with eyes and feelings mercilessly open. We witnessed the servile, snarling resentment of the kids in monkey suits who catered to tastes for which they had no empathy. We duly recorded the paternalist, saccharine tone by which the parasites made their needs known. The Australians had barked for Cokes all around. Fifteen minutes later, a tray full of "curds"—yogurt—was delivered. It was an innocent mistake: how were the Nepalese supposed to know better? But the Australians didn't treat it as one. They humiliated the waiters, first by laughing, then by shouting, finally by throwing up their hands in exasperation.

"Why don't we just eat the yogurt?" Iris asked. It didn't make any difference to her or me. We'd grown used to waiting an hour for a pot of tea and besides, we weren't the least bit hungry.

Yet the rest of the table found Iris' rather sensible attempt at tolerance to be quite irrational, very "stoned-out." The two couples thought such a gesture out of the question and clutched their ethnocentricity by reminding us, "That's dessert. Remember?"

Once they got the boys to reluctantly take the dishes back, the wife muttered, "Shithouse service again."

The rest of the dinner did arrive in sloppy waves. But how long had such three-course affairs been served in this country? It was during this same generation that the first palefaces had been airlifted in. Yet the American girl screamed in her best subway rasp when our soup was brought last.

"It's happened before," she confided.

Everyone laughed and shook their heads at this astounding bit of barbarism. Everyone except us. We knew that the Chinese usually served their soup last. They did so to rinse the palate. It seemed a highly reasonable custom. Besides, in sheer numbers, there were so many more of them doing it their way than there were of us doing it ours.

Iris and I hardly touched the fried rice. Yet we tittered among the monsters, were monstrously polite. At first, we'd felt awful about our inability to join their party; quickly, we'd felt worse about our inability to leave. There was an undeclared war going on in this restaurant, each time feeder met fed, weak met strong. Naturally, our heightened sensitivity enabled us to invest each petty skirmish with symbolic hues. But we didn't want to remain giggling bystanders. We wanted to disengage ourselves from these sightseers who killed the sights they saw as a hunter kills his prey. The Australians could not comprehend why they were not better served; we could not comprehend why these bridled children served us at all. Our companions came with a curse and paid with a curse.

On our way out, we noticed a private annex to the restaurant that was ashimmer with a blazing, primordial fire. Beside it, the guests at a catered party faced one another down a long plank table loaded with candelabras, pilafs, whole sides of mutton and game.

"Now there's a first class feed!" murmured the husband. It was a real pillage, more to his liking, and we lingered with him at the windows. We all snooped, without apology, and how could we help but? The folks inside seemed to be having such a good time. They were all white, white as their napkins, and young and long-haired besides. They were hipper than our gang, and showed plenty of savvy to have pulled off this beggars' banquet. They had to be old-timers, too—probably former Peace Corps people, importers and exporters, or well-established dope dealers. This unlikely bunch, gobbling away, was the seed of a new elite, a limited autocracy that was about all this miniature economy could keep in yak's wool, hash and carved masks. I saw at once that this party's "pig out" was fond, that the diners had taken the time to understand the culture they'd come to exploit. They were minglers, misfits, seekers. Had the British East India Company begun any differently? No doubt this was just the beginning: poor Nepal had so much to catch up on. In this rite that was undraped, unguarded, unrepentant, dark men still stood at attention in starched collars. Interlopers still ate and enjoyed themselves with abandon. The feast was spread before them.

It was just one more vision that made me thankful for an early retreat from my own race to the frigid meat locker of our hotel room. It was one among many tableaus of Kathmandu that I found myself able to scan, a little at a time, through the periscope of memory. All night long, as the brownie drug barred sleep, I tried to piece together my Hamlin, tried to see why I could no more qualify for a place in the fable than could the Australians or the hippie traders. But none of these concerns troubled Iris, who was happy to stroke my frazzled skull whenever I laid it on her lap. She, too, was up until dawn, oscillating to her own frequency, playing solitaire and whistling "Oklahoma!"

LOST IN THE HILLS

DAY TWO. We awake in the land of avalanches. Here, where we've chosen to trek, one loss feeds another. First, the French pair whom we'd counted on tagging after, skip their tea and skip out before we're awake. They know the value of daylight. Next, our mimeographed chart fails us, or we fail it. A dozen paths crisscross the knoll beyond Pati Bhanyang. The directions we clutch are vague, especially so in pidgin Indo-English. To find the "centre routing," we circle the first spur leftward instead of going straight over. Wishful thinking is our navigator; we're hoping we don't have to tackle such an incline so early in the morning.

Each time we pass a farmer in his sloping, tiered field, we call out the lilting name of our next destination, Taramarang. That's the gateway to the Helambu high country. One man points us forward, another back where we've been. The path is narrowing, but looping wider and wider around the hill. A spritely teenager in floppy gray tunic, white stovepipes and bare feet shoots past us like an Alfa Romeo on the Amalfi drive. He nods when we call "Taramarang," so we follow. But he shows no inclination to keep an eye on two laggards. Soon he is a hundred yards ahead, then a bobbing reddish speck. We are finally on the other side of the

167

big mound, but we've done it by way of a hollow that falls into another canyon and a range beyond. The "centre routing" on which we've gambled is now indistinguishable from the walls of mud dams through the terraced rice paddies. Our advance scout is already on the far side of the ravine, a blip in chest-high foliage. And we are not on any path at all, but zigzagging through some-one's staple crop. A team of leaf-pickers with oval baskets on their backs rustles against the distant hillside. "Taramarang!" we call. Perhaps the word is more than a place name; they do us a favor by declining to react. We unfasten our packs and collapse.

Half a day wasted by one wrong turn! We can't even calculate how to retrace our steps. Iris is grim. My brain is all blisters. We can return to Pati Bhanyang for the day, but being left for carrion seems more entertaining. We have gotten lost after all, at the first opportunity.

When I pull the first of many "I-told-you-sos," I realize I'm singing the proper part in our duet. I'm the eternal flake, the fifth column, an essential thorn in Iris' side. "Don't be cross as two sticks! Be a man!" Her despair is vented in anger against me so that it can give way to determination. I always let her win our test of wills because I crave further testing. I lag behind and watch her picking her way through the paddies, one dirt shelf at a time, until she's nearly back on the face of the hill we'd hoped to avoid. The sun is working toward noon, no arctic breezes here. While I give my shoulders another break from the straps of my pack, Iris scavenges farther up for unwritten road signs. She turns back to me, waving both arms. I lumber up to find she's enlisted a farmer who'll get us back on the true path. I can see the unsteady shed where the man is conferring with his wife. When he returns, he's more eager to point than to guide. His face is more wrinkled than an alligator bag. Iris hollers at me to get a twenty rupee note out of her pack. I do it, wondering if the peasant finds such henpecking any more amusing than I do. She waves the money, matador-like, but this old bull is not moved by red, or green. What can he buy with it? Still, the sight of cash helps him sense our desperation and we start off up the hill behind him.

The farmer turns out to be a fine old billy goat. He's anxious to skip up the mound and waltz back to his fields. His cragginess, and his quick step, make him the Nepalese equivalent of Walter Huston's prospector in *The Treasure of the Sierra Madre*. And I'm the Bogart character, Fred C. Dobbs, exhausted and cursing the old man all the way. The only difference is that I never possessed Dobbsy's initial arrogance or his greed. I'm not looking for gold, just distraction. I'm certainly finding it now. The peasant doesn't make any rest stops, though we've left paddies below and are tramping through a vertical desert. Bare boulders and spindly, globed bushes break the dust of the worn road. At last, just at high noon, we're on the top of the ridge again. We can look down on Pati Bhanyang, painfully nearby. We've logged four hours to get four hundred yards. Though the farmer knows no English, his language is visceral, acquirable as survival. He points toward Taramarang and offers a long, high-pitched cry that any listener could translate as, "Far, far and farther on beyond that . . ." He abandons us with his galling spryness intact.

After an hour's teetering on the ridge, the trail leads us back into the canyon we'd formerly passed up. Now down is as perilous as up. We get rolling like runaway snowballs. Down and down, alongside a water-carved rivulet that feeds a slope suddenly hinting of the Nepalese jungle: the dense, lowland terai that's still home to tigers. We are staggering toward a rocky, mostly dry river bed that's wider than a freeway. A good thing, because it will be simple to follow and what little water there is can replenish our jug. Packs of porters pass us as easily on the downhill run as they did on the lift. The path, our map shows, runs along the bluff above the bed. But we find no such turnout and scamper from the hillside onto the blinding, neutral expanse of gulley. At the bottom of the descent, an old man sits in a straw crawl-under supervising a stone water mill turned by a faint runoff. A water buffalo sips from the same stream, looking too meaty, too alive in the bleached river bed. Conga lines of women in black pleats to their ankles curve around ten-story boulders—an impediment even to the Nepalese—and show us the way downstream.

Once they've got too far ahead, we must use a process of elimination for finding a passable route. This bed, it turns out, is getting awfully lumpy. There are rocks to skirt and dead ends that lead us to charging flows of water we'd rather not ford. This game makes us feel we're being adventurous, cut-rate Lewis and Clarks. But it has few rules and no end. The sun passes over us and is blocked by the far wall of the ravine. In this colder light, the river assumes its true dimension. We're lucky it's not monsoon time.

We can imagine the Biblical-style floods that course through this channel of heart-broken granite. Occasionally, the sides of the canyon burst, lose their staying power, leaving immense slides of moon rocks. Industrial-sized pebbles have been rolled down by a Zen Paul Bunyan. Each stone is a monument, each tributary forms a dynamited chasm. Yet these terrifying proportions, or disproportions, are our best reminders of how close we are to the earth's highest mountains.

We are right in the midst of a glacial foundry. Luckily, the glacier moves slowly, but the day will be done so fast. The river, too, is gaining on us, sprawling over more and more of its bed. We scan the bluff constantly for some alternate path. Sunset is making the canyons blush. The boulders may be stolid, but where there is fertility, the hills glow eerily from within. With our forty-pound packs, we are astronauts landed on the wrong planet. We can't remember what misfired trajectory got us here. We must concentrate on reaching the space station at Taramarang. If only we were weightless!

Picking my way through the gulleys, I'm also resigning myself to a night in the wilds—even convincing myself it won't be so bad, though I'd never admit that to Iris. Could we face anything outdoors more ferocious than the Brahmin's sputum-clearing? The weather is hospitable, if the terrain isn't. And we're lugging the benefits of world trade on our backs: Portuguese sardines and Indian cashews and cheese from the Swiss-sponsored dairy that'll taste better to us than any curried mush.

The boulders are malignant now. We're not playing with skipping stones anymore. Each surface seems to expand as I step on it. I lose my footing crossing one of the thousand trickles of river. An instinctive balancing act fails to take account of the pounds on my back. I am slammed to the rock face, as if pushed. There is no time to break the fall.

"Iris! Whoa!" My glasses are smashed. Blood closes my left eye.

She's learned to ignore my squawking, but the blood brings her running. Back in Kathmandu, the equipper Pasong told us reassuringly about dramatic rescues made by porters who carry on their backs the victims of broken legs and appendicitis. My emergency hardly qualifies. Nurse Nancy patches the cut over my eyebrow with some gauze I'd insisted we bring along. Unwittingly,

I've justified my own dire forecasts. At my most embarrassing moment, an upstream traveler, mute bronze Nepali, pauses to perch on the boulder beside me, simply staring, sent to record the event for "This Is Your Life." He ogles as Iris completes the bandaging. He shakes his head sympathetically, then is amazed by my riches when I pull out a second pair of specs. I must see the rest of the mountains through this brown-tinted spare. But the injury has its satisfactions. It is a mark of my wanderlust, not just my ineptitude.

We must keep moving. No view of Taramarang's gold spires, emerald ramparts, neon. Iris concedes that we've barely enough light to pick out a suitable campsite. "Good work!" I scold again, this time without exasperation. It is my work, too. Now the canyon walls have leveled off, rice fields grow almost to the banks and low cushions of sand border the water. Iris sizes it up with an ex-Girl Scout's acumen. But where are the medals and the marshmallows? Later on, she may build a fire and sing traditional ditties about pine and whippoorwill, juniper and Jesus. I am supposed to be looking for kindling, but I keep casting about for the skyline, outline, any line of Taramarang. One more bend, I hear myself pleading. Just one more bend, though I don't know anymore what I'm pleading for. Certainly not my share of tea and another straw mat.

I hush up: complaining is not a serious activity and things are getting serious. The evening's purple fandango mutes into a somber blue fugue. We must settle for the next sandy alcove and lay our sleeping pads there. Iris takes charge of the operation, which is all I've ever asked of her. Together, we clear pebbles from where our spines must lay. We forage for the rare twig.

We've just begun to find our picnic area appealing, just had time to map its outlines in the dusk, when two peasant boys spot us from the ridge. Silhouetted against the frosty sky, they could be scampering Cherokee lookouts or maybe satyrs. Anyway, they can't be worse than the rednecks who like to plague campers back home. But they are coming at us, coming down to the other side of the river, carrying scythes casually on their shoulders. They start calling and motioning patiently. They keep pointing at something until we make it out: a shed, large enough to be a stable, behind them. It hardly seems worth it now to get soaked crossing the river, but we decide it would be best to accept the youths' invitation. We presume they'll take us in, feed us and bed us down by some crackling hearth. We congratulate ourselves for having stumbled on a bit of real life, a way inside. Besides, in this landscape where man is inherently weak, it would take quite a supply of hubris to refuse aid. It's worse to balk at taking than at giving— and those scythes look sharp.

We pack up hastily and help each other keep our sea legs across the chilling current of the summer run-off. The Nepalese boys don't approach the bank to greet us. They show no welcome wagon or curiosity. Perhaps they think of us as a source of contamination, for they keep their distance, like our erstwhile guide of the morning. We follow them toward the shed. We see them gesturing for us to set down our things. They keep going up the hillside. Wherever they are headed, we have not been asked along.

But then no one asked us to come here. No one told us to get lost in their fields. The shed smells of hay and manure. There's no flat dune on this side like the one we've just abandoned, so we opt for a roof. We will sleep in the dust and breathe the aroma of animals long overworked, long dead. It's still not the Mt. Everest experience, but it will do. With our flashlight, we seek another level spot for our bags. Instead of rocks, we sweep aside animal pellets. The winds are picking up, so we stay as far as possible from the square opening, that's just high enough for the leprechauns of the paddies. Still, there's plenty of room for us inside.

We're alone in the Himalayas. The outcome I feared most has come to pass, and it's almost delicious now, as if the fears were a seasoning. They make dinner taste fine. The keys on the sardine cans break before we can turn them, so we have to pry the filets out one at a time with Iris' Swiss Army knife. Cheese and chocolate have melted in our packs; they taste wonderfully the same. We've made garbage, but can find no sensible place to toss it in this pre-garbage setting. Though no one can possibly see us, we seek out bushes to squat and shit. We take our mildewed washcloths and plastic soap dish down to the water.

Rid of chores, we sit by the entrance to our latest home. Magically, the moon appears, just inches off the horizon, too full, too vivid, right over the river hurtling downstream. It's pluckable; distorted but harmonious. The moon's color is deep yellow—not a yellow of stain, of age, of cowardice, but a serene, alpha-wave yellow. At home, we'd call it a harvest moon. But this isn't fall, it's a summery spring. And the lunar glow proudly takes stock of fields that are largely chipped and busted gypsum. The pumice of the gods. I'm reminded of a Tanguy dream wilderness, or a cat's-eye moon from some Henri Rousseau vision. I hear the strains of Bartok's shepherd symphonies. I would prefer Tibetan bells. It takes me a long time to quit digging for reference points, to calm the noise in my head so I can listen to the river moving below us. Here, rushing waters are no accompaniment, but the only music in town.

Beside me, Iris purrs. I see her crooked, uplifted pug of a nose, her bedraggled bangs, her keen brown eyes open to full aperture. She has found her Asian vision. She'd been stirred previously by those unconscious gestures from a rickshaw driver or a silk weaver that reflected centuries of evolving selflessness in a second, but I can tell that this moment of moon-worship gets to her more. She doesn't have to say it, but I know she's seeking to recreate some lunar ceremony carried out by females of yore. She's digging up the oldest roots, the handiest symbols, for her "new mythology."

I won't tease her, not now. She's out to salvage humanity with this stuff, starting with herself. Iris' urge to conjure up innocence strikes me as more honorable than innocence itself. I reach for her hand, and we're soon glued together with sardine oil. The day's grumbles and whines evaporate. The Abominable Snowman ceases to shadow me. It's impossible to be "cross as two sticks." All sticks are uncrossed.

We know we should make love, but we're too sore and worn down. Besides, we've left all "shoulds" behind, along with Iris' diaphragm. "Was it too much weight to carry?" Iris kisses me. She likes her excuses, and likes me for allowing them. She aspires toward unattainability, and I whisper, "I've never felt better about being lost."

We slip inside our manger. Did the three wise men carry rented sleeping bags? We drift out of Nepal by the only means available. No customs inspection to pass in our dreams, no visas necessary.

Day three. Come to get their hoes, the tillers find us. Gathered in a semi-circle, they peer down bemusedly. They chat casually, they seem eager for us to be up and out, but otherwise mean no harm. Still, we feel like secret agents who've been slipped Mickey Finns, coming-to in the presence of our captors. Without my glasses, I count four women and one patriarch, all in matching red tunics. Peasants who could be parachuted down in a hundred lands, on a hundred types of poor soil, and start right in where the last sowing left off. And we, urbanites, ever out of place, squirm in our fiberfill beds. These Nepalis don't try to communicate, and won't be dissuaded from their eternal tasks. They just stare and chuckle until we're up on our elbows, then go their own way. And we go ours, having committed no trespass, no impasse, no impress.

Down to the riverside for a splash in the face. We aspire toward the Spartan, but our bones want out. The cultivators eye us while they stoop to coax slender shoots from their rocky patch. We don't dally by their shed, and we've little left for breakfast. Pledged to a "slow day," perhaps taking us only so far as we should have gotten yesterday, we set out. Iris sets the pace. How quickly we've established this hierarchy of the trail! But the morning is when I find it hardest to tag along. The backs of my ankles are rubbed raw again before there's time for them to scab. The soreness in my calves, thighs and joints won't pass until the body's been revved up to emergency function. The back is not yet resigned to more donkey service. The straps of my pack are two lashes.

Picking my way through the smaller stones along the river's shrinking edge, I feel like I'm walking on stilts. I'm Dobbsy again: the whiner, the shirker and the toad. A second-guessing defeatist is trekking along with me, and though he's hardly a stranger, I'm disappointed at how quickly he's asserted himself. But don't call him the voice of self-interest, an uncivilized ogre. No, my inner beast is highly bred. He wants his cigars and brandy after dinner, or at least an English muffin in bed. He wants to be spared all the trials that his "better half" has cooked up for him. He reminds me, incessantly, that while the mind may have a taste for self-improvement, the back doesn't. Yet I must, by any standards, be considered driven—for what other sort of creature would stray so far from his home and habits just to gain the wisdoms born of inconvenience? Or is all of this just my way to prove love and loyalty to Iris? The test I've been dreading is in progress, but the swine inside me doesn't care whether I succeed or fail. He knows what I won't admit: that Iris doesn't require such proof, that both of us could easily do without such an examination.

When a man has thoughts like these, he unloosens his burden, picks a nice, comfortable rock, and adds his tears to the rolling rapids. Iris, who's been brushing aside my pleas for a break, comes to fetch me for a second time. Her mind is crowded with the logistics of the hike. I don't care to add the logistics of our relationship, so the only way I can explain myself is to blurt out, "I can't go on. Maybe it's these damn boots. Every mile is taking us so much longer than our chart says it should. Let's face it, we're not ready. I'm not ready. . . . I can't."

"Don't say you can't," is Iris' slogan. "If you must, say you don't want to."

The difference appears semantic at first, but it isn't. She doesn't want a confession from me, or the satisfaction of having a scapegoat. She wants me to make it. To do so, I must not let my enthusiasm tire before my legs do. And each step I take from now on further disproves my "can't"-hood. Poor humans, saddled with the desire to achieve, bereft of the pleasure principle! How long ago did we lose it? Or was losing it what made us human to start? In anything of value we do for others or ourselves, the key word is "must"—even here, even in nature, even nowhere. My "can't" turns to "must" just as soon as baby gets its bottle, which is the moment Iris puts her arm around me.

As we confer, porters are sidestepping us. Their autonomic systems compute hillside and load, angle of rock, angle of sun. I must hide my puffy face from them, though they've probably witnessed such breakdowns before. They've even provided towing services for some. By the time I'm back on my feet, a whole troupe of Germans comes past in review. They move briskly and jauntily at the head of a line of rented bearers. How clean-shaven and masterful they look! The essence of Alpine! It's easy to look on top of it all when you've got ten men carrying your toiletries. Is this surfeit of hired hands what enables the sportsman to strike a commanding figure? At the famous Tiger Tops, south of Kathmandu, such men pay two hundred bucks a day to be guided about on elephants through a prerehearsed wildlife show. I feel a renewed sense of nobility about my honest, if badly planned, efforts. And the lads in *lederhosen* give us the news we've been seeking since yesterday afternoon: we're less than two hours from Tara-marang.

We reach it by noon. At the juncture of two canyons and their torrential drainage, a wobbly suspension bridge takes us over our river to town. It is hardly the yearned-for oasis: simple two-story houses made of thick, red-tinged lumber surround one curve of dirt a city block in length. Still, it looks like the Taramarangans are feting us with a parade. Main street is strewn with multicolored scraps of fabrics, embroidery work and remnants, frazzled tumbleweeds of discarded thread. This layer of woolen confetti isn't in honor of any heroic trekkers, just the continuous spillover from the several tailoring shops set up on front porches. Judging by the action on the treadle machines, and the quantity of merry garbage, this clump of life has the task of sewing all the clothes for the region. The town has also seen its share of sore-footed traffic.

Just off the bridge, we're tugged on the arm and beckoned with "Hallo, touris' man!" by a fellow with square head, smile wrinkles and goatee. The local version of Kathmandu's "K.C.", he's clearly trying to fashion a livelihood out of the stray foreigners who stumble through. Guided toward the house he's turned into a supply center, inn and canteen, we can see that quite a large family seems to be surviving on this man's slight acquaintance with English. We're comforted and exasperated to find the imperialist tongue has reached such an inaccessible point. At least, we can ask the man how tough a climb it is to Keul, the next notch on the ladder of the slope. He writes out the name of a tea-shop up there where we can spend the night. We pay for the information with lunch. In a cubbyhole filled with roosters and toddlers, we await hard-boiled eggs. They take the customary hour. We pick from the innkeeper's stock of tinned Indian fruit juices, which go at understandably exorbitant rates. Upstairs, we can see, there's a bare loft in which to throw our bags. A tiny, hand-painted placard wobbles from the peak of the gabled roof announcing the establishment as the "Pomp and Joy Lodge." There may be some joy lurking somewhere, but I see little pomp in Taramarang.

While the eggs warm, and we try to decide if we ought to continue, another party crosses the bridge and flops beside us on the lodge's all-purpose lunch counter and bench. One of the arrivals is a typically uncommunicative porter, but he has an excuse. This brawny Nepali turns out to be mute. His companion is a chipper, khaki-haired Canadian named Don, who's come all the way from Pati Bhanyang in this one morning. Don sports freckles and a crewcut that give him the look of an Eagle Scout mistakenly lost amidst Hare Krishnas. And, indeed, he's just finished a two-year stint in Yogic studies at one of the "bliss farms" in South India. He's trekking now, like we are, just to prove he can do it— and also to postpone a dreaded return to Vancouver. He's become part-Indian. We can tell that by the listless and overly patient approach he uses to bring down the price of some mango puree.

Now Iris is having trouble shaking her soreness. But Don is the spur we need to continue. With his offer to pace us the rest of the way, we decide to get a headstart on our final climb. Don will finish his lunch and catch up with us later. There had once been a highway for ox carts past Taramarang, so the path's clear and obvious. Iris and I share a great burst of vigor. We can even chat as we go, comparing notes on the scenery thusfar and agreeing we could do better driving through the Sierra Nevadas or the Appalachians. We're some three thousand feet higher than Kathmandu, but the vegetation is hardly mountainous. Will we ever get to the dominion of pine? Will we even glimpse snow or massifs? We must settle for vertical China-sculpted shelves crowded with wispy rice stalks, falling in semicircles toward the river. Where the land is not cultivated, the brush is dull brown. Of course, the air is resoundingly clean. But the gritty residue of poverty swirls around us each time we approach our own species.

In an hour, we come to the stone houses of Mahankal. For the first time, it's taken us just the time our printed schedule says it should! This prim, windswept village is out of the Swiss Jura, but there are no chocolate shops, or window boxes filled with geraniums. By a spring just beyond the town, a new, unadorned concrete schoolhouse stands. We can hear the class inside reciting in unison. We share the road with a few latecomers. Some of these children are potential Abe Lincolns, walking twenty miles a day to get here. Obviously, most children in these parts don't make it to school at all.

Don catches up with us just as our handout tells us to look for a plank bridge across the river. The bridge turns out to be a narrow chain hammock strung loosely over the boulders of the chasm. Iris and I cross one at a time, trying to use any techniques we can summon from our memories of circus tightrope artists.

Following the narrow, rotting boards laid over the rusting net, the bridge tilts and sways without warning. Don holds back, admitting he's afraid of heights. I'm beginning to think he's my kind of mountaineer. He chooses to ford the river, soaking his shorts. The trail meanders from the bridge until we can't tell it from the rungs of paddies. We're momentarily lost again, but the direction to go has to be up. Our chart tells us Keul is nearly two thousand feet above Taramarang. We forge our own path, skirt more fields, climb three or four mean ridges. The mid-afternoon chill prompts an unspoken urgency. When we ask several women in the paddies about Keul, they just stare back.

"Did they tell you stories in Kathmandu about all those warm, friendly Sherpas you'd be meeting?" Don huffs and puffs. I'm pleased by his willingness to admit that travel rarely feels the way it looks on a poster, particularly when it's travel by your own steam. But it doesn't seem fair for him to complain; he's made such good time. We are all disappointed by Keul. The town's just a lazy cluster of farms on the ridge above the river. There's no painted signs, no confetti. We surmise that the way station we're seeking is a whitewashed mud structure built right beside the main trail. The woman who appears at the door only scowls at us. The note we've been given by Mister Pomp and Joy means nothing to her. She squints at the Nepali script like it's a doctor's scribble on a prescription. We have no way to decipher it for her. Children scowl at us, too, from benches molded into the house's porch. They're the least jocular kids I've ever seen. Already posing in askew cotton caps, size one tunics and vests, they are their fathers in miniature. Barefoot and underfed—also general characteristics—they've learned to hold their faces in the communal mask. It's a caustic and remote look that reminds you these are people who are independent to the point of paranoia. They will take their time, thank you, about checking us out.

Their mother doesn't get more helpful. We retrace our steps to another house back down the trail. That's another half-mile logged by feet that have lost all feeling. But the word "Keul" brings orders from the farmers to return to the big white house. The second time, we grow desperate. Don motions for a place to sleep, I shovel imaginary food silently into my mouth. The answer is an obvious, sign language no. Several field hands wander over from behind the house to enforce the decision. We caucus, hungry and sore. A dust storm is blowing up. The next town cannot be reached by dark. I gird myself for another night outdoors.

Don's mute partner appears down the lane. The porter to the rescue! He no doubt passes this way regularly and everyone trusts him. Of course, he cannot speak either, but he makes a plea with gestures more effective than ours. He offers to stay the night with us, Don interprets, because he's not feeling well. Suddenly, we're welcome. The diffident woman nearly smiles. Her oldest daughter leads us to the annex, a converted space. However, suspicions remain. She holds out her hand. We must pay our dollar-or-so in advance. Equally dour daughters in long embroidered dresses begrudge us the evening meal. They ladle out minuscule portions of dal from a witches' cauldron.

The porter keeps eyeing our belongings as we unpack them. He keeps playing charades, too, until we've guessed that what he's after is some sort of painkiller. He knows that every Westerner carries drugs. Less afraid of them than we are, he demands his pill. Iris starts to rummage for codeine, but Don warns us that our medicines have a stronger effect on those who've never tried them, so she gives the porter a single aspirin. Sitting in a corner, head using drawn-up knees for a pillow, the porter is put into a comatose state. Thanks to him, we've gotten our lodgings, our required roof, complete with straw mats hosting fanged bedbugs and glassless windows that funnel the billows of dust our way.

Following Don's lead, we force ourselves to wash at the river bank before we sleep. The innkeeper and her man glare at us like we're loonies. The magnificent, white-bottomed river is seemingly no attraction to them. We end up lingering in the shallows. Each of us claims a separate rock and soaks our feet until they're anesthetized. We count stars as they emerge, listen to the current and reminisce. Where *else* have we all been? There are the customary exchanges of information about hotels and monuments. But the talk turns quickly from Asia to Europe to European food. "What I'd give for a slice of Italian veal!" I murmur. Don insists that he's been converted to vegetarianism. He's habituated himself to long fasts. Under the direction of a jet-setting swami, he's lived on lemon juice and water until this purifying combination was all that ran out of his other end. Yet he is already wavering in anticipation of his homecoming. "I used to head for steak 'n' lobster twice a week at the Sizzler," Don confides. "I was the genuine raw meat aggressive. I don't know if I can resist the old ways."

He certainly can't resist describing them. We begin trading memories to tempt the palate. The great meals: a four-course affair in Dijon, a Greek taverna's bounty. Then, favorite recipes: beef stroganoff, hopping john and corn pudding, spaghetti carbonara, poached salmon in dill. Our hostess is still on her porch, keeping track of us. Doesn't she ever eat? Can she know we're blabbering on like a bunch of starving dog-runners in the Yukon? The Himalayas may loom on either side of us, but before our eyes glitters a clean tablecloth, a basket stuffed with bread, a bottle of Burgundy and the *plat du jour*. We speak with our stomachs, via our hearts. Then we catch ourselves, laugh together, pull our feet from the natural Jacuzzi and start back up the hill, boots in hand.

Day four. Must this cat-and-mouse game be played out wherever we go? Iris is the one who made us go on this trek and I'm going to make sure she's the one who gives up. It doesn't matter that I've been craving such an outcome since we scaled the first unmoving escalator steps of the trail, or that I can barely make it across the sleeping room without bleeding into my socks. I won't be the first to point out that this past night has finished us off like no day could: awakened by a furious dust storm that choked off our rest, we'd been kept up and writhing by unrepentant bedbugs that others of our kind had deposited in the matting. Neither of us got any rest. Still, Iris has to throw in the towel. She makes the motion, I second.

To coax her into turning back, I continue playing navigator over morning tea. While Don rouses himself across the way—our mute sponsor is long gone—I spread out the topographic charts and explain why the next few miles have to be more precipitous than any we've faced. I do no editorializing. I let Iris show off her bedbug bites.

"I don't want to meet anymore of these critters. There's no need to go any farther."

"Are you sure?"

"Aren't you? Damn, don't be so passive-aggressive."

"Passive maybe, aggressive never. . . . I just want you to decide."

"You always want me to decide."

"But this is your dream, your baby." Now Iris snuffs it out with characteristic lack of anguish or ambivalence.

"All right. I'd say we've bitten off more mountain than we can chew."

"No regrets?"

"Quit it now. You win."

But I haven't. I tell her, "I just don't want to fail you."

"You can't. You never do, except when you try too hard."

She leans across the floor and the pile made by our mismatched boots to embrace me. Iris is my taskmaster only when I wish the role upon her, a point she's now proving by so willingly relinquishing the whip. The two of us can hobble down from the heights with a new sense of equality. Our journey, our whole lives, may be altered by this day's simple admission of weakness.

Perhaps our stay in the East is having its effect, too, because Iris and I seem to be trying to live within our limitations, even cherish them, as a means to live with one another. As of this morning, we are no longer here on a dare, we are here together. That established, we can look less at what's wrong with each other and more at what's right in the world.

Don decides to turn back as well. His legs are capable of higher altitudes, but the capacity alone does not make the prospect any more jolly. Downstairs, the Sherpa boys greet us with good morning glares, already disgruntled, distrustful little men. Seeing us setting out in the direction from which we've come, their mother now shows that a gloat is part of her limited facial repertoire. But surely, the three of us should elicit a laugh: loaded down with enough gear to mount Annapurna, yet maimed by these last few days into doddering submission before each ant-hill rise, the best we can manage is two staggers ahead for every giant step backward. Our first few yards on the march are shin-splinting enough to make me realize that Iris has just been necessity's prophet. It will take us half a day just to coast the few miles back to Taramarang.

On the way, we pass by now familiar markers, including the newly built country schoolhouse. If only every routing forced the traveler into repeat visits, one as blind groper, one as old hand! How much more ordered, less indiscriminate does the countryside now appear! How better able is the human eye to esteem sights it anticipates! The school's two-story shell no longer resembles a barrack, partly because there are students pouring out. Just as we've paused to drench ourselves at a water pump that's part of the new construction, the single class has gone into recess. These boys and girls are less diffident than their prematurely laboring counterparts—they know how to giggle and compare notes on the apparitions we make, though none dare approach. When their teacher emerges, he makes no attempt to greet us or use us as the core of his next social studies lesson. With waxed mustache and pleated white flannels, he looks elegant enough to have stepped out of an F. Scott Fitzgerald soirée. By now, we recognize him as yet another selfless but tellingly detached Brahmin, putting in his community service. He claps to get his pupils into two lines across the dirt playlot and leads the six-to-twelve year olds in one-size-fits-all jumping jacks before this academy without name or fight song, blazers or blackboards or desks. Forlorn on the school balcony, a one-legged boy leans on his homemade crutch.

By midday, we're tramping into Taramarang. The tailors are still working. But there are plenty of Nepalese men who are simply hanging about in the open-air tea shops, playing cards, smoking regally through mother-of-pearl cigarette holders and generally preening themselves. Most of the women are out tending the paddies that have somehow been rent from the surrounding ravine walls. We're no longer shocked by such a division. Women make Asia go, just like Iris has been making me go.

Only now we can stop. First, we drop our packs to claim space for the night in the attic room of the "Pomp and Joy Lodge." Next, we make it some twenty more paces to reserve three choice boulders along the bank of the river we've been following all morning and dip our feet in for some extended hydrotherapy. Even at noon, in the season when the mountains reach the limit of their thawing, the water is fluid ice. From our new vantage point, we can see how effectively this medieval trading post is hemmed in by brown canyon ridges, sealed off from history. The town is stagnant beside the currents in this Himalayan runoff. We can look back up our side of the granite channel, over the top of a communal garbage heap, and take in the village's entire ramshackle concentricity. What few people we see shunting about town seem to be imbued, as we are, with that most Asian sense of weariness and travail. Usually, it sweeps over everything at sunset, when the skin no longer knows whether to feel flushed or chilled, as human energies lapse while the heat carries on. Thanks to our hiking, we're ground down enough to share in this juncture's pleasantly bittersweet fatigue. Our throbbing ankles seem to say it; the stooped women grooming their thin fields say it; the measured haughtiness of the village elders says it; the packs of naked and fidgeting children all say it. What hard work it is to be alive!

Especially here, especially today. On cauterized paws, Iris, Don and I limp past the composting, pre-industrial dump, along the avenue of spent stitches and caked mud toward an unoccupied bench. We feel like we're waiting at a bus stop, but no rattling diesel can cross the terrain we've crossed. Bearing no cargo but our consciousness, our reward is to look, to conjecture, to judge. On either side, the tailors go on working, none too quickly, on their antique machines. A rare woman merchant—I figure her to be the town widow or perhaps fallen lady—sits dejectedly before her soda shop. She is searingly unhappy, with an agitated, distinctly contemporary air of disturbance, that sets her apart from the other townspeople. Still, she shows no compunction to make a sale, little response for the women who stop to gossip with her. The men next door ignore her and us, continuing with their variation of canasta or rummy. These idle dandies appear to be the guardians of Nepalese culture. Absorbed in their game, they seem oblivious to the rotting food and rooster ca-ca, the tumbleweeds of tangled thread and gay strips of cotton (the only gaiety in sight). There's no Strindbergian struggle here against "the filth of life." The filth has long ago been declared the winner.

As we gawk, an important personage arrived in the village. We can tell he's important because he wears a stiff, dark Western suit jacket over the traditional stovepipe trousers and undertaker's vest. He carries a well-polished walking stick. A retinue in more jackets trails him. And two equally distinguished colleagues are coming up the other end of the lane to meet them in the deranged woman's patio (though patio connotes far too finished a look). Rocking themselves in the high-back chairs provided, legs spread wide, canes planted as ballast, the men share tea, tobacco and talk. They may be landlords or tax collectors, but they impart a religious aura. They are priests in the service of hierarchy. My pet theory, tried out on Iris and Don, is that these are representatives of the panchayat, local assemblies that are the Nepalese stab at "democracy," as decreed, and occasionally abolished, by whim of the King.

They might also be members of Taramarang's ruling caste, since an event like this reminds us that hierarchies thrive even at such elevations. But we cannot split the core molecules that characterize this social prism and give it such indestructibility. The wealth of shades and textures displayed are but refractions; the real action passes us by. But the two leading strongmen try to let us in. Standing to take their leave in the pillowed street, they end their discussion with a butting of heads. They do this like goats, but don't lock invisible horns, just touch briefly, electrically. We've never seen such a custom before; the skull-bumping only points to the futility of our guesswork. The three of us on our bench can only make that gesture with *our* heads that we've been conditioned to find appropriate; we shake them in disbelief. The barrier of culture is so strong. It shuts us out of Taramarang.

We retreat to the river. I've regained enough strength to feel distressed by what looks like a general shortage of connective logic. Is it possible that the inductive process isn't innate but an invention that's not yet been imported to Taramarang? Don and Iris, back on their favorite rocks, pants cuffs rolled up once more, pooh-pooh me. But I ask them to observe the obvious gap between cause and effect in the way this village is run, or runs itself. Take the garbage. When I try to imagine how the problem is perceived, I come up with this: The garbage isn't thrown from second-story windows; it appears. Later, there is a bad smell; it appears. I can't verify any of this—I lack the language, alack, to know if the garbage is even considered a problem—but my intuitions are strong. I ask Don and Iris to observe the way our Pomp and Joy family is working to add a balcony. Their building methods are doggedly hit-and-miss. Instead of measuring the length of plank needed, they try one random stake of wood after another until one just about fits between the others. Yet they are hardly trying out some new design; they are copying a form built in the village a hundred times before. Iris scoffs at my generalizing.

"What's become of you?" she asks. "In the sixties, your battle cry was that logic was the enemy."

I stare at the torrents coursing past my feet. "Logic may be the enemy of this river, but it comes in handy when you're building a house."

After four months in Asia's jumble, I'm yearning more than ever for life to move sensibly, in the service of a design larger than my own. But this is a debate Iris and I have been carrying on for some years, since the days we were spokesmen for opposite factions of our political commune. While we'd argued years back over whether or not the men of the house should be forced to do their fair share of cooking by a schedule's mandate, Iris was really championing the mistrust of group solutions learned from her Texan oilhand family, while I asserted the primacy of collective solutions as taught me by New York intellectual parents. Iris believes in social change through individual gumption, example and Christian love; I hold to a materialist's view of man as a product of circumstance, transformable only through the influences upon him. We are coming to see that our disagreements are largely a matter of emphasis. What's the difference if she's buoyed by signs of an intuitive, feminist wisdom on the ascendancy while I sniff about for symptoms of capitalism's death throes? Both hopes bring us uncomfortably close to the realm of the crackpot, and both force us to concede that we need more than the life we've known back home to keep us human.

But how does Iris manage to get so damn rational about the benefits of nonrationality? As I'm pointing this out to her for the hundredth time, in the midst of our usual, delicious wrangle, a peanut gallery of teenage boys scampers down the riverbank. Like their fathers, they appear to have little to do but look pretty. They are quite accomplished at it, and, as a result, more eager to present themselves than the Sherpas we encountered higher up. Bright-eyed, cocky kids in natty outfits: they take up posts, squatting one to a rock, at the same respectful distance from us that they might have taken if they ever got a chance to look at animals in the zoo. They begin gabbing away. It soon becomes obvious that their mission is to make us squirm. They may wish to let it be known that our bedraggled and indolent presence on their turf is queer, unnatural, bothersome, and beyond that, emblematic of our power to roam and their lack of it. Or am I the paranoic this time? They taunt us without inhibition. They point at our T-shirts, Don's bandana, Iris' jeans, my bushy hair, enjoying themselves fully. The waters of the river glisten in their untroubled eyes.

"Bravado is a dangerous thing," Iris observes, beginning to stare back at this smug peer group, that no doubt reminds her of Texas Jaycees.

"Meaning what?"

"That ignorance needs encouragement. That it's hard to get really evil when you're by yourself."

"Also hard to get good." Our dispute over socialism and anti-socialism flares up in a new form. But I can manage no defense against the Taramarang boys' derision, needing words for protection and feeling naked without them, while Iris knows just how to respond. She begins to perform the same vaudeville bit. She aims her mockery back at them, getting Don and me to join in. The boys can't tell that our buzzing is pure jabberwocky, our castigations badly overdone. Our primal rank-out contest, this acknowledgment through mutual revulsion, is gaining these adolescents' respect—just as it might have done in some sweaty junior high corridor. A truce held in place by hairy eyeballing gives way to alliance.

Now that we're equals in intolerance, the kids want to know everything about us. Their only means of investigation is a random grab at what we carry. Their favorite find turns out to be my wristwatch. "What is this strange contraption?" they seem to ask. But how can we talk about time with our hands? Maybe Einstein could, maybe some grass-skirted hula dancer can. We don't know how to reach an audience whose conception of the moment is inapplicable to ours. The oldest boy professes to know how to read the dial. The others see through his boast and so do I.

How often I've hungered to be like these prisoners of a single canyon, to cast off what impels me, to stop the gears, to be late for all appointments, to give up measuring the immeasurable! Observing the result, I feel vaguely nauseous. Here is life in its eternal essence, the dream of every utopianist who ever dreamed of going forward by going back! Here people are most decidedly "in harmony." Do they dare to hold the mirror of consciousness to themselves? Is their pride just a shield, does their work entail any accomplishment? I would like to think they are liberated from envy. Then where would they get the yearnings that might carry them beyond their current condition and knowledge? On what magic carpets would they fly over the nearby ridges? Or don't they need to? Were I one of them, I probably wouldn't strain myself to see Nepal, or anywhere else. I wouldn't wish to travel a single step outside my domain. But wouldn't I be losing something? Or am I placing too much positive value in people seeking to be different from what they are, since that's all I've ever known?

And how can I know what these boys seek? How can I claim—how can Iris presume, with all her "mythology"—to speak for the man who watches the water wheel?

He leaves his post on the far side of the river at sunset, and so do we. There's one thing we have in common. Without Edison's incandescence to show the way, there's no nightlife in Taramarang. Since we're hardly in shape for galavanting anyway, Don and Iris and I settle into the Pomp and Joy's crawlspace loft. Reclining once more on the straw mats, waiting for the biting things that reside here to start their work, we talk once more about home. This time, however, we manage to omit reference to foodstuffs, neither caviar nor Arby's Roast Beef, since we've just been served double helpings of rice and curried potato mush. For the first time since we've met up, Don tells us about his yoga training. He's hesitant to do so, and certainly makes no attempt to proselytize. Cantankerous as a country doctor, he seems incapable of assuming any sort of holiness. I find it hard to believe that our accidental companion has just gotten his walking papers from a "bliss farm" near Madras. Yet he has stories to prove it, all about proceedings aspiritual and kinky. Don's guru, who would fly in from Monte Carlo on his own Lear jet, specialized in an obsession with the fecal. After long fasts, the sunglassed swami would instruct his devotees in the pleasures of coffee enemas that set off spasms of energy all the way up their evacuated metabolisms. Such cheap thrills were always in the service of "cleansing the body." It doesn't take long for Don to get us to try his patented lemon juice treatment once we'd finished our trip. Guaranteed to flush out the world's impurities! For starters, before he retires, Don stands on his head for ten minutes and urges us to try it. Soon enough, we take up his dare. What else is there to do in this town? But the loft cannot accommodate our antics. We leave footprints in the lodge's soft roof.

While we're still in compromising positions, a young Australian climbs up the hatch to join us. He's hiking in rubber thongs. No Vibram soles or aluminum frame pack—and that's the tip-off. We don't have to ask, but groan together when he tells us he'd set out from Kathmandu this very morning! Like a good Newar porter, he gobbles his rice and sleeps instantly. Iris soon follows, but Don and I are restive, too swiftly recovered from our previous soreness and lack of resolve. It doesn't faze us that another dust storm is blowing down from the Helambu, the region we'd hoped to see, powdering us with a grit that pushes its way through the loft's many cracks, finally forcing us to shut our eyes. Don has to prepare himself for his postponed returned passage to North America and can't help quizzing me about TV shows long canceled, sporting heroes long lame. He's a true pal by now, the first I've found on the journey. Around me, he can own up to his homesickness; around him, I can spill all ruminations regarding East versus West, confess my disquiet over the unblinking cruelty of much that goes by the name "tradition." As the high country winds whistle their lullaby, Don stays up with me. I can almost hear him hearing me out. Obviously, Hindu eons have passed since he's met anyone who could get so eloquent about the zen of heartless freeways or John Coltrane solos or Reggie Jackson's extravagant home run pokes. At the same time, he's astonished to find someone so resistant to the charms of Asia's many decorated tyrants, self-proclaimed seers, opium daze epiphanies, spiritual quests. Playing the swami himself, Don says goodnight by assuring me, "You are one person born in the right time and place."

If that's so, why have I come so far to find out?

❖
FOREIGN MATTER

T HAT LAST WEEK in Nepal, we'd begun a contest to pick the most Easternized Westerner. Which meant the phoniest—and we had no trouble turning up qualified entrants. The saddest part of it was that those dollar-a-day Buddhaheads who were most sincere were also the most implausible. The kids who'd turned thoroughly Sherpa or Hindu or Han, from cloth-capped, hash-dizzied noggin to chappal-sandaled, road-powdered toes, were the kids who'd actually changed the least. While these blissful vagrants had tossed aside their competitive wits in scorn of European ambitions, Asia's edge-of-survival game had served to revive, even glorify, their baser instincts. A change of costume merely helped establish an Oriental *mise-en-scène* in which the Occidentals could act out whatever they liked, offend who they liked. Our contestants were wolves in monks' clothing.

So far, the candidate for top honors was a vision I'd stood beside in the Poste Restante line of the urine-scented Kathmandu "royal mail" office. Though the light was poor to nonexistent, I noticed that this youth was not satisfied with the usual Indian pajamas, but had dyed his velveteen vest and his cheesecloth bloomers a translucent pink. He'd even doused his curly hair with henna to color-coordinate his Little Bo Peep coif with his outfit. His shoes were gold-braided Sultan's slippers, with toes curled like flames and pointing up as he pranced. Both arms, and his neck, were a gallery, displaying one of the subcontinent's largest private collections of ivory bracelets, Shiva charms and holy-eye pendants. Over his curls, he'd planted a lopsided shepherd's skull cap, also pinkish. As a finishing touch, he clutched a full-length Biblical staff, which he rocked like a baton while he chanted, *"Shanti, shanti"* until I began to suspect this was the name by which he was getting his letters from home.

The pink prancer had nearly been matched by the lost Christian Iris had spied one morning doing his ablutions with outcasts in the sunken pit of a Nepalese public bath. How pale he looked beside his fellow scrubbers, how much more of him there was to scrub, stripped to his loincloth! And so raw and newborn, so foolishly pure, amidst the blackened spigots and sandstone statuettes! What could these people, and their sculpted deities, have made of his grappling with toothpaste and Prell shampoo?

Returning to India, we would soon find more entrants thanks largely to the Indian border patrol. Awaiting the midnight shuttle from the Nepalese border to the Indian plains along with a medium-sized village that slept, ate and presumably multiplied in the shelter of our first Indian railway platform, Iris and I were girding ourselves against the scramble for seats that was the station house populace's recurrent form of uprising. Just as the train arrived, pulled by a steam engine, we were beckoned by a single, hyperskinny constable. He was truly a figure out of Gilbert and Sullivan, shrunken inside an outlandish sailor's suit, pointing at us with his umbrella. He plucked foreigners off the platform like a garbagepicker plucks old paper in the park.

"You will follow on after me, please!"

"But we've got to get on this thing . . ." Already, as the train slowed, whole families were catapulting through the windows of the second-class carriages. And we'd fought through three swarming queues just to get our tickets!

"Yes, yes . . . have no concern." We were led, against the human tide, toward the front of the train. The policeman, or whatever he was, deposited us in an empty, European-style compartment with two wooden benches facing barred windows. I was sure this had to be some sort of rolling pokey, and Iris bridled at being segregated from all that folklore in the other cars. But we were just the first victims of the round-up. In order of appearance, came a shaggy blond Dutchman in homespun vest and blue jeans, a swollen-eyed, big-hipped girl in overalls who turned out to be the daughter of the Mexican ambassador to somewhere; a New Zealander who puffed a corn-cob pipe and dressed like a Boy Scout; and a set of lanky twins, with red hair in pony tails and Irish brogues, outfitted entirely in the floppy white winding sheets favored by the inhabitants of the region. While the rest of us sat meekly on the benches, these yogic Dubliners spotted sagging nets above us and clambered up, quick as mountain lions. Using their knapsacks for pillows, they stretched out for a comfortable snooze.

"That's a smart way to use the luggage racks," Iris commented.

"Loo-gage racks?" sneered the louder of the twins. "These aren't loo-gage racks, Missy. These are the bogies. You know, the sleepers, me gal. That's all the Indian railways ever provide, unless you're a maharani. Good to bring along a bed roll, except you don't need one in this heat, do you?"

"No," I answered. "And you won't have much time to sleep."

"How's that?"

"We'll be changing trains." I was eager to spout the information that had taken me an hour to squeeze from an indifferent clerk. "From Raxaul transfer at Muzaffarpur, take the Evening Mail to Siliguri, transferring to Local for Siliguri Junction, transfer point for Rayna, transferring once again for Patna Junction, thence by steamer across the Ganges to Patna Central . . ."

"Ay, the time-honored roundabout."

"It's labyrinthine," the second echoed with a whisper. "The ol' Minos and the Minotaur bit."

"Muzzy-froo-froo!" The Dutch hippie came out of his stupor. "I wouldn't take a bath in Muzzy-froo-froo!"

"But who was kind enough to make us these reservations?" the Irishman wanted to know.

"The porkie pies," his alter ego answered.

"Handy of them."

"But why us?"

"Don't ask why." The voice of the veteran.

Still, rumors were exchanged. Broken English was no obstacle. "Maybe they isolate us. Like a cancer," said the Dutchman. "Like foreign matter."

"We've been kidnapped by a white slave ring!" suggested the Mexican number, who's name was Rita. "It's *muy* exciting!"

"No, no, dear child, they simply have orders to protect us," the New Zealander explained.

"They don't want us to lose our stashes," the hippie joked.

"Ay, that's it!" confirmed the spokesman twin. "We heard about robberies along this line. Lots of pickpockets, I heard tell. The tourist bureau's just keeping us out of harm's rather large way!"

This theory was confirmed by the officer when he rejoined us. But some doubts were left because he answered all questions with that characteristically Indian twist of the neck that meant yes and no at the same time. He was practiced at being noncommittal. With his bobby's demeanor and gold epaulets, he belonged in the River Thames Patrol. His eyebrows were massive, his skin the color of a rubber ball, and he was so wizened he looked as though he'd been stuffed, at birth, in a crawlspace between two tenements. However, when Indians frantically tested the heavy door to our berth, the officer shooed them away with a hummingbird's trill of Hindi and a general waving about of his closed umbrella. Before the train pulled out, an hour late, he was joined by two stockier men gripping ancient wood-barreled rifles. Rejects from the Ghurkas, perhaps.

As the tracks curved, I could see hairy legs dangling through the windows of the cars behind us, plastic shoes slipping off, braceleted forearms snatching for air, corners of attaché cases. I was relieved not to be in that wriggling midst, but also disoriented. Unpopulated, unproblemed, what was Mother India anyhow? Just another plain to roam, another verse of "Happy Trails to You." But if we weren't part of the Indians' India, we were in another one that was just as genuine, that served as a great haven for castoffs and scroungers, the India that was their vast stage.

The Dutch fellow beside me was an unabashed performer. The favored English words in his dialogue were "joint," "pipe" and "roach." They were his *raisons de voyager*; he was returning from Kathmandu well supplied. He kept pulling perfectly rolled, hash-dosed cigarettes from his vest pocket. He seemed completely oblivious of our armed escort, but it turned out he knew something we didn't. After passing the smoke around, he got up and presented a fresh one to the border patrol. The offer of "ganja" brought out their first crooked smiles. They smoked the joint like pros. When the first sergeant's rubber face cracked, all decorum vanished. His troop got the giggles.

Their tipsiness only added to the confusion of our many switchovers. Each time, we replayed a worn melodrama. Suspense was provided by the fact that no one seemed to know where our next train was coming from. How many tracks did we have to hop in the middle of the steamy night? Was it right that the police chased Indians off the platform benches so we could sit there? Would the Indians notice if we refused to take their places? And would our escort be looking after us on the next train? Did we want them to? The wait was always longer than scheduled. The policemen would procure us our bench, disappear, return only after the next train had sat and shuddered awhile and we'd gotten prepared to pile into the dark caverns of cars. We would count the bodies sleeping in their wraparound dhoti sheets and surmise the train was already full-up. Then the police would usher us to another empty mail car near the locomotive. In the meantime, the Mexican girl would regale whoever would listen with an account of her many roadside liaisons.

"It was so hard to leave him there in Pokhara! Those nights on the mountainside, I'll never forget them! *Amor* Himalaya! *Mi querido!* We know each other too briefly, we are like the wind, no? . . . But it is good to be free also, like the wind."

"That's our credo all the way," said the brash twin.

"I am much woman!" Rita took her cannonball breasts in her cupped hands. "My boyfriend's waiting for me in Delhi, but you know what I say? 'While Juan's away, Rita will play!' "

"Have another hit of this," the Dutch boy encouraged. "It will make you shake hands with oblivion."

"Ay, it packs a karmic wallop!"

"Yummy! . . . I told myself, 'Rita, be strong. Don't cry. It's not worth it to shed another tear for a man in this lifetime, Rita.' I want to be reincarnated as a tree or a flower. Something pretty, but without sex! . . . There was this Italiano boy I suntan beside at Paradise Beach. That boy in Mykonos was the worst. He made Rita cry so much—and I only know him two days! Two days in the sun! We did not need clothes. We did not need words. This time, it was not so hard to go."

At each layover, the Irish partners busied themselves at the refreshment carts that soon surrounded our bench. A wobbling kerosene lamp lit a pan filled with month-old oil in which a bearded vendor kept various forms of rigid dough floating. The Indians went ape for these greasy turnovers. "Pure Ghee Products!" the signs in town always boasted. "Lovely Sweets! Most Fine in Bengal! Try Once, Return Forever! Sweets!"

"Mmmmm! Quite tasty, ay?" The Irishmen compared notes through the night. None of the rest of us dared touch anything so thrice-fried. "Remember the puri in Bombay? Ay, the South! That's where they really cook things up!"

"Yes, India's a goor-met treat, it is! It's a rolling banquet!" Apparently, changing trains every fifteen minutes was how they got to see the menu. "It's a goor-met treat for the four-star tourists and tchai-shop set alike!"

I preferred the approach of the New Zealander, who, between refilling his pipe, asked for sips from my iodine-dosed canteen. But I grew uneasy when he started in, "The Brits left the railways, all right, but they didn't bother telling the locals how to run it. . . ."

"It can't be all that hard." I'd learned that "locals" was just the postcolonialists' euphemism for "natives."

"No, but they've got a knack for complication," he mused, without having to say who "they" was. "This your first time on the subcontinent?"

"Yes. . . . But I've already been in Calcutta."

"Right. Nasty heap, that is. . . . Did you go and queue up for one of those student discounts?"

"Uh-huh. Took us all day."

"Ever seen so much paper stacked in one room, and so little being done about it? It's no surprise they don't have any to spare for wiping your arse."

I wasn't quite sure of his logic, but it was three in the morning.

"You'll be grateful to the Brits by the time you're through."

"How so?"

"At least, they built things. At least, they left something behind. Otherwise, what would there be?"

"Just Indians, I guess. And a few thousand temples."

"Yes, that's about it—if that's your cup of Darjeeling. Of

course, there wouldn't be airfields, or railways, so I don't know how you'd get to see them."

I didn't know why he was here, a fifth column among the idolators, unless it was to tamp down his pipeful and feel superior. I didn't have time to find out, either, because our final baton pass of trains turned frenetic and sloppy. The umbrella man had his assistants round us up and follow him toward the front of our latest steam-drawn city. While we counted the boxloads of snoring bodies from the platform, the doleful sergeant moved through the darkened cars at the same pace as our chain-gang shuffle. He was doing a bedcheck, and soon called for the aid of our honor guard. They trotted through the pajama party, rifles at their sides. We waited obediently for their return, senses dulled, with nowhere in particular to escape. We watched them flush a newcomer out of the bogeys the way hunters flush out a pheasant.

"Vast is it?" This bird knew how to squawk. "Don't touch me, crazy *polizei!*"

Their prize catch was wrestled onto the platform, though neither he nor the Indians put much serious effort into the tussle. His name, we'd soon learn, was Rolf. He was a large-boned Swiss with fierce eyes and a stiff, unwashed shock of black hair. His lumberjack's build and swagger were particularly conspicuous beside his Munchkin captors. Though Rolf was dressed like a saddhu, the quilt of sewn handkerchiefs that made his pants and vest were stretched to bursting by his milk-fed frame. His clothes were but doilies atop a volcano. From the little else Rolf carried, it was obvious that these homespuns were his only set. They would no doubt be traded somewhere down the road for any new disguise that was appropriate to the local climate or religion. Tonight, he was a gunsel in angelic robes.

"Vat you do with me? You take me from good sleep, understand?" The Indian *carabinieri* first recoiled from Rolf, then attempted to bound him in with shrugging shoulders. "Ach, you vant to protect me, is dat it? From my dreams, ja? Ach, I vas sleeping good. When I go to toilet, I ask Indians to vatch my bags, ja? I been in India long time. Never got a thing took. Not even a cigarette, you hear?"

Whatever the time of night, Rolf wouldn't go quietly, like the rest of us, especially when he saw that he had an audience. Besides, he knew these patrolmen would gladly kick their fellow countrymen about, but would never dare raise an umbrella against a European.

"Why you can't leave me alone? Why you not let me sleep? Dis is crazy, man. You know vat is crazy? Fucking policeman." Still, they nudged him in our direction. "Ach, come on now. You vant to be crazy, I let you. I go vit you, okay? Rolf is good boy, ja! . . . Only I never got a thing took. I don't got suspicion for Indians like you got! Ach! Come on!"

Any hopes I had of staking out a quiet spot for some shuteye in our next cattle bin were dashed when Rolf met voluptuous Rita. They were a perfect match, with years of global gossip to exchange. It was hard to say which of them had been away from home longer, if they could be said to have a home. Rolf was conversant in every subject Rita raised: home remedies for malaria, the least crowded beaches in Goa, the best villages to score dope in Gilgat and Swat, the right price for a bottle of Johnny Walker Red in the black markets of Rangoon. The *chica* in coveralls didn't mention any of her former lovers; perhaps she was thinking of Rolf as her next victim. But he wasn't looking for anyone or anything, just looking around. Rolf was complete. He had to be dependent on the world he'd left behind only when the pages for visas and customs stamps in his Swiss passport were filled. This was his one complaint in life.

"Cheap Swiss bastards don't give me enough fucking pages! Let me see yours. Ja! You see dat? Six more pages than me. And Americans get as many as they like. They know how to use the staples, man. It folds like an accordion! Now I'm running out again. Got to make a big scene at ze consulate. Otervise, go home again. Lucky I vent to Lumbini to cross border to Nepal." He'd detoured a hundred miles and several days' journey from the usual entry point. "Ja, I remember from the last time, the customs stamp it is smaller in Lumbini. I vas right! See dat? I save half a page, ja!" Lumbini was also Buddha's birthplace.

"You're *loco*, boy," Rita was batting her lashes. She preferred to talk about her latest case of "Delhi belly" and tease him with implications of how the ailments had restricted other activities in her lower region.

"Ach, I don't care!" And he didn't. "I eat anything! I trink everything! Hand it over, man!" Rolf's words were blown from his mouth. "I vas never sick. Just like I never got nothing took.

If you are living amongst ze people, ja, zen vat can happen to you? Only vat happens to the people. Ach! I am happy."

He pronounced it "hoppy" and I believed him. Rolf was comfortable no matter where he was because he was an overgrown pup, a perennial child who saw the world with a child's easily replenished amazement. Despite his protests, he was tickled by the way he'd been pirated from his berth; it was one more delightfully illogical gambit. He bridled over the escort service only because he wanted back in the absurd playpen. "I travel every place. Never had no protection! I see everything. I need to eat and zen sleep. Othervise, I need nothing. Except ze fucking passport!"

Dawn was coming. Our last leg was also the shortest. We knew this route had run out of trains when the police stayed behind; after all that official coddling, they shoved us out through the window. But we hadn't reached the end of the line. To get there, we had to cross one formidable river and to do that, we had to let ourselves be carried along by a morning commuters' stampede. Down a well-trod gulley we all slid, toward an antique steamer with two decks and the same number of charred smokestacks. The quay was no more than series of gangplanks that bowed under the hordes and didn't seem capable of holding them all. Rolf acted as leader of our pack, holding his walking stick in the air so we could keep near it, and clearing a path toward the ferry as though his free arm was a machete. Aboard, Rolf led us up a set of stairs that no one else seemed to be testing, then onto a covered upper deck, with glossy hardwood floors that made it look like a dancing pavilion. There were luscious, tasseled red armchairs placed generously about, just for us. With Rolf there, we thought nothing of falling into them. He didn't check his ticket, or care what sort of contraption was now conveying him. He found a local English-language newspaper on the galley by his lounger, as if left there by his valet, and started to declaim from it: "Yesterday forenoon Madame Home Secretary Sri Devi Nanu Ram addresses ze All-Bihar Women's Conference concerning ze governmental program aimed at smashing area-wide ignorance of birth control methods and vas received cheerily. . . ."

I had a perfect seat for my first look at the Ganges. It was being revealed in a murky, purple light. The surface was shallow and unbroken. The granulated water showed no current at all. Yet a single oarsman at the prow of a crushed slipper of a barge was working his way slowly, slowly against serious resistance. He was far up shore, nearly stilled, as I tracked his progress, mesmerized by the oar he drove through the river like a musician drawing a bow. No, the musical equivalent of the Mother Ganga and its navigators was not an instrument of pluck but of drone: the tamboura, harmonic ground of the ages. At the rate he was going, it would take the oarsman all day to move up the riverbank a thousand feet.

Somewhere near Patna, downstream, they were supposed to be building a bridge. Later, in New Delhi, I would be treated to a documentary film all about it. The work had begun with enthusiasm. Only the second human attempt to span the Ganges! Squadrons of barefoot women built up the pylons with buckets of mud. Slowly, so slowly. Gangs drove the supports into the shallows with well-timed heave-hos. Slowly, so slowly these human pile drivers worked. And where was the bridge now? I saw only long, low dunes of Himalayan silt. Slowly, slowly, said the Ganges. How dare I be bothered about having lost one short night's sleep?

Predictably, a team of conductors, or bo's'ns, came and asked for our claim stubs to the easy chairs. We were the only occupants of the first-class section and none of us had first-class tickets—only white skin and audacity. Again, Rolf was pried from his coziness. This time, he was not alone. We had to push our way toward the back of the ferry and find space on the aft deck. No armchairs here.

The old coal-burner started up. For over an hour, we drifted toward Patna. All that time, the tireless Scottish engine dumped its Victorian soot into the breeze and down onto the second-class passengers at the stern. The soot fell on the freshly starched kurtas and neatly kept account books of the spectacled clerks. It fell on the lavender rags of the beggars. It fell on the painted limbs of a family of naked pilgrims, interfering with the daily cleansing they effected through a shuffling of the few brass bowls and cups that were their only possessions. It fell on the Indians' seering, staring, scowling faces. The faces told me, "You see! The coal furnace's discharge can't get at our souls!"

But the atmosphere was less clouded by imported pollutants than it was by desires gone nowhere. The cross-legged commuters on our ferry's back this day carried with them the delicate dreams that were the oldest expression of man's elevation from beastliness. Yet they were still forced to live like beasts. The Indians I met loved to talk glowingly about their great, wise civilization, but none of that grandiloquent respect for the whole seemed to be accorded to the human constituents. The people bore every indignity for the sake of their culture's continuing cohesion. It wasn't a fair bargain. What did all the touted spiritual pre-eminence do for the Indian flesh? My own life may have been riddled and ruled by objects, by possessions. These people's lives were riddled and ruled by the lack of them. It wasn't just the scarcity of water that made the Ganges sacred. It was the pervasive filth of existence. Anything that refreshed momentarily, that tore off the dirt of living near the earth, was worthy of worship. At the very least, non-being was preferable to being because it was *clean.*

I cast about for my comrades, for the comic visions of the night. They'd been separated, dispersed, gone as silent as the river. Even Rolf had crumpled into a pile of World War I life jackets. Our group status had vanished. No armed guard, or color barrier, protected us. Foreign matter no longer, we were a dilute in the turgid stream of India.

Already, the day was a kiln. Nothing could escape its slow burn. The stares pointed at me were black, blacker, blackest. The insistent dust had to be constantly flicked away. So, too, did the light. The great Indian light blew like glittery grit from one victim to the next. The light: capricious and uncomfortable like the dust. The light: refracted and tortured like the people. The light: cleansing and purgative like the river.

We eat, we breathe, we die. In that sense, each society purports only to its own expertise of eating, breathing, dying. Why had I come to see this one? The holy men were so busy painting themselves they almost forgot to be holy. It is their task to be holy. The babus and the desk clerks smirked. It is their task to smirk. They do it for the benefit of all, though in order to smirk so effectively, their task includes being against the benefit of all. Dawn on the Ganges had afforded me a moment of pure, uncorrupted sight. A veritable karmic wallop. Then came the Indian questions: Who knows what you see? Would someone else see it the same? What does it matter in the long run? What, after all, is the *good* in seeing?

Portrait:

❖

DWARKOJI

Dwarko, now you proceed to Bodh Gaya Samanwaya Ashram and reach there on October 2. On your way at Gaya, purchase a spade. When you enter the Ashram, go straight to the fields, dig and turn a spade of earth and then approach the Ashramites to say, "I have come from Gaya to work on this ashram land." After that engage yourself in your favorite Kanchan Mukti (liberation from wealth) programme. —From the brochure, "Experiments in Harmony"

BEFORE his simple quarters on the ashram he's tended for much of this life, Dwarkoji awaits the sunset. On the elevated wooden pallet that serves as deck, dining table, meditation mat and loading dock, he sits cross-legged, tapping one fat toe. His thick hands rest for the moment, one on each knee. His posture is firm; he is balanced as a stilled ball. He is wrapped from the waist down in folds of overstarched cloth. His skin is nearly red against the layers of toga white. His hair is shorn so close to the scalp that the blackness has been taken out of it. His eyes are brown and laconic as a bullock's. A few white strands circle exposed tits, but the rest of his body is eunuch smooth. Dwarko's torso is plump enough to connote authority, muscular enough to confirm continuing vigor. This sunset, however, he drowses.

Dwarkoji—as he has become used to being called, the "ji" an honorific that his countrymen like to attach whenever they are given the least excuse—could be an exiled Mogul prince holding court in his perfumed garden; he makes a splendid imitation of a champion Sumo wrestler, trying to regather his strength between matches. Sometimes shooing off gnats with his squat fingers, staring into the deepening haze over the papaya grove, Dwakoji is imposing in the Indian manner: patience is the hallmark of his militancy, inactivity deepens his activism, a dazed humility signifies his leader's calling. He is a zealot of endurance, thriving on self-sacrifice. Seemingly unaged by his wait, by all these sunsets, Dwarko makes an effective advertisement for a life without meat or sex. In another time or place, he might be considered too old for giving orders or showing himself half-naked. In another time and place, he might find it easier to move, to rage, to digest. But this time is late April, hottest month of the year, and the place is Bihar province, hottest in India. It is a time and place to which a man must yield, even stolid Dwarkoji.

From his hard perch, Dwarko takes stock of his sanctuary and working farm, his spiritual retreat and Gandhian boot camp. Again, the combination is peculiarly Indian, and so is the languor of its growth. The straw boss looks out over the accomplishments of his current incarnation. He counts one threshing machine; one milking goat with kid; several acres of vegetables and fruit trees, badly in need of better irrigation; four cement barracks with open chinks where there should be proper windows and doors, which house a dozen or so ashramites from throughout the nation. A few of these volunteers are faithful to ideals as well as discipline, and a few is enough for Dwarkoji. He likes to tell his guests, "The business of change is slower than any other business, and in India, that is very slow indeed." Dwarkoji watches the nanny goat, tied contentedly to a fence, munching a bundle of fresh-cut wheat. One of the girls who works in the kitchen, a comely one in tattered pink sari, makes a game of chasing the goat's offspring and finally cramming the yelping thing inside a straw basket where it must spend the night. The girl and the kid: India's future. Dwarkoji allows himself a laugh. He thinks of the students at the ashram's nearby school for harijans—"God's children," Gandhi's name for the untouchable caste. Thus contented in his discontent, Dwarkoji is not unlike Gautama Buddha, who sat under the bodhi tree but a few hundred yards away and there attained his Buddhahood.

It is because of Buddha's tree that this town is called Bodh Gaya, and because of that thousands of devotees come here every year, and because of that Dwarkoji's ashram must serve as a showcase. It must represent all the ashrams begun by the followers of Vinoba Bhave, a saintly figure who walked fifty thousand miles across India getting the rich to redistribute some of their land to the poor through the power of prayer and nonviolent witness. But Dwarkoji himself refuses to become a showcase. Where the spiritual is the political, this leader respects his own delicate spirit and remains himself. He may have the job of a salesman, but never the demeanor. He carries on with his pleasures, and claps for his supper to be brought with the dusk.

Dwarkoji does not eat with the others; he never even sets foot inside the communal scullery. He lives in a separate building and maintains a separate toilet. Despite leading a movement aimed at overthrowing the system of caste, he accepts the caste of leadership and the leadership of caste. It is an inequality apparently unapparent to the Indian eye. But the many travelers housed by the ashram are unclassifiable in the Hindu scheme: often, they are friends of friends of foreigners who once did symbolic work on the ashram. So, each evening, the girl in the pink sari summons Iris and me from our assigned room, stifles her giggling and leads us to Dwarkoji's pallet. We are allowed to eat with him. We, too, can sit cross-legged on the slatted wood planks, though we are not so good at it. We must keep shifting our beatitude lest we cramp up.

Dwarkoji knows how to live like his goats. He has fed himself, and his recruits, only off the orchards he now surveys from his front porch. Self-sufficiency is the Gandhian watchword, for the movement has always moved by example—and has little money in any case. Self-sufficiency, curried with pride, can also have a most pleasant flavor. Dwarkoji hopes we can taste it. Another girl, head lowered, bears three portions on round silver platters and pours water from a tin beaker into tin cups. We dare not refuse this water or inquire about its purification. I do not tell this half-saint that his cups remind me of my childhood's TV glasses, with pictures of the Flintstones around the handle. Dwarkoji doesn't want conversation yet. He's devouring the daily ration of curds made from the goat's milk, some rice mush and vegetables with chili, all of it sopped up with the flat wheat cakes called roti. Dwarko does not find the ashram's bill of fare monotonous.

"We call these lady's fingers," he informs us, without looking up from his dish. "Delectable, yes?"

"Mmmm," Iris assures him. "Where I come from, they're called okra. They are grown in the American South."

"Soul food," I can't help adding.

"All food sustains the soul," Dwarko concurs, plunging on.

I just nod, exhausted at the prospect of properly explaining my remark.

"Yes, and there are many foods for the soul," he begins, rubbing the bronze tub of his belly to polish it. "And there are many fertilizers for that food. Not just the kind that the cows make! Hardship, for instance, can be a splendid fertilizer. No, in India, we do not lack for fertilizers."

"Then you are pleased with the output of the ashram?" I find myself asking, though the word "output" seems to imply a relentlessness that would be impossible here.

"We must take the long view," Dwarko starts in at once, his dreaminess disappearing with my proper opener. "If one gramadan program is successful, we might get the landowners to turn over some holdings to the peasants in five or perhaps ten villages. We do this through moral persuasion. It is no quick affair. Yet there are at least a hundred thousand such villages in Bihar state only. In all India, who can tally? We have fifty million sightless in our country. The families who send children to our school often do so unwillingly, with great suspicion. There is much ignorance among these low caste elements, who are forced to live half the year on weeds and wild berries. A successful graduate, for us, is one who becomes a laborer, or a farmer, who can simply feed himself and write his own name."

Now Dwarko's pallet has turned lectern, and we are sharing his seminar under the stars. The stars, too, seem to pulse more slowly in the tropical sky.

"It is hard for us to comprehend. In the United States . . ."

"Ah-cha!" he interrupts at once, clicking his teeth and bellowing the all-purpose Hindi word that is simultaneously "Okay!" and

"I see!," "My goodness!" and "So what?" "Of course, of course. Material wealth and spiritual wealth are divided on this planet. You possess many things we are wanting. And we, too, can offer much in return. Didn't we provide the example for your Martin Luther King?"

With this defense against attacks unlaunched, Dwarko dismisses his obligation to the West. For him, there is only India. What Indian has lived to see or rub against each of India's borders, or even one of them? Like a sitar player seeking a change in tempo for his raga, Dwarkoji taps the platform with the full side of his foot.

"The lasting solutions will come from our historic way of life. Man must first be at peace with himself, then with his neighbors."

Perhaps it is because I am so unused to seeing anyone "at peace," I confuse it for indolence. Perhaps this is why it seems to me that Dwarkoji is secretly comforted by the immensity of his task.

"But there are basic institutional questions that have to be tackled, right? There are problems which can't be solved through meditation."

"And that is why we grow food and run schools!"

"The man who does good for others, does good for himself?" Iris asks, repeating a schoolgirl's homily.

"Very good, my dear."

"Then why is there still so much inequity here, so much more than in our own country? And so much suffering that goes uncomforted?"

In the darkness, Dwarko appears to pout. I scramble to amend my statement.

"It's not just in India, but all the countries we've seen. From one to the next, the only difference is the face of the local dictator. . . ."

"This is not of great significance over the long haul. Power will always be exercised for the few. And power can only be used for evil, never good."

"We came to Asia to gain faith in what you say," Iris tries, rather meekly, "but so far, we've lost it even further."

"No, no, you mustn't. Just look at the number of you who are searching for that faith! We take the coming of all these young vagabonds to India as a great sign. They are looking for something that their own society, with all its riches, cannot provide."

And what do they find? Only the stars answer. Staring up at them, I realize how sweetly the Indian night covers the tawdriness of the Indian stage, so glaringly lit by day. The night is a seal that binds up human efforts and temporarily completes them, no matter how piecemeal they really are. Bereft of the West's ongoing electric hum, this night is charged solely with the machinery of living needs. Night is the time when underdevelopment shows its advantage.

"I hope you're right," I tell Dwarko, wondering if it is my fault or his that our colloquy has sounded so naive. Not a jot about balance of payments or the colonialist mentality.

"But your being here proves that I am! That the world will be made whole!" Dwarko knows how to shout calmly. "Your lack of hope is merely hope in reverse."

And what is your hope, Dwarkoji?

He claps his hands for the girl. "More curds, more roti!"

On June 1, 1972, when Dwarkoji completed fifty years of his life he heaved a sigh of comfort and relief at the work done in this Ashram which stands as monument to hard work and dedicated service in this world-famous pilgrim centre of Buddhists to whom it is sacred by Lord Buddha's roaming and enlightenment. As Vinobaji once said when complaints were received about ashram working, "I am not worried about the ashram, as it was not started by me; but it was inspired by God and it is His creation!"

In the morning, one of the ashramites appears at the open cutout to our room so that he can show us "speciality sightings of Bodh Gaya." He does not look particularly pleased with the assignment. This young man shows an older man's furrowed brow, permanently mussed-up black hair to match a wrinkled black kurta. He escorts us with a quick worrier's step. It is hard to guess what he's worrying about, since he's obviously given the tour many times before. We gather little about him or the town from his Hindi-laced English, but we can refer to our Fodor's. First, the bodhi tree. It's easy to see why the prophet stopped here. The thick canopy of branches provides a good spot for meditation, and besides, there are few such opportunities for shade in the parched province. It is a landscape that many have sought to flee through hallucination or illumination. Near the tree where Buddha was first struck with his Buddhahood, a five-story stupa now provides more shade. This Oriental version of a "historic marker," already historic itself, is strikingly like an Aztec pyramid, chiseled with functionless portholes and ledges. Around the grounds are the usual smaller stupas, granite phalluses, solid bells that ring out word of the former presence of something transcendent in this place.

Where Buddha paused, a few stands offer "the pause that refreshes," but a Howard Johnson's is still some eons off. Beggars line the path leading out of the garden. Squawking, *"Babu! Babu!"* they don't even offer trinkets or carved replicas of the tree. Bodh Gaya's tourist office has been closed for lack of funds. Yet down the dusty trails that fan from this shrine, each Buddhist country in Asia has constructed some memorial. It's Buddhaland, with free all-day admission, though the outcropping of temples are often unmarked and unguarded. The Tibetan pavilion upstages the rest: a high-ceilinged fun house painted on all sides with a flaming vision of a prophet who consumed fire and was finally consumed by it. The artists' imaginative fire is fanned by mountain winds that have never braced these lowlands. The Thai contribution takes us back to Bangkok, with its gawdy, gold-flecked roof shaped like a pair of ascending wings. The Burmese exhibit is characteristically remote and giddy with gold leaf. Naturally, the Japanese have constructed a flat, cantilevered roof supported by underpinnings of black steel. This could be an exposition hall for robots or refrigerators, but the rice paper walls bear an inky chronology of the Buddha's travails. This last version of the man who made himself immaterial is a Samurai in shin guards and shoulder pads, with exposed rib cage, hobo whiskers and a maniacal, bloodthirsty grin. Examining the drawing, Iris and I get to kneel on the floor of the shrine. It is marble, the coolest thing around.

Relieved of his duty, our guide drops too. I ask him, "How long have you been in the ashram?"

"Ashram? Me?" He holds up two fingers. Then he goes on to explain in a long stream of Hindi. He can't figure out that we can't follow him.

"Your work? What do you do?"

An answer in Hindi, then his first smile of the day. We shake our heads. He struggles to get out the word, "Doctor."

"Doctor! Ah!" Iris and I try to communicate acknowledgment, then wonder. We cluck like proud grandmas to show we're impressed. When I glance over at Iris to suggest I find him too young and unkempt to be a real doctor, her glance answers with a shame-on-you. He smiles again.

"Yoga doctor."

"Oh! Yoga doctor."

He is off again in Hindi, and we're ready for a siesta. Even the marble is starting to feel like an electric blanket.

"You can cure with Yoga?"

"Cure? Yes." More Hindi. "Ah . . . many sick. Cure all." He shows us how he does it by taking several deep breaths through one nostril. He does not look worried any longer. He is about to reveal his true self.

"Do you cure at the ashram?" Iris wants to know.

He only points to the walls.

"What are you doing at the ashram if you are a doctor?" I ask more pointedly.

He keeps pointing to the walls, about to tell us something urgent.

"Buddha!"

"Yes, yes. We know." What does he think we've been looking at all morning? "Buddha."

"Lord Buddha old Hindu priest. Hindus love Buddha." Then he looks very earnest, the furrows re-forming. "You . . . Hindu?"

"No, no."

"Many Hindus in America?"

"No, not many. Very few."

"Yes. Very many. I read. Many ashrams." He has not heard us. "Hindus grow big."

I imagine an American downtown filled with naked saddhus, a freeway clogged at rush hour with ecstatic, chanting drivers smeared with red dye, a gargantuan balloon of Ganesh, bloated elephant god courtesy of Goodyear, next to Dumbo in the Macy's Thanksgiving Parade.

"You . . . Buddha?"

"No. No religion. No believe."

I am not surprised that he doesn't understand.

"I believe," says Iris.

"Don't confuse him even more!"

"Then why don't you tell him what you really are?" she prods.

"But I'm not really . . ." I'd vowed to keep quiet about my ethnicity on this trip in search of ethnicity, particularly as we neared the near East. I didn't want to run into any trouble over something I couldn't define. "All right, I'm a Jew."

The guide still waits for an answer.

"Jew!" I point to my own chest, in a gesture of self-incrimination that reminds me powerfully of the lines for condemned and reprieved at Auschwitz.

"Joo?"

"A Jew. Jewish."

The Yoga doctor doesn't know what to make of it. I give up, relieved that I suffer no punishment worse than the usual invisibility.

"We go now back to ashram?"

"Yes. We go."

The Ashram has always set an example for cleanliness. All the inmates together clean the premises daily which is part of their morning manual work. The Ashram has constructed latrines which are an example to outsiders. Even now Bodh Gaya with its temples and monasteries remain insanitary. Good credit for this role of the Ashram must go the unique personality and marvellous work of Dwarkoji!

First, Iris is unable to attend Dwarko's open-air lecture, and by the next night, I can't either. We would get notes from the school nurse, if there was a school nurse in residence and not just a "Yoga doctor." Our excuse is bona fide: we are having our first bout of dysentery. I must struggle out in the morning, between episodes, to cross that invisible line between Dwarkoji's compound and ours to inform him of our problem. In New Delhi, the billboards call it, "The Embarrassing Interruption."

On the ashram, at this model of the disease-free India to come, it is almost a biologic repudiation. I dare not suggest where we got it.

"Perhaps the food on your journey." Dwarkoji is very concerned. Apparently, I am right to suspect that the matter carries symbolic overtone. "Did you imbibe in the train station?"

"Just tea."

"Then perhaps you were hosting it for some time."

"Perhaps."

"It is a demerit against all of us," he admits wearily, in that curious schoolboy's lingo that educated Indians never outgrow.

"No, no. We foreigners just aren't very hardy. . . . We're not used to all the curry, even the goat's milk."

Dwarko's face goes utterly cold.

"Everything here is absolutely pure and hygienic. We drink our own well-water. . . ."

"Of course. I just thought, we might not be ready to handle raw goat's milk. We've never had it before."

"I see." When Dwarkoji says that, it means he does not see.

"I am sorry."

"Please. We are the sorry ones. But you will find the ashram excellent for recuperation."

"That shouldn't take very long."

"We will see to that. We will give you a cure." Dwarkoji bounds from his platform and scurries, best as he can, toward the kitchen. He does not enter, but remains in the unpaved courtyard, clapping. Another girl appears at the door and he gives her orders in Hindi. I stay silent, like a good guinea pig, though I was about to start both of us on a regimen of antibiotics. Iris would never forgive me if I passed up this chance to go homeopathic. Holding back more cramping, I wait with Dwarkoji on his pallet until the girl brings a handful of grain in a mortar.

"This is flax seed. Traditional cure. Ayurvedic medicine, it is called. I shall mix this for you with curds. Take the mix right away, again tonight. Take only lemon juice tomorrow. You will be well."

He takes the seed in his fingers and sprinkles it like wheatgerm over the yogurt. He mixes the ingredients lovingly. "This will solidify you," he assures me, and I can see why. The yogurt is a congealed brick.

But we are not solidified. Iris is much worse off than I am— serving her right for her culinary daring. She has a night of fever and delusions. She learns to navigate by moonlight on the path to the latrines. They are no longer maintained at Gandhian standards. The porcelain footstands and the holes that funnel wastes some

few inches into the mud are always sprayed with the products of
the last few users. Iris is in too much pain to mind the sight or
smell, but it bothers her that the community has such a ready
means to monitor our condition.

"I wish this damn cure would start to work, before I leave a
permanent stain. Awful rude of our intestines, don't you think?"

"I think you'll get better quicker if you stop feeling guilty."

"It's a deal."

The cure hasn't worked by the next sunset, but Dwarko ad-
vises, "Stick by it."

Maybe he prefers to eat alone. Or perhaps he's applying his
well-cultivated forebearance to the struggle against microbes as
well. Certainly, he's shown patience with one of the ashramites
who's cooped up day and night in the room next to ours. After
watching other volunteers bringing meals to him, we learn he's
seriously ill, and has been for nearly his full two-year tenure. What
we can't learn is why he's not in a hospital, what he might have
or if he'll ever stop having it. But no one appears to begrudge
him his room and board.

"I know we must be a drain on your resources," I tell Dwarkoji.
"I was hoping we could have seen your school by now and moved
on."

"Please do not trouble yourself. Tend to the girl."

Iris' delirium has passed, but she does not have the strength
to leave her bunk. Moaning each time she moves, Iris' still form
is shrouded in the pointillist drape of mosquito netting.

"That canopy makes you look like a princess, or a famous
courtesan . . ."

"Dying of the clap."

That is the closest her pioneer's ethos allows her to get to a
complaint—so I know she still must be hurting. I tune in the
"Voice of America" for her, like I did the last time in our Balinese
hut. A panel discussion reminds us that the Wisconsin Primary is
over and that somewhere in the universe, someone cares who
won. Lord Krishna 8, Jimmy Earl Carter 0. I remind Iris of all her
pledges to outdo me in good health.

"Just think how you've let them down in Berkeley. The weaker
sex, and all that . . ."

"You've had so many imaginary illnesses," Iris groans back,
"you don't have to get the real ones."

"That's the best part of being a worrywart."

"You're not worried now, are you?"

"Now? Now is too late."

"I'm not," Iris whispers, with some military firmness. "I think this is the very best place to get this, better than some hotel."

To prove her right, the pretty girl who's been serving us meals, whom we figured despised us as an added burden upon so many burdens, appears outside. We beckon her in, and through more sign language, she inquires about Iris. Almost instantly, she sits on the edge of her bed, pulls back the gossamer cage of netting, and starts stroking Iris' forehead with spidery yet confident fingers. She soothes faithfully for an hour; she doesn't seem to have anywhere else to go. To amuse herself and Iris, and perhaps promote the healing, she sings a spiraling, wordless plaint for anyone who will listen. I do, though I'm fidgeting about the room like an expectant father. For the first time, I feel welcome in the ashram. The dysentery hasn't just made us vulnerable, it has also robbed us of the pretense called purpose. I should have known we didn't need any to find a welcome. I should have realized we didn't have to be writing a report on underdevelopment. We are here—whatever the reasons, the fewer the better—and we will be nursed.

In the middle of Iris' third night of urgent evacuations, she gives in. I get her to choke down the antidiarrheal pills the AMA prescribes. At breakfast, I am able to tell Dwarkoji that our conditions are much improved. He beams with pride. Yet I can't leave that pride intact when it's based on false information, false security.

"We are also taking some medicine of our own," I blurt out.

A look of gentle yet irreversible disappointment spreads over Dwarko's face. We have not betrayed him, because we never made any promises. It is simply that we will never find the way.

Before independence, we used to think that foreign rule is the only obstacle in the development of our society. Once we are free nation, every problem will be solved. But after independence, we found the problem in clear shape. We have to work hard for the weakest section of the society if really we want to enjoy the fruits of freedom.

—Dwarkoji.

Once we're recovered enough to see the school for untouchables, no one is in any hurry to show it. One evening, Dwarko cancels the ten-mile expedition due to "staff insufficiencies." The next time, he postpones again because he must host some well-connected fundraisers. Of course, they never arrive. But Dwarko must stand vigil, just in case, and finally, on our last day in the ashram, he packs us, guideless, into the Land Rover that shuttles between the two projects. Of course, the jeep is crammed full. Iris sits on my lap in the front seat. The coach vibrates like a paint mixer and the doors won't stay shut. Conversation with the squinting and single-minded driver, a long shot at best, is made doubly impossible by the rattle.

Soon as there are no temples, there is no town. Instead, we find fields that are dotted with stooped women but little sign of their crop. Stumpy palms form an arcade that leads to the paved one-laner that is the main trunk route across North India. Bullock carts share the highway with the nation's truckdriving convoys. But India's Peterbilts are merely mechanical howdahs, cabs and trailers festooned with baubles and irrelevant rows of lights and those wide-eyed, purple portraits that make Krishna and Shiva look like two more forlorn children in ads for CARE. Road signs don't bother to tell the miles, as that might be too discouraging, but instead convey Mrs. Gandhi's New Year's resolutions: "The Need of the Hour Is Discipline!" The oxen pay little mind, moving at their most reasonable pace no matter how often the drivers flay. There's plenty of flies and mange on these good servants' flanks, but the eyes up front glisten and implore like those of the most emotive movie starlets. I get to stare back as they fade off, since our driver does not hesitate to pass any animal or man in his lane. He dares the ultimate karma of collision, offering clues of our position by continuous toots on his Clarabelle horn. He keeps the horn going as if that's what keeps the motor going.

This doesn't look like the India of mangoes and monsoons; it's more like a replay of ancient Egypt. I don't scan for *Kamasutra* carvings, but for pyramids and sculpted Pharaohs and a desert that must be nearby and poised to creep over everything. The road crosses arroyo after dry arroyo. Water holes have turned to unlubricated craters. The villages, too, look Sahara dry and transient as sand. They are clusters, almost heaps, of straw and fired mud, a huddle of flimsy peaked roofs full of grass cowlicks. Also cow patties, finger marks dried into them, stored and baking on every available surface. Close to the huts, groups of lanky, burgundy women pound laundry and grain. In what passes for a town plaza, gaunt grandfathers in senatorial robes ply ancient trades: healer, malingerer, indentured gofer. Their costumes are shockingly white because everything else is brown: the brush, the river beds, the pitted earth, the village rooftops, the people, the sky. Life has surrendered to the sun, and the surrender flag's color is brown.

Predictably, the first bridge we approach has collapsed. A detour has been ground out, truck after truck, through the former river trench but, just as predictably, a palm tree has fallen across the detour. Our Land Rover slaloms around all obstacles. The half-ton loads going from Calcutta to Delhi cannot. We pass a line of stalled vehicles miles long. Stationary, they look even more like overdone carny booths, badly frosted cakes, or war canteens strung with Christmas lights and beaten silver decals. Behind them, off the road, the turbaned teamsters fraternize, play soccer, bathe. They appear oblivious to the 45° Celsius. They look like they've been trapped here for days, waiting for that single tree to be removed. For the first time in this country, I see faces that nearly look calm.

Since our drive has lasted more than an hour, we figure the school can't be much farther ahead. We get there over dirt trails that wander like mad seers across an utterly level, utterly growthless plateau. A helluva spot to stick a school—especially since the school, like the ashram, is largely a farm. No land could be more stingy than this, no landscape less hospitable. Yet a group of concrete bunkers appear, salt and pepper shakers on the brown tabletop. As the jeep pulls up to the first one, and before it's quit shuddering, a wiry old gentleman in sandals and homespun tunic rushes out to greet us.

"Welcome, welcome. How good of you to come!" He speaks English like an Old Bailey barrister. I half expect him to ask us in for tea and crumpets. He even carries an umbrella, hooked to his forearm. No doubt it is for shade, but it looks like he may be expecting a sudden London fog. "Was the ride satisfactory? Good, good. You are fairly primed for lunch, I'd say. But first, I will exhibit our papaya groves. Also, the three wells that support us. You see, the school is entirely self-sufficient. That's the watchword. We have no one to look to for aid or credit but ourselves."

We race off in the midday heat behind our host, cooled solely by his bristling enthusiasm.

"The children here learn everything by doing. We are forced into this method of pedagogy by our circumstances, as I'm sure you can note. Each age group takes responsibility for a different crop. They learn their mathematical rudiments this way, you see. They must know how much seed to sow, what their yield per hectare will be, and so on. And they must not waste one kernel." We can see why. The papaya groves are skimpy and leafless. "The children work here half the day, and in the classroom for the balance. Of course, for these unfortunates, any sort of learning is a great advance. . . . And now, the dormitory for older boys."

We are led inside one of the boxes plopped down on this wasteland. There are four perfectly square rooms inside, each with concrete bunks built into every wall. The only dormer who's home is a composed woman in an impeccable sari, attempting to make cozy the corner assigned to her. A few thin bedspreads block the window, and are strung so that they can approximate curtains across the room at night.

"One of our instructor's wives," the barrister tells us. She blushes and nods. We can see the couple's tiny charpoys, like drawers in a morgue, placed to catch the infrequent breezes. On one cot is a black attaché case, the teacher's companion in all countries. But this one does not contain lessons alone. It is so overloaded that it has popped open, a dying vinyl clam. Inside, there are utensils and a pan, several shirts and worn socks, a pair of Sunday shoes. The attaché case contains the couple's worldly belongings.

Iris and I do not have the words to praise, or even assess, such stunning sacrifice.

"You see, this is a twenty-four-hour task they've taken on. Most assuredly, yes. They must supervise the boys here as well as try to drum something into their heads."

"Are there girls at the school, too?" Iris asks.

"Not enough. You see, there is still great suspicion surrounding the school. Sometimes, we have to more or less pinch our pupils. I won't say steal because that sounds dreadful. But it's the only means to convince the families to let us have a go at them. They can always run away. And some do. It is a particular problem with the girls. Recently, we had our first wedding here at the school. This was a very auspicious occasion for us. It is considered a positive omen amongst the villagers. Now we shall get more girl students."

The vigorous old man keeps chattering away, though our eyes are on the woman, the bunks, the clutter made by so few belongings in so little space. Then it's off to another stop, straining to keep up, hoping he doesn't notice us sipping from our water bottle. After far too many papaya groves, we're dropped at the mess hall.

"Our fare is rather simple here. You've sampled our lentil dal, I'm quite sure."

"Mmmm. Every day," Iris tells him. "We're not tired of it yet."

"Good!" Lunch is dished out along two hallways lined on both sides by children in near-lotus position. No tables to eat off, just well-scrubbed floors. The teachers are at the head of the lines, supervising the ladling out of the dal. We get cross-legged at the far end and sit with the harijans. There is some pointing, some tugging at our jeans, and some unabashed gawking, as there would be at any school, any time. The students are all grade-school age, well-behaved and more pleased to be in school than I ever was. None are fat. We eat, as they do, with our fingers; we talk, as they do, with our eyes.

After we've slurped down our helpings, two intense, barefoot teachers summon us. They don't speak English, but show their welcome with smiles that turn downward instead of up. In their bare classroom, in the next bunker, it is nap time for all, including teachers, but before they stretch out on the floor, the class comes alert at the teachers' instructions. Standing at the back of the room, hoping to be unobtrusive or at least give the appearance of being educators, we expect to be taken through a model lesson. Instead, the children gather in a circle, none taller than the teachers' knees. These kindergarteners are forming a choir, and out comes brash, high-pitched singing. Their first number is a local folk tune, the universal harvest ditty. The second, our send-off, is "We Shall Overcome!"

This may be a heartwarming ploy that's performed for all visiting dignitaries, but it sure does the job. Iris clutches my arm. We are stunned. The children sing forcefully, and with evident joy, though they have learned these strange words by rote. We beam at them and exchange careful glances with the teachers. They are bemused to see that so simple a gesture evokes such a visible response. We are grateful, flabbergasted, uplifted. These children are not only reminding us of their inherent goodness, but of some goodness that's been imported from our homeland. We've been brought back to the schoolhouses, the sharecroppers, the struggles of Mississippi. We thank the children with bows and pranams, the clasping of palms. Each time, they blush. The prospect of brotherhood frightens them as much as it does us.

The children keep up their shattering gospel refrain, but the jeep driver is at the door. Our visit is ending before it's begun. As we head toward the door, the choir breaks ranks. They want to touch us before we go, just to make sure we're real. They are so tiny and goo-goo eyed, with wide brows exposed by crew cuts. We cannot help patting them on those brows, cannot refuse them a grab at our ready-made clothes, our pale arms and odd, stringy hair. It's impossible for us to remain unmoved.

This does not mean we pity pupils or teachers. They are committed. Their paths are set. But what will be our purpose, our dharma, our worthy trap? Where are our barren fields?

The old headmaster, umbrella and all, is chasing the jeep.

"Ta-ta, my friends! Please return often! . . . I hope the lunch was satisfactory. Not very palatable, I know. But we Indians have learned to eat anything! . . . Oh, yes. That's so, isn't it? We Indians can digest a stone."

Much disillusioned, Dwarko wrote to Vinobaji, "I came to you with a great dream to realize Gandhiji's Ramrajya in India. But I find no difference in the villages where you and the others have been working for a long time. The same dirt, the same ignorance, the same inertia and indifference exist in Suragon or Sevagram as in my village in Sind." He received a reply to his third letter as Vinobaji could not get the other two due to postal vagaries. "Your letter is very thought-provoking," wrote back Vinobaji. "However, I shall reply to it at the proper time."

"Do you know how we are so certain that nonviolence is the way?" Dwarkoji asks, beginning our summary session under the stars. "I will tell you how. There is the story of Stalin I must use to illustrate. Yes, this is that most violent Stalin I am citing. When our ambassador to Russia was being recalled, after much dedicated service there, he sought to have an audience with Stalin. This was during the ruler's last years, and the Indian ambassador had never once socialized with him on a personal basis. Only now he was told to appear straightaway at Stalin's private quarters in the Kremlin. In a large, empty ballroom with just two armchairs in it, the ambassador was met by Stalin. Their talk was courteous, the usual formalities, until Stalin asked a curious question. He asked the ambassador what the common man in India felt when he heard the word 'Communist.' As the ambassador was a liberal and well-meaning man, he replied that Communists were viewed as dedicated, conscientious persons who sought to eradicate the inequities of society, and so on. Stalin was amazed, genuinely moved by this report. And tears came to his eyes! It was as if this old man, wearing his medals and titles, had never heard a kind thing said about Communists, or himself, in all his days upon the earth. As though there was another man inside the uniform. As though he did not live in his Kremlin palace. He kept pressing the ambassador to go on, with questions like, 'Can this be? Is this really so?' Stalin, who was reaching his end, began to weep like a child."

Dwarkoji pauses, daring us to interrupt.

"This gets 'round to my point, you see. Stalin, too, was like other men, like all men. He wanted more than anything to be loved. No matter how powerful, how greedy, cruel or exalted, each man secretly wishes nothing more than to be loved. And to be loved for himself and his best, God-given side. And these wishes are our weapons. Is this not so? Nonviolence is the way of love, and other ways bring us nothing but sadness. They are rejections of ourselves. Nonviolence is love on a mass scale, and love is the best encouragement for an individual or a society to grow."

We cannot argue.

"Tonight, we ask you to join our prayers. You may do as you wish."

Dwarkoji rises from his pallet. We follow, at first grudgingly, because we, too, have become used to the lulling sunset regimen with its melting horizons, its view of crops on their roundabout way to ripening, its stillness accentuated by the contentment of the ever-munching goat—and its serving girls. Yet this last invitation will finally give us a peek at how the ashram's "other half" lives. Too bad we don't get to see Dwarkoji's room, though it appears tiny. He leads us into an immense, unfurnished space, made more immense by the dark. It has the feel of a barn, just the right size for a square-dancing hoedown. But the ashramites who file in behind us have something else in mind. They gather in a close circle at the center of the hall's smooth floor. Dwarko gets no special place. In supplication, he is an equal—just one more source of an anonymous, atonal hum. Almost before we've all settled on our haunches, the chanting starts, informal and without the posturing of a performance. If there is a leader, it is the young giggler who has been bearing our meals. Her prayers are most feverish, most piercing. She seems to be the one to shift the mumbled phrases first, then the others follow in an unmetered round. For once, Iris and I see Indians who are unified, ardent, overflowing with resolve. But the notes they produce, strident in their a cappella thinness, are meant to go upward. And they do. There's hardly an echo in this big room, only levitation. The jasmine night absorbs all the "thank yous" we can bestow.

IMMATERIALISTS

HAD I REALLY come to know any Indians, they would surely have been disappointed in me. Here I'd taken it upon myself to make the pilgrimage to Benares, now called Varanasi, which claimed to be the world's oldest continuously inhabited city and was certainly the holiest. Yet I remained heretic. The scorching heat did not prompt me to seek the escape of prayer; the colorless, sclerotic waters of the Ganges hardly seemed antiseptic enough to purify me. The closest I'd come to enlightenment was a certain lightheadedness produced by an urgent, painless diarrhea. And all I could think about was that the date of our arrival was May Day. That most secular of holidays! On May Day, the working class marched and picketed and died to exhibit their faith in the tangible, to insist on their just rewards in the here-and-now. A little more bread, please, no rupees in the sky. This May Day, I would not be on call to rally or sing along with the chorus of "Joe Hill" or advance the cause of the proletariat by an hour's wages. Instead, I was trudging down to the local River Jordan, and paying my homage, however unintentional, to that most successful and enduring symbol of the masses' opiate. This was one highly revisionist way to commemorate the Shirtwaist Factory Fire, the Haymarket

Riot, and all the other milestones in the martyrdom of labor, and
my godhead—whether Jahwe, Vishnu, Karl Marx or John L. Lewis—
chose to punish me for it.

Iris insisted we get to the Ganges at dawn, which was the time
when the pyres along the funeral ghats would be stoked to full
capacity. I didn't particularly care to see corpses, but, in Benares,
this was "the thing to do," akin to sampling brioches in Paris.
There was some appeal in the prospect of near-coolness and the
anticipated duet of light between the brightening, rippleless sur-
faces of water and sky. The rickshaw ride proved a bonus. We
coasted gently toward the riverfront through an evaporating pur-
plish dew that enveloped the iron grillwork and stone disrepute
which was India's part-Victorian, part-Baroque version of modernity. Silent figures in mummy wraps seemed to skate figure-
eights across the streets' smoky patina.

Everything might have been in its travelogue place had it not
been for the man who pedaled us. How could we ignore him on
this day? This unorganized, disorganized, worker had been outside
our hotel all night waiting for a fare. He had fought off several of
his colleagues with louder cries and a better rate. He was to be
paid but a few pennies. No wonder he ignored our instruction to
drop us at Dwadaswamedh Ghat, main hiring place of the boats
that plied the embankment. He had no material incentive to take
us where we asked to go, so he didn't.

He kept trying to tempt us into being cycled toward "Muslim
area, buy silk saris, no tourist prices"—an offer made by every
driver in every town—and finally stopped at the top of a steep
mud gully that ran into the river. There were no bathers here, no
paved steps crowded with fortunetellers and alms-seekers, no free
and competitive market for boat rentals. At this makeshift landing,
there was a monopoly: one boat, one price, one oarsman who was
obviously a crony of our rickshaw driver. "This Dwadaswamedh
Ghat?" The driver insisted that it was. "Boat man here friend to
Americans. You see corpses, I wait. Then go to Muslim area."

"No go Muslim area, no wait!" We were handing him our
money, too much money, just to get rid of him, but he wouldn't
take it. He wagered it all on the prospect of further commissions.
He wasn't listening when I commanded, "No wait! Take us to
Dwadaswamedh Ghat!"

By the time we got there, it would no longer be dawn. Already, the sky had turned from a bloodshot backdrop to a coarse yellow blanket that itched everyone.

"No wait!" Iris was screaming. She had gotten awfully good at standing up for herself, at casting off the inhibitions that had once gone by the name of "showing respect." At last, our driver took his fare, shaking his head as though he'd never witnessed such stubbornness. Then he returned the money at once, but for a different reason. It was torn, microscopically, around the edges. This was the main rule of a giant hot-potato game played throughout the country. All the paper money was printed on shredded wheat, yet one shred made the bill uncashable. Everyone was constantly trying to slip their bad bucks past everyone else. We had learned to do it, too. But all this haggling had set back our early start! We were so annoyed that we didn't even hear the price for a trip upriver quoted by the anguished, liver-colored, buck-toothed oarsman. Our rickshaw driver watched us pull away from shore, proud of his acumen, nodding angelically to assure us that, after all the shouting he would be there when we returned.

He had taken us, literally, for quite a ride. We were rowed more than a quarter-mile before reaching the main stretch of ghats, with their worn brown planes of step, sometimes catty-cornered, falling in stages to the blessed flow. On some of them, laundry was being done. Unfurled to dry on the steps, the yards of beige homespun made banners without slogans, flags that belonged to the nation of drudgery. "Arise, ye prisoners of handicraft!" Farther upstream, the skyline of Benares came into view: onion-shaped cupolas of temples, eroded lookouts of palaces lodged on the man-made bluff of staircases.

This steep gradient to the Ganges, descended by so many near-nudes, was really an ascent to worthiness. But the way was broken in a cubist jumble of slanted balconies and crooked landings, all of one sandstone piece. Under Sanskrit-embossed umbrellas, priests recorded in ledgers the names of the bathers. Such bookkeeping was the Hindu's only tombstone, the lasting proof of an individual's existence. So many individuals moved to and fro on this stalled down escalator: waterfront orphans, yogic stuntment, body painters and trinket hounds, double amputees slipping from step to step like Slinkys. Crews of eight-year-olds jostled for a turn to push off rowboats or pull out the infirm, these children most assuredly workers, earning their livelihood off the others' soggy faith. Only the river's languid mirror stilled the hubbub.

Smashing that mirror were the pilgrims, come for their pre-fatal flops, their do-it-yourself extreme unction or baptism in reverse. Some of them bobbed up and down in place, like greenhorns getting their first dunk at Coney Island, others dove and spun and gamboled, taking all the consolation they could from Mother Ganga. Some were fully clothed, some in loincloths, some with faces all powdered for the plunge. Many of the bathers grasped beads, chanted or clasped hands together in gestures of prayer that cut through the tide. Others drank from the water, shampooed, laundered what stuck to their backs, but all pursued their individualized rites with the abandon of Huck Finns down at the swimming hole. It was Iris who pointed out why the sight looked so queer. "They're actually happy!" she cried. It was one of the only times we'd seen Indians en masse (how else could they be seen?) in such a condition. The results were infectious as the water. Goaded by the exuberance of those flushed with their preparations for a cleaner, preferably cooler next life, Iris confessed, "I'm aching to climb in!"

But I did not have to restrain her this time. She was learning to concede that the ache was all good conscience required of her, and that it was no more possible for her to become a hundred-yard breaststroking Hindu than it was for them to become only-on-May Day materialists. Perhaps it was unfortunate, but Asia was teaching Iris to look before she leapt. When she did, she couldn't help but see that the Ganges had been muddied by more than turbulence. It didn't matter that a team of Indian scientists had completed a study which showed that the river possessed properties unknown to any other body of water and somehow purified itself every two hundred yards. For them to report otherwise would have been like the United States revealing that hamburger meat caused increased aggressiveness or the Cubans admitting there was anything unhealthy about sugar. And try as she might, Iris' eyes, like mine, discerned hazards and divided nature's neutral flux into kind and unkind microbes, making her squeamish in the face of salvation. Unable to dive.

Other tourists passed in dinghies like ours, or grotesque double-deckers, the better to gawk. But we noticed them no more than the bathers did; Iris and I were working up to rapture. We'd even uncovered the secret charm of the Ganges' far bank, which was nothing. As at Patna, this city, no matter how long it had been in operation, had disturbed but one side of the sacred flow. Low sand bars the color of oatmeal were what formed the other side of Benares' eternal crush. The only echoes were the laments of dune birds and empty-handed fishermen. All the way across to nowhere, the river seemed taut, as if at meniscus. Like the flaw-erasing mirror of the Venetian lagoon, the Ganges spread light too thinly across its surface, remained underpainted primer on the canvas for a composition that never appeared.

Just when we were about to ask the oarsman to steer us toward that invitingly unholy bank, he turned without warning toward one of the slender boardwalks of dock and grazed it just long enough for a young man wearing a dashing crimson scarf to jump aboard. Our cruise was no longer our own; we'd been thwarted once more in our futile attempt to hold the Indians at bay. They just wouldn't stay put and let us glorify them. Indeed, India was a great teacher, constantly reprimanding us when we were tempted into the slightest disloyalty to our western ways.

When we protested to the oarsman about the unscheduled pickup, he just shrugged. And we did not protest too long, since our new passenger pulled a wooden flute from his kurta's breast pocket and announced, "I am music student." So he wasn't just hopping a ride, he was going to serenade us. We realized such services weren't included in the package deal, but the music that came from the man's flute had no price. Its beauty was offhanded, such a forthright enhancement of the river's sad slow lapping. It was like all Indian song, a call that did not appear to come from the shoddy player or his roughhewn instrument but from some far kingdom, some distant epoch of gentility. The music student cast his eyes discreetly away from us, perhaps knowing that the hollow bottle he was blowing into was us; that his notes sounded beneath the skin.

He played just a few bars, grew dispirited, and quit. I began reaching to make a donation, but the music student brushed it aside. "No, no. You must look!" We had come to the funeral ghats—and indeed, a bit late, for they were uncrowded, except for a few official pack rats who stood close by the stokers of two pyres, stationed to swipe the jewels or rags from the sodden black cores of those human logs that caught fire easily, but didn't burn

all the way through. The outcast women and children who scav-
enged the corpses were but another breed of laborer. Yet they
looked awfully scurrilous in their nose rings and ash-stained cuffs
and callous pawnbroking, truly animal in a brutal way that animals
never are. They were far more engrossing than the sets of feet
jutting from the weak flames.

"You must not take pictures," the flute player cautioned, though
I had not even bothered to raise my camera. The boat turned
downstream. With the current, our return trip would be completed
much more quickly. Iris proposed that we escape our rickshaw
driver by disembarking one ghat early. At first, the oarsman tried
his best to keep from understanding us, but he eventually com-
plied. Judging from his glintless eyes and drooping jowls, he had
no particular loyalty, not even to himself. We were free! But we'd
forgotten about the music student. He'd already sailed beyond his
starting point and passed it with us. Now he hopped onto dry land
close behind us, tapping me on the shoulder while we picked our
way past the first row of meditators squatting on their candy-
striped "Raj-Tex" blankets. Again, I started to tip him. "Excuse
me, one moment, please!" he whined. "See famous silk sari factory.
Gold brocade. Just have a look!"

The world of concrete needs clung to us, even in ethereal
Benares. We could escape but briefly those economic imbalances
that had enabled us to be here. Yet we, who knew all too well
about such realities, had to try and ignore them, in the form of
this "music student." Iris and I had to climb the stairs briskly,
instead of lingering amidst the piety as we'd hoped. No use, he
was following close behind. "Please have one look. I show you all
Benares. Famous silk sari factory."

Ignored or ignoree: who knew which was more debased? I
made the mistake of turning to see our shadow. Once acknowl-
edged, his presence was all the more difficult to eradicate. He
didn't hear me when I shouted, "We don't want to see silk saris.
Please leave us alone!" He only cried louder, "Just this way, please!
No price for looking. Just one minute away!" He was private
investigator Third World tracking two prime suspects in the Case
of the Unfavorable Exchange Rate. He kept up with us in the
narrow, pre-automotive alleys of the old city. No invisible tail he,
we heard him clomping on the cobblestones. We had no place to
hide in this world crouched in upon itself, where we could prac-

tically look into the second-story bedrooms, where commerce was conducted in doorsteps, the wares for sale little more than charcoal-singed curds in clay pots and leis of jasmine petals. Holy cows had the right-of-way; tourists didn't. "Please, right this way! Just around the corner! You will see!"

The flutist had begun to tug at our shoulders like a brattish child. His eyes were tearing up and tried to look stung. We would have to be the tolerant parents, humoring him to end the nuisance. "Oh yes, you will not be sorry!" Was it a pun? "Beautiful brocades, famous work of Varanasi! Look! Look!" He shoved us up against some barred windows at the back end of a blackened sweatshop. Inside, several looms were going at once. Strand by strand, young girls built up the colorations of endless yardage. Were they in the ILGWU? Did they get coffee breaks, baby breaks, or sickness-unto-death leaves? It was refreshing, for a change, to see Indians who were so duly and thoroughly employed. Yet what did our guide have to do with this place? He did not try to coax us into the showroom, but merely kept us in position at the windows. We were speechless. How could we file a consumer's complaint when all that had been for sale was a glimpse at a wisp of a product? The music student bowed. "Oh, thank you! Now you must come to my house! Just moments away! See many saris! I invite you!"

Now his appeal had come down to the personal angle, as though there was such a thing in this ocher mud labyrinth. We chose our own direction, any direction, in those lanes dotted with god's eyes, hexagrams, and the flower-laden ledges of private shrines. Our guide kept coming, kept moaning, until Iris had the last word, the only word: "No!" She was disciplining a puppy. And he came not one step farther, though we could hear him going on where he froze, "You must come to my home! No charge for looking! I give you Coca-Colas! Only a few minutes further on!"

A few minutes "further on" and we were completely, delightfully lost. We were no longer in Benares or anywhere we could name—the whole point of making pilgrimages—and that proved the most pleasant sensation of the day. Still, we had to keep working our way through the laboratory maze, not just because noon was approaching, but because potential guides lurked in the narrow passageways. Further tests were planned for us rats. We found accidental refuge down one cul-de-sac that opened onto the court-yard of a ruined palace, now claimed by squatters taking midday naps. At the far end was the back of a false facade, eaten away with moss, crisscrossed with runways that led to the ramparts overlooking the river. We were drawn to this ravaged perch by the view, but remained to explore a series of rooms without ceilings, each housing curious stone forms: a huge circular stand in one, or sometimes short stairways that led only toward sky. Every crude dial or granite sweep was calibrated by the tarnished brass trim of gigantic yardsticks. A worn-out plaque revealed that this untended site was the observatory of Jai Singh of Jaipur, a sixteenth-century eccentric who was India's first astronomer.

Along with New Delhi's Jantar Mantar, its larger and pinker counterpart, this observatory was one of the few sanctuaries in India for whatever went by the name "scientific." There was no way for us to guess the former use of this Maharajah's neatly measured cones, spheres and rhomboids; his instruments were now reduced, or elevated, to pure sculptural form. Just as they charted the stars, they graced this one castle wall of Benares with a calming order. At least, it calmed Iris and me, ambivalent yet representative members of a culture that put premium value on ordering, mapping, manipulating, explaining. India's more esteemed artifacts—its cave scrawls and torrents of erotic carvings—all flung themselves down before natural forces, appreciated them through subjugation, but this relic was singular in its detachment. It was quiet, austere, shady, forgotten.

Here, in this roofless aviary, we could flutter. In this materialist haven, we could get spiritual. Appropriately elevated from the bathers and mortality's well-greased wheel, Iris and I could ponder the topics that should have been pondered in Benares. Not exchange rates or rickshaw fares, but what was wrong with this knobby-kneed human race. It seemed that we had fled newfangled cruelties to find old ones, traded atom bombs for blight, the indifference bred by alienation for the indifference bred by caste. In the West, a posed disillusion disguised a pillager's zeal for the future; in the East, a monopoly of faith fronted for a crippling obsession with the past. The choice was between catastrophes organized or random, between murders gradual and swift. Yet I could not go on without presuming that people, at their core, were good—even if that was a leap of faith as wide as believing the Ganges rinsed off all sins.

"But why doesn't that goodness find some organized expression?" Iris asked.

"That's the question all history tries to answer. The verdict on human nature."

Human nature, I now had to admit, included sneaking to the front of a line when the line got too long. It was spreading out full-length on an unoccupied bench while hundreds slept in the dirt beside you. It was developing the most inane prejudices, like hating a man for the shape of his toes—just because one hadn't been properly fed that day. Our very assumptions about human nature were themselves possessions, savagely guarded by those who did not stand on lines, sleep in the dirt, miss their daily feedings.

"But why do we have to label everything?" Iris asked at the Ganges, returning to her favorite theme. "Human nature doesn't have to be good or bad. It just is."

And, looking at her hair blowing across eternally ruddy, eternally optimistic cheeks, I had to add: "Human nature is also never admitting why one really loves something." It was always having to justify our least justifiable passions.

"That's true," Iris said, though she was not thinking of her and me. "We haven't been told that the Ganges is timelessly beautiful at dawn. That it just *is* that way. Instead, we get all that malarkey about how the silt from upstream gathers at the rate of four cubic feet per second. . . . That's not what makes it holy!"

"I know. The guides boast that their city is the most ancient, the most prosperous, the most loved. Founded in 1168 by the Emperor Aurangzeb. . . . Nobody can bring themselves to say, 'I love this place because I was born here and must die here and because man has the capacity to love that over which he has no choice.' "

"But we can't just come out and admit that about the U.S. of A."

"Or about each other . . ."

Iris and I shared a good hug—not admitting anything, mind you—and came down from the ladders to heaven. In too short a time, we fledgling immaterialists were back in the world of capital. Out of the maze, we funneled into a British-style "circus," whose diameter was clogged with fruit vendors and horse-'n'-buggy traffic.

On the far side, we returned to the older quarter by filing down a series of whitewashed steps through an arcade lined with the usual brass goblets, painted wooden soldiers, bolts of silk in over-abundance. This subterranean bazaar ended in a square where walls and pavement flamed white. Here, veiled women sold vivid pyramids of gray, saffron and fire-engine red powders, poured out on blankets. We'd never seen the ceremonial dye in such quantities—only in blots on millions of foreheads—and at first didn't know what it was for. I had the urge to sweep my hands through the tactile piles, to muss up their volcanic points, to see the lurid dust swirl and go flying off with the breezes my fingers could make. The women who knelt beside these temporary mountains were equally still, perfectly measured.

Admiring them, we were approached by an old man in tortoise-shell glasses. He introduced himself as a priest of the Golden Temple, whose limits we'd reached, and his black robes, scholarly bearing, and eyes beyond lust were identification enough. Since non-Hindus weren't allowed to enter the central altar, he led us to a second-floor landing above the continual press of worshippers. For once, we got above the Indian parade, found ourselves on the reviewing stand. Our escort might have thought we were appreciating the architecture, but my eyes, and Iris' too, had turned to sponges these last months—and kept soaking up impressions of the multitudes, of these extras in the epic of overpopulation. We forgot the priest was beside us, until he asked, "Ganja? You buy ganja?"

Iris had to laugh. Even he was in on the action. "But you're a priest, aren't you?"

The old man cowered. He was so humble. "Of course, priest." But then every man was a priest in Benares. "How about change money? Very good rate."

And all this inside the temple grounds! But I could see Iris was tempted. I'd been keeping her from trying out the black market in every currency, and besides, this fellow appeared harmless. Maybe we'd also been softened by so many previous bombardments. Iris inquired about his rate, and he pulled his unofficial bank's deposits from under his clerical garb. As soon as actual bills were in view, it all happened quickly, as disasters tend to do. Iris took fifty dollars from her money belt; the priest counted out an awfully generous amount of bills, untorn. They exchanged wads, and then the priest shouted, "Police!"

"Where?" Both our heads turned, so briefly, until we realized that there could be no police in the temple. The old man was gone.

And the thickness of bills in Iris' hand had magically shrunk.

"He took us!"

"Shit! How?" We stood on the landing and kept reviewing his every gesture. His act was remarkable, except when we considered that we were in a land where survival itself was a sustained trompe l'oeil. We had chosen the wrong place to try and get an edge.

"Damn it, I.! There goes a week in Pakistan."

"You wanted me to try it, didn't you?"

"Maybe."

"Come on, now. We both did it." She was a veteran now, taking the worst in stride, since the worst was what you got most practiced at. "I guess we've been initiated."

It was true. The only real point in traveling was to make money valueless, to swap it for the currency of more time, to get rid of the terrible stuff. We were full-fledged travelers now.

"But could we be so dumb? And so greedy?"

"We've got some human nature in us, too."

I couldn't stay mad at Iris. I couldn't keep worrying about my own wad, my own hide, on this *primo maggio*, this occasion for solidarity.

"Let's drown our sorrows in some mango lassi," Iris suggested. "Then we can go back down to the river and kiss our greenbacks goodbye."

"Not all of them. I'm hanging on to my return passage."

"Come on. We'll hire another boat."

And this time, we strode right up to the front entrance of Dwadaswamedh, where we'd hoped to get all along. It was flanked by a permanent convention of beggars, who took advantage of the custom which dictated that the pilgrims give alms before their dip. Squatting in neat rows were the quadriplegics, the lepers, the sense-stripped blind deaf mutes, who were no more self-enveloped than me or Iris or the rest. There were probably quite a few frauds among these handicapped, too. Competition was brisk; a survival of the weakest. Why hast thou abandoned me, Charley Darwin? What's with this place, Papa Karl?

But we didn't pause; we'd already made our donation. When a dozen competing rower boys approached us, we learned that we'd also given more than we should have to the oarsman of the morning. The starting price here for the same trip was one-tenth of what we'd paid before, and we hired one of the boys by offering one-half of one-tenth of that. We were back to our fiscal caution. We were obliged to guard our privileges, this class conscious May Day.

It ended with a sunset intense as the dawn, though the filter was now red-hued compared with the morning's harsh yellow. At the funeral ghats, just one pyre was going. The same attendants prodded the carcass to keep it going. Yet even in its final moments, the being that lay there was protected by the light it gave off. How obvious that last mystery! It couldn't be lessened by any modern Prince Singh measuring it. And how oddly consoling to see proof of each person's combustibility!

"This holy place. No photograph." Our young boatsman had learned the speech. But he had learned something else, too. "You give me *baksheesh,* you photograph. Okay?"

So he too was a priest, granting cut-rate absolution; so he too was a worker, trying for every penny he could. Why did I keep expecting these desperate people to behave more nobly than I might have, as if they should compensate for the lapses in my own morality? That was the conceit of all Westerners "searching" here. Yet it was hard not to keep looking for saintly people to go with the sainted light. And hard not to keep asking: If this poverty really is some demonic test, do the Indians fare any better at it than would you or me?

When Iris and I returned to the Uttar Pradesh Tourist Bungalow, our morning's rickshaw driver was at the gate, expecting us to begin all over again.

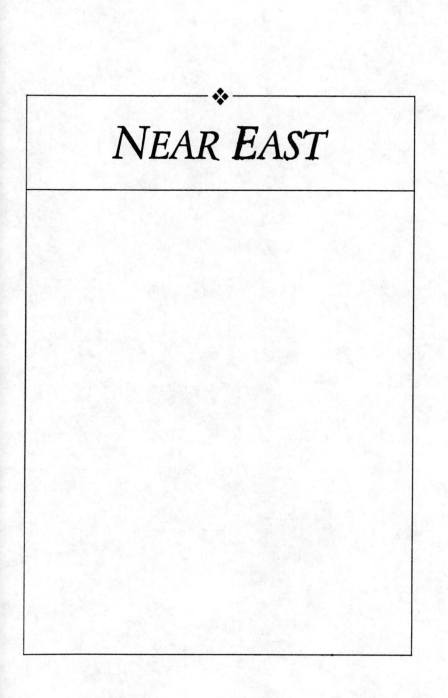

NEAR EAST

❖

PASSAGE TO AMERICA

T HE WORLD had to be round, since we were going around it.
But weren't those deluded, unscientific ancients more accurate, truer to the compasses of our hearts, when they declared it
flat and square? Iris and I were willing to attest by whatever oath
applied: this thing had definite edges. Yet once we'd peered over
the side and found that a leap toward the unfamiliar was available,
it became unnecessary. One glimpse of land's end was reassurance
enough; our intention, after all, was mostly to find, and not to get
lost. We didn't have to parachute off the side.

And this planet had to have corners, despite how it may have
looked from outer space. Iris and I knew this was so because we'd
just turned one. Somewhere between the Helambu (when we'd
determined the farthest point about sea level that our feet would
take us), and the decision to forego a thousand-mile detour through
Kashmir (when we'd quantified the outer limits of our wanderlust),
Iris and I became aware, without actually having to concede it,
that we were heading back—no longer away but toward. No matter
how slowed by heat and circumstance, it appeared we were doomed
to a speed that kept us from adhering to Asia; no matter how great

the cumulative delay of tardy train arrivals, we were hardly fore-stalling our return home by a single station.

There were always too many ways to return. Movies were the most accessible means, especially when Asian ticket prices and cavernous, nickelodeon palaces made each show seem like a Saturday kiddie matinee. But this version of our homeland had been out on the circuit too long, chopped into too many bluing prints with unreliable sprockets. "The Sting" in Penang, "Jaws" in Bangkok, "Spartacus" in Singapore, only heightened the jump cuts our lives took once we were back on the street. Coming attractions of Kung Fu stunts—Bruce Lee demolishing a dozen roadside touts—struck us as a better reflection of our low-budget travails. In India, we sampled widescreen musicals that ran to six hours of eyeball-rolling, neck-bobbing lip-synching. As a respite, we were willing to search out an "art cinema" in a diplomatic enclave on the out-skirts of New Delhi for an Alfred Hitchcock double-bill. But what did the highly skilled slalom toward some unforeseen climax have to do with the sights that greeted us at reels' end? Naked masons waited in a lot across the street for their new bricks to dry in the sun, unacquainted with the concept of suspense.

Reading provided a smoother route out, and books became the staple diet required by our homesickness. In Singapore and Delhi, we were able to load up on as many orange-bound Penguins as we could carry. In between, the drought caused us to drink up whatever we could get. From Mickey Spillane to Erich von Dan-iken, the books came to us willy-nilly, forming a commodities market in omens, with ever-climbing rates of exchange quoted along the overland trail. Was it any wonder that local, merchandise-starved shopkeepers treated English-language books like dia-monds in the rough? Every souvenir shop had its shelf of soggy paperbacks, every guest house its impromptu collection. Like our fellow consumers we grabbed our first volumes with an eye to read them quick and trade them quicker. But once they became dead weight in our packs, we never could seem to find any takers. The two of us bequeathed Marcel Proust to Punjabi chamber-maids, jettisoned Charles Dickens down properly nineteenth-century plumbing or just sold off low to the same sort of peddler from whom we'd bought high.

At least Iris and I could alternate selections as we moved. We read on train rides, or, more often, waiting for those rides to begin.

We read through evenings when we tired of exotic entertainments, nights when we didn't want to know where we'd deposited ourselves, keeping the terror at bay by huddling beneath the single-filament bulbs in our fifty-cent rooms. A few times, when we lacked other apparati of distraction, when we just couldn't face anymore of the "out there," we stayed in bed the whole day, reading.

Wouldn't it have been thriftier to have gone browsing in our neighborhood branch library instead of India? What was I doing devouring all the gossip I could about Joe Willie Namath's gimpy knees, glued to *Cosell by Cosell* in Chiang Mai? Or Marshall McLuhan in Bali, where the only media in sight, hot or cool, were papier-mâché masks?

Isolation drove me to new heights of literacy, but Iris was accustomed to just such a dynamic. Growing up in bleak oil company towns, she'd discovered at an early age that books were a quick ticket off the refinery grounds. As an awkward, dreamy Bohemian amidst cheerleading yahoos, she'd learned to take refuge, and a measure of superiortiy, in "the classics." She'd hid her few pimples, and many strivings, beneath the bookworm's pose. As a result, she was always coming up with Latinized words that she mispronounced. Her vocabulary was stretched with written words, the kind she'd never heard crop up in Panhandle parlance.

At first, the two of us tried to enhance our vagabond's erudition, plucking up every Asian title. Even the Bhagavad-Gita! We dove into *Freedom at Midnight*, hoping we'd come to know India, but winding up with Gandhi's toilet habits instead; Ved Mehta's family cameos served as a more intimate introduction. Edgar Snow's *Journey to the Beginning* suggested that the only opportunities for true adventure came when social upheavals drew nigh. The closest we came to our Yenan was an eery station identification on my short wave: "This is the voice of the Malayan revolution. . . . This is the voice of the Malayan revolution. . . ." Forster's *Passage to India* was more poignant on location, and Doctor Ali's colonial bind proved a mirror image of our own. The eras had flip-flopped, and we now sought to cajole and forgive the subjugated as they'd once done for us. Yet it was a book set in Brazil that told us the most about what we could, or couldn't see in Asia. Claude Levi-Strauss turned out to be our most articulate ally, whose respect for the savage was tempered by his weariness at ever understanding

him, or himself. *Tristes Tropiques* became our true guidebook,
turning travel into science, science into myth and anthropology
into the work of unearthing the present.

We soon wanted to read about anywhere else but where we
were. Asia was already too all-inclusive, a test of will that couldn't
be shirked for very long—but America had been transformed into
a harmless wisp. A-mer-i-ga! We were starting to say it like Asians
did, starting to picture it as they did, which was not as some greedy
ogre, but as a place distant cousins had gone to earn more money
than was imaginable. And just as months of watching strangers
struggling to understand us had made us hyper-aware of the stuttering rhythms of our own speech, we now found special joy in
the lingo of the American epic. With London in Alaska, Steinbeck
in Salinas, Faulkner in Mississippi, we rediscovered the realm of
the heroically restless. Only that ultimate expatriate, Henry Miller,
was as colloquial as we craved. After days in Delhi and Lahore,
we were quite willing to accept Franz Kafka's *Amerika* as our own.
The Great Gatsby made no less sense in Afghanistan, just a suburb
of status-conscious East and West Egg. Every best seller and pot-
boiler became a treasured morsel of our homeland's gooey cake.
Every page was a well-smudged component piece in a social machine we could better dismantle from a distance.

We had sworn never to be caught in the various American
libraries run as showplaces by the Embassies and the U.S.I.S.,
a/k/a the Department of Disinformation. But the need for more
reading matter wore down our resolve. Besides books, and month-
old *New York Times*, these oases offered air conditioning that
bordered on refrigeration and water fountains that were certified
safe to sip at. The snack bars were replicas of corner luncheonettes,
as if shipped from Peoria and reassembled piece by neoprene
piece. But the hamburgers were far off the mark: ground mutton,
ground buffalo, ground yak, judging by the taste. What made these
institutions most enjoyably American was discernible only to
American eyes. Every chair was in its place, every carpet vac-
uumed. The decor was sterile, expertly overdone, full of posted
rules and wisecracks, prefabricated cheer. A motif—be it corn
stalks or bald eagles—was carried over from the wallpaper to the
bookmarks to the napkins. In the midst of Asia, such outposts
struck us as culturally thin, visually transparent, readily sprayed

clean because they hadn't been imbued with any of the local mysteries.

But the libraries also provided us with an opportunity to turn the tables on our tormentors. Once inside the State Department's deodorized jurisdiction, as delineated by a blue-eyed Marine at his watchdog podium, we were the ones who knew the ropes, the slang, the Dewey decimal system—and that we didn't necessarily have to salute. While the Asians had to grapple with our forms and regulations, Iris and I went directly to the head of the class, or the line. The preferential treatment we were granted was sometimes an embarrassment, but we accepted it as a counterbalance against the other kind we'd been getting. While Sikhs in New Delhi waited obediently for immigration information, stunned to be turned into butcher store numbers to be paged, a high-caste librarian took his time exhuming, at my command, a decade's worth of *Sports Illustrated*.

I didn't have to explain why I needed to know the scores and the standings. I never lost that need. Back home, baseball had been my sturdiest umbilical to American mass life, the form of participation in my society's rituals that I reckoned cost my conscience the least. Now that I was away, it could be made to serve the same function—no less urgently, though with more difficulty. If I carried about a religion of my own, a vehicle for transcendence, then baseball was it. The gods this sport made me worship still wore gentlemanly knickers and chewed tobacco and came in all shapes and creeds on bubble gum cards. Baseball, from afar, was even more emblematic of the America for which I longed. The America that might have been and the America that never was: an infinitely expanding field of green, bathed in underpopulated calm; a hallowed place of quiet in history's rapaciousness, punctuated by the harmless whack of fungo bats; a melting pot that still left stylish Italian shortstops and Irish showoffs and Caribbean dandies and sharecroppers' kids and even Jewish southpaws unmelted; the innocent summer of mankind.

In truth, I missed the latest "stats," the earned-run averages and the franchise-shaking trades more than I missed the sleepwalking routine of my former life. I could not unhitch myself from baseball's reliable seasonal clock. It was torture when spring training overtook me, in Calcutta, where I couldn't possibly find a

Sporting News. How might I get the latest Cactus League scuttlebutt from my listening post in the boondocks of Nepal? The scent
of hot dogs was overpowered with curry, the splash of some rookie
phenom upstaged by yogis who weren't named Berra. So I was
forced to become my own commissioner, inventing my own teams,
stocking my own eccentric lineups: "Vishnu Kowalski 1b, Rico
'Benny' Benares 2b, Catfish Abdullah lf, Vida Blue Mosque p."
Through these managerial flights, I continued to forge a meaning
out of the trivial and mundane,which was the whole trick to creating cultures, including the ones we'd been admiring at each stop.
I had to keep practiced at this sporting cabala whose significance
was no more comprehensible to the Hindus (or Iris, for that matter) than the Upanishads were to me. Was I any different, having
my view of the cosmos severely altered by the news that Reggie
Jackson and Ken Holtzman had been swapped for Mike Torrez
and Don Baylor, than the gaggle of boys on the grounds of a Jain
Temple who'd tittered at our strange dress and "abnormal" ways
just before going prostrate so they could take swipes at the trunk
of some "holy tree"?

In moments like those, Iris and I had each other as reference
points by which to check all perceptions and claims. As such, Iris
made an unwitting ally in preserving old ways she professed to
abhor. Together, the two of us could conjure up a gingham tablecloth laden with cornbread and candied yams, or the more
barren bounty of traditionless highways that were ours to cruise.
This America wasn't exactly waiting for us, but we knew it would
be there all the same (with its big league rosters slightly rear-
ranged). We were well aware that America never missed us as
much as we missed it, and that we would miss America most of
all when we were in it.

Was there any more American way to feel? At home, we were
lost. Abroad, we were walking apple pie: our speech a broken
record of twanging "okays," our dress two sets of sneakers, stubborn denim, T-shirts advertising chocolate shops and lost causes,
our attitudes simultaneously golly-gee naive and promised land
righteous. Iris and I found it easy to miss the country we wished
to inhabit because we had never been there. Iris and I found it
easy to come back because we had never been away.

Portrait:

❖

MERCIFUL SISTERS

"**T**HERE IS SOMETHING in us that seeks this aridness," says the one sister, gazing from the train at North India in summer.

"Quite," says the other sister.

"I think we've grown skittish of too much green," the older one observes.

"It's rather too easy, all that," the younger agrees.

"We were supposed to be home nine months ago."

"We keep putting off poor Mum one cablegram at a time."

The two sisters cannot be more British. Shoved toward the windows and nearly out of them by the skeletal specimens claiming each inch of bench and racks for the night ahead, these very young women sit upright and comfortably work away with knitting needles. They pause to wipe their brows or admire the view, as if they were riding a big taxi through Regents' Park. The two sisters' thin hair is twisted in buns that neglect not a strand; their cheeks are blemished only with freckles, their skin is scrubbed and starchy as the muslin dresses that they wear partly because of the heat, partly as uniform. Sharing our compartment, they could be nuns,

239

these sisters in white. They are nurses, the descendants of Florence Nightingale.

"Helen was a year in Luzon with the WHO. Ricketts and polio, mostly. That's the Philippines," says the second.

"And she did a stint in Bangladesh," the first adds cheerfully.

"It was marvelous. I had my own pup tent in the Chittagong hill tracts."

"She wanted to stay on, but they'd run out of funds," the one sister boasts on behalf of the other. "She'd have done it for free, but they all thought her daft."

"We just signed on for a whim. We'd both taken our degree and weren't ready to keep charts for some Mothers of Mercy ward."

"Or sharpen pencils for fair-haired Cambridge boys." The younger one turns to her mentor. "Do you think we'll ever see the River Cam?"

"We've already seen it, haven't we?"

"That's true. But what can Father make of us?"

"It can't be explained. We just had to wait out those weeks in Agra so we could see the Taj by full moon."

"Mmmmm."

"And Kerala was enchanted, wasn't it? All those festivals. Bloody marvelous!"

"And we didn't want to miss Sarah's wedding—she was one of the nurses—up in Simla, so close to the top of the earth. We just couldn't miss that."

"Nevertheless, I don't ever want to marry," the younger sister insists, for the record.

"And what about the bells in Mandalay?"

"Didn't Father serve in Burma?"

"No, he never got farther than Ipswich."

But these children of England couldn't be contained by their home isle. Their predisposition to roam is an extension of a former imperial spirit, though they aren't about to create more carnage, only tidy up a bit.

"They made us give a hygiene lecture in Rangoon."

"I preferred Phuket Beach."

"What about Kota Kinabalu, love?"

"It's because we can't see too much at a time, can we? It's our maidenly fairness. We simply mustn't take the sun."

"We've had to keep indoors, you see, from eleven in the morning until three every afternoon."

"I never thought I could play so much gin rummy."

"It's just that we've been issued the wrong epidermal equipment," says the younger sister without complaint.

"We take after Mum. I do miss her."

"Home is always there. . . . But isn't this lovely?" The older sister is talking about the sun being squashed into the horizon's permanent rim of dust; she is following the path of a lame boy across scorched bean fields; she is seeing the thatched huddle of his village as she thinks he sees it. She is speaking sincerely, because she knows no other way.

"We used to help trim the hedges in Kent."

"I don't care for hedges."

"They are just polite barriers, aren't they?"

"Only those who have seen the disorder can appreciate order," says one nurse.

"Only those who have breathed the foul air can know the fresh air," says the other.

"Perhaps we shall lose our way altogether."

A rare vendor is distributing hot meals. The sisters take the pewter trays. They put down their needlework, reach into their purses for napkins they stick in their collars like bibs, cross their legs and lift the lids. They pick from the thick bowls that fit into grooves of the tray. They eat rice, yogurt dip, curried greens, chutney and chappatis with their right hands. They don't spill a grain.

"Absolutely splendid," says the first sister to finish.

"It's the balancing of flavors."

"It's just like attending a nutrition class."

"But now, for the fun . . ." The younger sister rummages in her sack for a Cadbury bar. She shares it with everyone in the compartment. The older sister busies herself with a larger contraption.

"Our indulgence," she calls it. A portable gadget for purifying, and then, carbonating water. They have a cup of seltzer with us. The Indians who are still awake have a cup, too.

"Now we're ready to rest." But they must do it sitting up.

"I'd prefer some gin rummy."

"All right. We've only got a few hours more."

"What's the name of our stop?"

"I've got it written down somewhere. It's before Jaipur. We take a bus ride two hours from the station to the Bird Sanctuary. There are bungalows right in the jungle, and there's nothing to do in the day but walk about. Magificent variety of species, they say. Brilliant plumages. I want to stay for at least a week. . . ."

The sister is interrupted by a conductor. There is a man in the next car who is having chest pains. From the way the conductor is talking, they are not the ordinary pains engendered by too many hours on the hard benches, too many years in the degenerative heat or by the lumbago of poverty. "Please, have a look, Missy . . ."

The nurse does not panic or groan.

"One moment, brother." She stands on the seat and reaches for a first aid kit that someone is using as a pillow. "Will you excuse us?"

Her sister has already risen for duty. "Perhaps we'll meet in Kashmir. We're going to rent a houseboat."

"Do you have the stethoscope?"

"Of course." The younger sister finds it at once in the kit, then stares up at us. "If this keeps on, I don't know if we shall ever get back."

"Come along, love."

The younger sister looks at the older sister. "She's a terror, isn't she?"

"Don't talk rubbish."

Both sisters are smiling as they hurry from the compartment. Between cars, I can hear the younger one say, "I'm certain that Father mentioned Burma once."

OVER THE HUMP

IN NEW DELHI, I bought a varnished walking stick carved from a piece of knotty Himalayan pine. Though it gave me the jaunty appearance of an experienced hobo, I was carrying this club for Iris' sake. We'd heard admonitions galore concerning the countries we were about to traverse that suggested we use any prop at our disposal to discourage marketplace molesters. The Muslims, we were warned, treated as fair game all females who did not cast their eyes continually toward the ground. And Iris was hardly the docile type, though, as a concession to purdah, she did start wearing a full-length wraparound skirt, one of those export cotton prints stamped with elephants. Now it was goodbye to the elephant, hello to the camel!

But the Middle East began, for those of us bucking the historical tide, well into India, at Agra. From here, the Moguls had once commanded Hindustan, and, as beleaguered emissaries, distilled the customs and aesthetics that came with their armies from Persia. The monuments left behind by that courteous empire became the symbols that most tourists associate with India, yet they were as little a reflection of today's Indians as they had been for their predecessors in peonage. The Taj Mahal, and its companion marble valentines, remained aloof as the Shahs who built them, encased in limpid gardens, unstained by contemporary Agra's chaos and mud. These were not examples of "faded glory." The Mogul tombs and monuments were anachronisms the day they were put up, and, as such, could never be viewed as relics. Here, the fade was built-in, the glory tempered by an awareness of mortality and impending loss. These monuments embodied what has been termed a "nostalgia for the present." Today as ever, they could not help being stone calling cards for Islam.

It wasn't easy to make a close inspection of the edifice that was justly renowned for appearing ever to recede—combing the Taj was like poking one's hands through a laser holograph. When we finally got close enough to verify the solidity of its seething whiteness, Iris and I found the marble etched with words. A Scheherazade in Morse code graced the pelvic cupola, trimmed this ultimate pedestal. But these were not Hallmark homilies for the dear departed Miss Mumtaz Mahal. No, blazoning from the portals were the hundred names of Allah! Up to the noontime parchment sky ran our first sight of Arabic script, looking the way the oceans' waves would write if they were literate.

As with most romantic objectification, the lady who'd been the cause was unable to appreciate it. All the beloved got out of her last relationship was the coolest spot in town for her casket. As befitted this sexiest of structures, the inside was even better than outside: an enfolding honeycomb of chambers, a progressive winnowing of daylight into more flattering shadows through the partitions of marble reduced to lace. Guides called out shrilly to demonstrate the dome's echo; one moan from the beloved, one sigh of assent, could resonate for centuries here. By dusk, and again by sunrise, as we were drawn back to the passive facade, the grounds cooled to match the builder's unrequitedness. The reflecting pools shuddered, the hexagrammoid base blushed.

Would the mirror image in black, planned for the opposite side of the Jumna River, have achieved the same effect? Black is bitter black in all lights; only hope is capable of shadings. Shah Jahan was lucky his tribute remained asymmetrical. Instead, he went on to commission the Shalimar Gardens in far-off Lahore and other projects that suggested this emperor's real passion was not ladies, but buildings. Such a predilection marked him as a true son of the Mogul line. From the polished cigar box of the nearby

"Baby Taj" to the abandoned court at Fatehpur Sikri and on to Delhi's Red Fort, we let their architectural signposts lead us toward Mohammedan turf. Gone was the Hindu temple's anarchic cabins, its finger smudges and motley forms: the precise, crystalline patterns of Mogul tilework were neither static nor intolerant but lifted eyes and soul toward a logarithmic heaven. Nature, like society, was made of exponential components and the point was to balance them. Strict measurements kept men from toppling over onto other men, and so did strict faith in Allah. Suddenly, there was one god again, and He wasn't a scourge or a dancing goat but a careful surveyor—offering a comforting fatalism born of the systematic.

Was this Muslim detachment, this mathematical whimsy, what made for so startling a change of atmosphere when we crossed from India into rival Pakistan? The transition was eased by a night's free room-and-board at Amritsar's Golden Temple, within the placid, incense-swathed Mecca of the Sikhs, a religion and nation caught between the other two. Beside us for our last flop in India was one of the Irish "goor-mets," whose twin had come down with hepatitis. Ay, what a treat!

It took the entire next day, half a dozen bus rides and stages of suspicion, to cross from one colonial sibling to the next. Once we made it through an arcade of mimosa that served as the final, nationless tightrope, Iris asked our first Pakistani official, "How long is my visa good for?" and he chortled, "For as long as you like, pretty lady!" When she asked a border guard where she could find a toilet, he faced her with a pained incredulity, then pointed with a chivalrous sweep of arm toward open fields on both sides. He seemed all too happy to admit that the whole country was a toilet.

It was the most reliable information we'd received in weeks. Pakistan was for passing through, despite the opportunity it gave us to watch Hinduism's agonized introspection being replaced by Islam's iconoclastic shrug of the shoulders. In Lahore, there would be no lilting rhapsody of Shalimar for us! The Sikh's free meal had left me with a fever-provoking tapeworm, and Iris didn't want to explore the Walled City without me—or was it the protection of my cane? What was one more bricked casbah, one more mélange of rotting meat, dejected peddlers and cheap plastic goods? It wasn't worth the risk, like the one taken by a French coquette we saw at the station where we were catching an overnight train for Peshawar. From our compartment, we watched helplessly as this St. Tropez creation, braless in neutral tank top that grew more revealing as it sopped up her panic sweat, was cornered by most of the men on the platform. Summoned by the girl's reckless affront, that made plain the command of her sex, the pack offered its backhanded compliment. They set about vilifying her for the power she held over them. Our train pulled out, my walking stick at my side. By dawn, Iris and I were riding a horse-'n-buggy toward the outskirts of Peshawar and the first bus that would take us over the Khyber Pass.

First, we had to choose between those riddled metals shells, with treadless tires, engines warming toward constant misfire, sacks of feed strapped to the roof, Arabic flourishes scribbled all around. To help us, competing jockeys in caftans screaming "Kabul! Kabul!" until they made certain each seat on their run was thrice-sold. The bejeweled heap we picked was one of the few that didn't have local passengers riding up top with the cargo. The Afghanis appeared to enjoy the trip more from outside, squatting on the luggage racks with their white trains of turban unfurled like mail pouches behind them. Seeing how confidently these tribesmen sat astride their latest, bucking form of conveyance, I was reminded of their fabled equestrian passes through the Central Asian steppes. What Atilla the Hun would have given for a tank!

The Pass itself was not spectacular by American vistoramic standards. The Khyber's bare peaks had been whittled down to pencil stubs. They were small enough to be hurdled straight on, without banks or bends. Yet this progression of brown sand castle drippings had been one of the ancient world's most formidable barriers. Whole ways of life had been shaped as a result of this short obstacle along the trading route. Was that why there were still so many forts along the Pass when the landscape revealed practically nothing to protect? It took some practice to distinguish these homemade ramparts from crags along the buttes—many were little more than stone fox holes, camouflaged lookouts, former cannon roosts, or nomadic filling stations. Shelters, bivouacs, hideaways, who knew? There were no historical markers or guided tours of styrofoam replicas. "Authentic Fort Khyber" was still in use. Smugglers and pirates and various brands of patriot lurked in these old strongholds, these stitches of rock that fit so well into this scarred range. But the pillaging hordes I'd been dreading since Berkeley made no raid on our semi-extinct Leyland bus.

Over the hump was the Afghani customs house. We were given a generous rest stop there, not because the border enforcers were too conscientious with their rubber stamps, but because all the luggage had to be untied, brought down from the rack for a prodding, then retied again. No tea shop here, this was one country where you were expected to carry your own supplies. We soon saw why: there was only a minimal descent on the Khyber's back side. We had reached a plateau that was decidedly Alpine. After India's heat and dust and overcrowding, Afghanistan was a breezy, granite romper room. Along the northern horizon was the snowy Hindu Kush, and wide arms of untouched, double blue lakes were outstretched beneath the highway. This country looked studded with enough deep wading pools to cleanse the Ganges' pilgrims once and for all. There were only occasional settlements, signaled by irrigated fields and dark, wind-combed clusters of cypress.

No less than the cooling breezes that bore down from Tashkent, those trees startled me. They were the first visual components of the coming Levant, of Genesis One—underscoring the fact that we had indeed made it over South Asia's Great Divide. Down one slope, flowed Indus, Ganges, Brahmaputra, with their sluggish brand of fertility; down this new one trickled Biblical waters toward the Mesapotamian mess, the first settlements of Greco-Roman wheat eaters. Such a moment was enough to make Iris and me start our own good book. Here, *we* came out of the desert. Here, we quit wandering. Here, we could thrive instead of subsist. Here, we could be learned and not just crafty. Here, where there was still so much room, a new strain of man might be grown.

Threading our way through the Kabul Gorge, we found further tokens of civilization to come: American-built tunnels through hillsides, Soviet-built dams. The fruits of geopolitical bribery, they were nonetheless striking to us as actual engineering, audacious interventions that the Indians could not yet pull off. Sunset neared and the canyons showed red veins beneath the olive tinges of the shrubbery. Our bus pulled over at the side of a canyon bottom coursed with charging Hussars of water. Unexplained stops had meant trouble in India, but Iris and I were soon relieved to learn that the driver merely wanted to perform his afternoon prayers.

Across the road, in a gravel turnout, he faced Mecca and went prostrate. That gave his passengers time to roll up their pants' legs and wade into the current. Everyone began drinking, and though Iris and I knew perfectly well that this was still hepatitis country, we drowned our parched faces, rinsed our gritty hair and slurped up the gorge's benevolent milk.

Our will to continue was equally refreshed by the appearance of a new pridefulness. The Afghanis actually boasted, actually raged, actually laughed! (Indian rage was always pro forma, resigned to pointlessness, Indian laughter a misfired cough.) Despite their layers of swaddling, these people could not hide their ultra-human bravado. Did the credit for this also belong to Islam? As with the welcome breezes, the grateful traveler couldn't look too hard for sources, or quibble over damaging side effects.

Stopping for an extended dinner (and prayer) break in our first Afghani town, Iris and I wandered away from the ramshackle coach house that offered tea in blue enamel pots and charred strips of shish kebab seasoned with clouds of flies. Drawn to a feverish side street that turned out to be a trading oasis for enough guns and knives to launch a modest holy war, we were soon encircled by three large fellows who would have made convincing stand-ins for Bethlemen's wise men at any kindergarten Christmas pageant. Underneath their hooded robes, Iris and I could make out flared nostrils, gray beards, furry eyebrows sewn together with squinting annoyance. Or could it be curiosity? The wise men carried old wooden carbines, but then, so did most everyone else.

They took up positions around us, their expressions not so much menacing as expectant. Unlike the thousands of pests who'd come before them, they did not speak English. Why bother when they had such an advantage in armaments? They had nothing to sell, there was nothing for which they pled. But clearly, they were after something which they admired, since they made sure, smiling all the while, that we were surrounded. Iris and I smiled back, attempted to shake hands. Their hands did not reach toward ours, they reached for my Indian walking stick.

The traders each stroked at the handle, clucking, then passed it around while I kept a tacit grip at the bottom. They had not asked permission to make this inspection, they had grabbed. It was so flagrant, I wasn't quite sure at what point their fondling turned into a heist. So they were not after Iris, but my protection for her!

But I'd grown attached to the stick as well. Why should I let the infidels have it? For the first time in many miles, an appeal was being made to *my* pride, and not just my guilt, rousing me pleasantly. I was hardly ready to go to war over the cane, but maybe just a little tug-of-war. It quickly got nasty, though all of us kept on grinning diplomatically. Iris joined in, not out of jealousy for having been overlooked, but because I was losing the battle. The entry of a female into the fray did not spark chivalry, but goaded the Afghanis to work harder. Iris and I traded dumbfounded looks. Could these bearded seers really be doing this? In this land of fortresses, what was yours was only what you could protect. The rules were clear, the test immediate. A crowd was gathering to see how this one would turn out.

Fortunately, the grappling ended with a blast from the horn of our bus. Combined with Iris' unexpectedly steady force, the noise distracted our opponents long enough for us to wrest back the cane and start barging our way through the gallery. The way our pursuers were shouting and waving their fists, it must have looked like we'd just tried to pinch something from them. Perhaps we had—by brandishing a weapon that I was unprepared to use. One of the frustrated thieves emphasized the point by shoving me off with a gratuitous swing at my shoulder.

"Fuck you!" Iris screamed at this obvious foul, fully risen to my defense. The words sounded so strange.

"Fuck you!" I mimicked. Why not? Surely, they couldn't understand us.

But they did understand. The three brigands were instantly twice as enraged, and answered in kind, "Fa-koo! Fa-goo!"

Welcome to Afghanistan! No doubt, the glorious epithet had arrived on the South Pole, too.

"Fuck you!" we corrected as we escaped, finally good missionaries.

"Fa-goo!" The chorus went up again. "Fa-koo! Fa-koo!"

Iris and I retreated under the hail, gripping each other and our prized stick, laughing laughs that nearly liberated us from ourselves.

Music:

❖

OUR LEADER

NATIONHOOD is a kind of organized secret. As a homeland becomes more "developed," the secret is more efficiently dispersed. As the general will is more firmly consolidated, the more badly is the secret being kept. Until the day comes, crowded with unknown soldiers and intermonetary debts, when not one citizen can conjure up the secret anymore. Individuals no longer feel they are receptacles of anything that can be of general value. Their human currency has been too frequently devalued. They have lost the knack of hoarding those private ways of doing and figuring and astonishing which make them most resemble each other in public. For their own good, in the name of getting their hands on what those other nations have, they have tattled. But in Afghanistan, where the links between men and their state are as tenuous as telemetry to satellites, and the apparatus of acculturation makes no fuss, conspires behind mud enclaves, the cause of nation cannot be rended from stubborn heredity. There is a secret in every face.

I saw it first in a sepia photograph, taken as a trophy of the old raj: the commander of the British garrison at Kabul posed with the prominent representatives of the heathens, on the night before the Afghans rose up and routed their conquerors, slitting the Brigadier's throat. He is the only one smiling in the photograph, but he is not the only one who is smug. Under their askew dishtowel headdress, these chieftains are keeping counsel. They are staring down the imperialist lens and leaving it smitten. They are steadfastly refusing to figure in anyone's plans but their own. Plunked down in the path of ancient trade routes, this Afghani posture has always taken practice, always involved danger. They risk what they must to keep the planet at bay.

While their conspiracies give rise to the most specific of secrets these plotters are equally faithful to the generalized kind. There is a set of instructions that hold the Afghans to being Afghani. It is never told, though often flaunted. This code can't be broken, only broken down. It is in the way these tribes choose to doll up their horses with garlands of carnations, red and white; in the infinite grid of their carpets; in the springy tread of octogenarian mullahs, their wooden rifles slung over their shoulders à la Davy Crockett and their bridesmaid trains of turban trailing behind. in the wobbly minarets that still rise where the rest of their mosque has vanished, bowlegged smokestacks left in an orchard, attesting to the constancy of ruination; in the unhurried gait of boys who wheel their carts of camel's wool gloves and socks, vending embroidered comforts like Good Humor bars; in the wild array of caps (one man, one crown), studded and velveteen; in the whispers of veiled women, and the men trying to tell them apart by their toenails, the sexuality that becomes a secret within a secret, a love that exposes itself through revenge; in the careful triangle stacks of new potatoes and wreaths of leeks and apricots sold fresh from sacks saddled on donkeys; in the half-moon gleam of knives that have yet to cut, piled up in the markets; in the national crouch, that has nothing to do with a cower, which makes every hard rock a divan and every patch of dust a dining table for dipping yogurt and lovingly patting the football-shaped sheafs of brown nan, a bread torn from the grip of round underground ovens that bake enough for a caravan in minutes; in the talk that is swallowed by the bubbling of samovars, the one eye peering out from the side of that steaming silver shield, in stone that wants to stay stone, cities built to die; in the blue tiles on the holy turrets of Herat that challenge the sky's infinitude and win; in the homosexual leer of Doctor Aziz and the strapping boys drawn to his supine pool table; in the dove which is chained to the old-fashioned camera with draped eyepiece on tripod so that your portrait can be taken with freedom on one shoulder; even in evidence along Chicken Street, that thoroughfare of shops manned by and for hangers-on, where the traders haggle all day over the price of an Afghan coat, throw tantrums, storm about and sulk, but in the end, when a deal is struck, insist on sipping tea with the purchasers and inviting them to their homes for kisses and pledges of friendship for life.

It is caught in a more current snapshot, too, which memoralizes the devious countenance of King Daoud. A face that only a mother could love, if he hadn't killed her. What a bald, demonic fist of authority, sprouting from a necktie! He's displayed everywhere, by decree, omniscient and omnipresent yet never there, a million miles removed in his haughtiness so that Iris and I dub him "our leader." This tenacious silhouette makes Spiro T. Agnew look meek, effeminate and even earnest. A strongman for strong men, he took power by offing his brother and marrying the brother's wife, or some such Hamletian plot. Later, he would get a Shakespearian comeuppance from Babrak Kermal and the "revolution" that was just the intruders' latest ruse. No sweat. The secret's indifference to most brands of terror encourages more terror. The secret dares itself to be dislodged.

The secret is used to fleeing into the mountains. It is there now. It explains why a country of nomads never needed any roads, didn't want their moon plateau lassooed with highways, was wise enough not to encourage the progress of new conveyances and eventually troops. The secret can be transported without asphalt. It survives where it must and prefers sleeping outside. It has swift justice for stoolies. And it is what brings all manner of vulture to this brittle, empty tabletop of a land. They don't really come to secure their borders or oil; they do not come because it is "strategic." Since there is so little else for outsiders to covet, they must be in search of it: it, a wink, a flower, a gesture, a pattern in the weave, a piece of bitter ground to lie on and graze, our leader, what keeps the Afghan Afghani. These mechanized invaders, these modern eavesdroppers, have their secrets, too, and the main one is that they must bombard secrets and make war against everything they can't understand.

THE FAMILY JEWELS

W E had been forewarned. But was there any place we'd been that hadn't been stickered with some tale of disaster? The rumors of dire outcome were hard-earned trophies of the road, displayed as often as possible, recounted merrily by those who wanted to tempt us into going where they'd gone so we, too, could tell others never to go there again. This time, Standard Fable Time, we'd been assured that the border we were about to cross had once been closed abruptly due to an outbreak of cholera on the Afghanistan side. The closure had been so sudden that it trapped a group of travelers in the high desert between the two countries. As potential carriers of the disease, Iran would not admit them. And the Afghanis wouldn't take them back without proper visas. Where in that no man's land could they be issued such papers? Stranded thanks to an especially tidy Asian boondoggle, the travelers began to die of hunger. Or was it thirst? Or was it sunstroke? Several days, or several weeks later, depending on who told the story, a brave vanguard in the army of tourism made a desperate charge at the Iranian patrols. "We're coming through, creeps!" The cry was not translated into Farsi. The first wave was shot dead. After that unfortunate incident, tents and canned soup were sent to the others who were forced to sit out the cholera scare. And the story stood. Why not? The more fantastic, the more easily it could be said to mirror "the real Asia." The word spread: Don't fuck with the Shah.

But what would Reza Pahlavi, he of the Peacock Throne, want with us? First, he wanted to shove a Dixie cup's worth of antibiotics down our throats. Was this verification of the cholera fable? More than likely, it was just the twentieth century greeting the twelfth, and rushing to sterilize it. No distance we'd come was greater than these last few miles, from a stone hovel, where tribesman swathed in blankets and rifles had looked into our eyes before granting us free passage out of their beloved territory, to this prefabricated truck stop and precinct station where a team of hefty automatons in freshly issued khakis studied the fine print and shoved us through their hygienic induction. We had left the realm of humming silver samovars and now waited in a Formica cafeteria for the next bus to take us down a road that was paved all the way to Paris. The rigs that waited here to begin another trip down that line were no longer battered shrines, fringed with rows of lights or lovingly painted-up with icons and harvest scenes. They were Mack Trucks and Benzes, corrugated boxes that bore nothing but the name of the company that owned them, said nothing about the favored deities of the man in the cab. We were back in "the West," even if this far Eastern outpost of oil wealth looked entirely unnatural, imposed. The sleek orange modules of the royal customs house— including, no doubt, an interrogation room—clashed with everything in this rough nomads' turf, especially the last gnarled clumps of Afghani frontier enclaves, native structures which looked like fungi risen direct from the soil. We were back, and I couldn't tell if it was that fact, or the pills I'd just been forced to swallow, which made me nauseous.

I felt worse in Teheran. Stumbling down the capital's endless boulevards, its tree-lined ramps to the Caspian, Iris and I simulated two immigrants having their first look at New York. These facsimiles of Fifth Avenue had outdone the original; the Guccis and Tiffanys were well represented. The skyscrapers were cleaner and glossier. However, the secretaries who worked there did a neat trick unknown in the Big Apple. Emerging in high heels and miniskirts, they soon wrapped themselves mummy-tight in traditional, full-length black shawls. This concession to Islam looked sincere enough, but illustrated the confusions of a forced leap. Too quickly, Kabul's fruit-bearing donkeys had been replaced by supermarkets; the flower-laden horsecarts by Mercedes; the feudal vengeance of "our leader" by the systematized coercion of the multinationals. The frenzied prosperity that awed us, and no doubt stunned the Iranians, was like the black cloaks on the secretaries: unnatural, imposed.

The corporate world's greeting for us was a sneaky sort of quarantine. Combing the usual, one-star side street hotels, we were refused at every one. Such facilities, the desk clerks told us, were for Iranians only. If we wanted a room, we had to try the Amir Kabir. It seemed that every foreigner who couldn't afford the Hilton was bound to end up there. And at first, it didn't seem like such a bad place—even if it was located right over a Goodyear tire warehouse in the middle of the automotive supplies section of town. The circular design of the hotel, and its many windows, suggested that it had once housed tires, too. An odd place to put a hotel, but the burly and slightly irritable crew that manned the front desk gave us quite a welcome. They grabbed our packs— for "safekeeping"—and handed us a room key before we'd even said we were staying. We were urged to consult the handy schedules, posted everywhere, and in all conceivable languages, for every bus and train headed to other lands. A few left from right in front of the hotel.

In the meantime, we were urged, forcefully, to please enjoy the facilities of the Amir Kabir waiting room. There were already many disgruntled guests doing just that. But, to our eyes, this was quite a find. What other such dump on our whole journey had offered television, couches, and a snack bar that prominently displayed a freezer full of chocolate milk and German sausages? However, there were services the Amir Kabir did not provide. Most conspicuously lacking were any maps or information about tourist attractions in Iran. It took us a few hours, and some mingling in the waiting room, to realize that the Amir Kabir was SAVAK's answer to the hippie problem. The conveniences offered were all designed to hurry you out of the country. And while you remained, this was the closest a law-abiding traveler could come to protective detention.

Most of the kids in the waiting room didn't seem to mind. They were on their way to more exotic realms, and warned us that Teheran was all "hassles": the people closed off, the restaurants few and expensive and serving the ubiquitous "chicken-rice," the motorists properly maligned for their disdain of traffic lights and pedestrians. Besides, the Amir Kabir was the best attraction in town, because here those going East met those going West. Few dared to inspect their opposite number too closely, lest they glimpse something they didn't like. Iris and I seemed to be exceptions, the returning survivors, and quietly relished our status. We sat in a corner and made bets on who was going to make it and who was going to turn tail. The Amir Kabir crowd looked so untested, awfully spoiled. They seemed to take it for granted that there'd be plenty more delicatessen cases, lots of pasteurized milk, where they were going.

An uprooted motorcycle gang, German-speaking, claimed the bench next to ours. They were the last of the Rockers, perhaps on the road in search of some Mods. The men were in denim to their toenails, their belligerency punctuated by hobnail boots and studded riding chaps. Could this have been why they found the Teheranians less than cordial? The motorcycle chieftain's swagger seemed sure to be eroded by dysentery and the quick work of some Indian come-hither man. The power behind his throne was the only woman in the band. She looked straight out of last year's *Vogue*, and I caught her name: Monique. Her hair was dyed white, bordering on the metallic, and cut with fringed bangs to suggest true outer space androgyny. There was nothing androgynous about her tight riding britches tucked into spiked boots, or the way she toyed with her beau and his bodyguards. Would the boots last the trip? Who would do her hair when it grew out? Or would she soon be modeling a sari?

And why were any of them going? It wasn't really fair of me to ask, since I was already on my way back without a concise answer. For some, sadly, a simple advantage in exchange rates was enough. And people like Monique would get all the attention they craved. Iris was just prodding me to make a break from this transcontinental holding cell, when I spotted a familiar face. He wasn't that easy to identify, since he'd changed costumes and nationalities. The sleeves of his Indian smock had been crookedly chopped off and torn threads covered his brawny shoulders. A few kerchiefs covered with "Om" signs had been sewn together to make a perfect Lawrence of Arabia burnoose. He'd grown a King Faisal goatee.

And the straps of his rubber flip-flops had been broken and replaced by pieces of thick, soft cord that added to his oasis trader look. Obviously, he'd gotten here via the southern route, through Karachi and warring Baluchistan or maybe Bahrain. But he was buoyant as ever, chatting with anyone who would hear him out. It was Rolf, the happy wanderer we'd last seen on the ferry across the Ganges.

"Ach! Hello! . . . Ver vast I knowed you from? Ach. Kashmir? Mrs. Colaco's? Ach."

"The train from Raxaul, remember? When they rounded us up?"

"Ja, ja. Ass-licking *polizei*. I vas sleeping so peaceful. Never had nothing robbed! . . . You go now to Istanbul?"

"Maybe." So Rolf might join us on the next leg.

"I go to Black Sea. Take ship from there."

"Oh yes, we'd heard about that. But we don't know the schedule."

"Schedule! Ach. . . . Ven I gets to Black Sea, I take ship. If I wait a day, if I wait a week, I am happy." He still said "hoppy." "If I waits a year, it makes no difference. Ja."

Rolf was the model Asian traveler. The Indian Tourist Board should have asked him to do their ads.

"And what happened to the pages of your passport? Did you get more?"

"Pages? Ach. . . . First Turkey, then Switzerland. I already got into Pakistan with *baksheesh*. Ja. No fucking pages left. No money neither. . . . Maybe I sell old passport on ze black market."

Maybe he could give it to one of the itinerant innocents beside him who could return it to India and scatter the passport's ashes to the wind at Benares. The Amir Kabir was getting us down. Teheran couldn't be any worse and, remarkably, the bouncers at the door let us through. At our own risk.

The Amir Kabir's scuttlebutt proved right on many counts. The drivers were indeed maniacal, the sidewalk survivors harried and preoccupied. The restaurants did serve that single, drab poultry dish. But Iris and I soon found a sandwich shop packed with junior salesmen on their lunch breaks. These Iranians were as friendly as any strangers could be and soon feted us with non-Islamic hot dogs and the most succulent dill pickles outside Israel. When we asked them what we should see on a quick visit to

Teheran, they all answered "the jewels." We did not have to ask who owned the jewels. After giving us directions to get there, the man who bought our lunch added, with equal doses of patriotism and resignation, "We have been ruled by kings for ten thousand years."

The latest autocrat kept his baubles in an enlarged basement vault of an ordinary, in-service branch bank. That seemed rather casual treatment for a deposit that was said to be the foundation of the country's economy. But the Shah had more than one Fort Knox; he probably kept his best stuff around the house. And there were plenty of electric eyes and plainclothesmen surrounding the rest. This surplus of karats was beyond the scope of my assessment, the precious metals were astonishing in sheer bulk alone. Encased in burglarproof cubes were pans of emeralds, rubies, diamonds yellow and clear. The rocks were loaded on, like turkey and ham at a buffet. They reminded me of the old-fashioned arcade game in which a dime got you a chance to work a scooper into a pile of cheap trinkets; these were, indeed, scoopable piles. Then there were sheaths for swords and daggers, ceremonial orbs and crowns, every surface crammed with stones. The artisans of past epochs must not have been able to come up with enough projects to clear out their inventory. At least, they did not have to be hampered by false humility. One man-sized globe represented the oceans in gold waves, the continents with more cast tundras of emerald. Center stage in the vault was occupied by the many thrones. Vacant, glittering, they struck me as hot seats, as permanently glowing electric chairs. These were, indeed, the family jewels, exposed by a monarch who was confident that no one else would be able to come up with a set that was bigger or shinier.

Was the Amir Kabir's waiting room the best he could offer us? Were the thugs at the door really his loyal henchmen? The only thing to do before bed was watch television, which looked unnatural in its own right after months without it. What made it more incongruous was that it was tuned to a station run for and by the American community in Teheran. A rerun of "Gunsmoke" was followed by a weather report, complete with isobars and a goofy, crew-cutted announcer who drawled, "It's a go-do-it weekend for all you lone rangers out there. A high pressure ridge's moved in over the Persian Gulf, and the extended outlook for Shiraz, Isfahan and the greater Teheran metropolitan area is fair and warmer. Whooo! Ain't it warm enough for ya?" Presumably, it was also good weather for drilling that crude.

Like many of the Amir Kabir's honored guests, we surmised that it would be best for us to get out of the country, quick as we could. This was, of course, just the conclusion urged upon us by the friendly staff, but neither of us had the stamina left to stick around just to be spiteful. On sagging cots in our insufficiently draped glass cubicles, so much like observation cells for unruly inmates, we daydreamed of a return visit. One day, Iris and I vowed, we'd see the real Iran, whatever that was, whenever it emerged from the black cloaks and the terror. One day, we'd wander the perfumed gardens of Omar Khayam instead of sniffing stockpiles of Goodyear rubber. One day, when a new Persia had arisen, we could linger and poke about in the ruins of old Persepolis. One day, we knew we'd be truly welcome—when our corporate countrymen were not. In the meantime, we made reservations on the next freedom ride to Turkey and didn't dare grouse about our accommodations. We didn't fuck with the Shah, accepting the moral of that tall tale we'd heard back down the road. From the shouts and haranguing we heard coming from the front desk, we were inclined to believe the latest one. Ask for a change of room at the Amir Kabir, rumor went, and the staff beat you up.

ALLAH HIT ME

"TURK GOOD," our first Turk mumbled. I presumed he was referring to Mount Ararat, the pride of Armenia and legendary resting place of Noah's Ark, which was framed through the portals of the customs gate. It certainly was an impressive sight, one perfect round nipple of snow. Too bad he wasn't talking about that. He wasn't even talking to me, but to Iris. "Turk men good."

This bear of a fellow then demonstrated what he meant by moving his middle finger in and out of a female socket made from his other hand's thumb and forefinger.

Iris gave him a laugh harsh and husky, the kind that might be provoked by an obscene phone call that's too much fun to hang up on. I knew that she'd be able to handle this direct proposition, after enduring several incidents of filched ass-pinching and bizarre bazaar *frottage*. I'd learned, too, that there was no point in my being jealous of the whole world. What for? Iris and I still weren't saying that we were "in love," but all that had counted for such a long time was that we were traveling on the same ticket.

"You want ficky-ficky in the toilet?" The burly fellow pressed his case, since he could see our bus was almost reloaded. "Good ficky-ficky. Turk good."

I gave her the nod and we started toward the coach we'd been on for nearly a day. The *urso* in black vest followed, waving a sheath of Turkish lira. Driving off, I helped Iris calculate the value of his wad, in dollars. She, too, was getting seasoned. The only thing that troubled her about the encounter was that the Turk's offer had been insultingly low.

It was already midafternoon, but our first stop across the border was for breakfast. This wasn't surprising, since the trip from Teheran was already running ten hours behind schedule. Our first samples of leavened bread and baklava almost made us forget. So did a new crew of drivers who'd taken over the Mercedes-Benz bus. One of them, a stud who wore his shirt open to the belt buckle and flashed a smile full of gold-capped teeth, became their spokesman.

"Ladies and man, I am Kemil. All problems, come to me. We go now to Erzurum. No stoppage. . . . You see. Turk men good."

Yes, yes. At least, we had Rolf to entertain us. He'd been awake all night swapping yarns and insults with an American cowhand who'd been padding his savings account as a construction worker in Iran. They were a great pair because they'd yet to be spooked by any sight they'd seen. They compared notes on the one train across the Baluchi desert, which took three days and offered no food or water. There'd been plenty of rebels, however, who swooped in periodically on their camels and aimed machine-gun fire at the train.

"Ach. Dat is Asia." When Rolf said Asia, you realized the word had three syllables. "I vas dreaming the whole time of sauerbraten!"

"You go for that mangy stuff?" the American asked. "You must not be wrapped too tight."

"Ja. I am sick of rice and tea." It was a shocking admission. "Give me some fucking meat and potatoes. I say, I vant some fucking meat on ze plate!"

He was always playacting. This time, he spoke for some time to an imaginary waiter. He might have gone on for a hundred miles if the cowhand hadn't given him competition.

"Yeah, an' gimme a juicy rib-eye steak, butter-basted, with

home fries and A.1. sauce, an ice cream sundae and a few triple-thick slices of that Texas toast . . ."

"Nah, nah. German food it's best! I am sorry!"

"No, you ain't sorry!"

"Ja, ja. I am sorry. The German food ist best. Schnitzel. Ach! Spaetzle. Ach! Bring it over here, man, and hurry vith it!"

Across the aisle, a party of overweight Iranian Fuller Brush men was enchanted by another young American. They didn't know that he was a draft evader in permanent exile. All they knew was that he spoke perfect Farsi. Leaning forward in their seats, sweating in their rolled-up oxford shirts, they cooed appreciatively, called others on the bus to witness the spectacle and gazed at him like he was the Messiah, or at least Zoroaster. It was some feat on the American's part to silence these gabby, expansive men. They'd been feeding the whole bus with slabs of bread, onslaughts of apricots and pistachios. Most of them were bald, but their faces were young, still straining fervently to meet the next new word, new sale, new insight. They made me feel like I was among my relatives at Passover. And why not? After all, the whole Middle East was Semitic, and so, it seemed, was I. In the salesmen's continual throwing out of arms, I recognized a familiar attempt to encircle the world, hug it close and thereby control it. I was at home with the giving, giving, giving that verged on bribery—wasn't that a little like what I'd been trying with Iris?

An hour or so after Kemil had promised "no stoppage," we did just that. There was no apparent reason for it, but the crew scattered before we could ask them for one. They abandoned us and the bus on the side of the road by the outskirts of a Turkish village just big enough to boast a mosque with single minaret. This was one pit stop too many. Outside, the sun dipped toward Europe and heated the stilled bus. The Persians untucked their wrinkled shirts and snoozed. The rest of us wanted to get off, but to do so, we knew, would encourage the drivers to dally longer. It was enough to put Rolf in a fighting mood.

"Vat ze fuck ist with this death ship, eh? Ve start beating on our seats, ja? Dat's it. . . . Vun, two! Vun two!" I followed his instructions.

But Rolf and I were soon distracted by the increasing number of children from the village who were skipping out from their houses to catch a glimpse of the strange creatures in the bus.

Obviously, our unscheduled stop was a big event in this remote
town, and getting bigger by the minute. The kids bobbed up and
down, ogling us through the tinted glass. We ogled back, because
they provided a Turkey in microcosm. Even in this happenstance
setting, the girls and boys were strictly segregated. The boys were
stubborn little men in black vests and flat caps that kept their
hairless faces pale; the girls were little homemakers with glossy
kerchiefs tied modestly around their hair, wearing shapeless print
dresses not yet filled with the bulk built by bread and olives and
pregnancies. The boys tried to impress us. Naturally, it took the
form of fighting. I saw more slugging and horseplay in ten minutes
by that roadside than I had seen in my supposedly "rough" New
York childhood. This was a culture of bullies. The smallest boy
was being hit by the next smallest who was being shoved about
by the next largest. The pecking order was a major form of social
expression. No wonder Turkish history was so militarist; no wonder Turkish living looked so black-and-blue.

After half an hour without a sign of the crew's return, we
descended into the tumult. Close by were a few chicken coops
and some rutted fields. Beyond, against a distant blue range, was
a habitat most distinctly Balkan. Already we could sense the sooty
fringes of Eastern Europe. The houses were dense, airless things,
all stone and chimney. They were built for insulation, not looks.
They went down in an earthquake like executed prisoners into a
common grave.

Still, the children who lived here were properly rambunctious,
and Rolf loved it. He was the first to join their sport. He organized
a game of tag and chased them all about. In his burnoose, he was
a sheik playing linebacker. Or was he a runaway Arabian stallion?
The boys were scared of him—he was so large—but they chan-
neled their fear into taunts and "ficky-ficky" gestures. Then they
tried their obscenities out on the women in the bus. They goaded
each other into bedlam.

The little girls, on the other hand, were too well behaved.
They were maids-of-honor who'd been hoping all their short lives
for such a fairy tale procession to come waltzing through. Gathered
in prim circles, they were less overjoyed than starstruck. We were
pages torn from a celebrity magazine, signposts of a life the girls
knew they'd never get near.

Iris was equally spellbound by them. Their longing looks touched a chord in her that sent her back to the forlorn make-believe of her rearing in towns of the Texas Panhandle. She was drawn to her sisters in lonesome prairie pining, and I stayed behind her. As soon as she showed them the least attention, these ladies-in-waiting formed a kind of court around her. They almost curtsied and bowed. Still, none of them smiled. One girl, more carefully groomed than the others, better behaved, cracked a magic wand over the maidens. She controlled their adulation, keeping the rest from grasping too feverishly at Iris's dusty, yet fashionable, denim skirt. It was a grim, curious ritual, clouded by a frustrated romanticism that belonged to Iris as well.

Behind us, Rolf and the cowhand were rolling in the ditch beside the road with five or six boys on their backs. The games had gotten a little nasty for me, but when I got a few stinging jabs to the shoulder as a greeting, I had to face my attackers. I, too, had to put in my bid for bullyhood. When I refused to return the fire, the boys' looks got even more piercing. I had betrayed them in some unspeakable way.

It was sunset, and rumors floated that our driver was visiting "a friend." Rolf and his new-found gashouse gang had meandered far enough up the road to discover a three-story brick building. It had the look of something institutional, a school or hospital maybe. Rolf came back to round up a posse that could barge in and demand an explanation. But the brash spokesman in the continental get-up ambushed us from the other side of the bus.

"We will explain all." He was infuriatingly calm. "I am Kemil." We knew that. "And what, please, is your names?"

Rolf didn't bother answering and neither did any of us. Some of the larger boys disengaged themselves from the melee and challenged the driver. Kemil threw a few solid punches without losing his breath. He was the king of the hill, the biggest bully of them all. His stature was made even larger through his association with foreigners. And he had plans to build on that, no doubt. Now I knew why I'd disliked him from the beginning. He looked set to put in a round or two of sparring, but thought better of it. The village kids were easy pickings, but now he would have to deal with Rolf.

"Vas ist dis, man? How many fucking hours ve must wait?"

"Please, no worry." Kemil didn't answer the question, but a grimace erased his obsequiousness, warning us that he was about

to get educational. "Turk men keep word. All Turks Muslims."
He announced that like none of us could possibly know.

"Very religious, good Muslims. Must be good. Keep Muslim rules." And what about keeping schedules? "If I bad Muslim, when I die, go to heaven, Allah hit me."

Iris and I couldn't help laughing. The hierarchy of fisticuffs rose into the sky. There was only one bully and his name was Allah!

"Yes! Yes! That true!" Kemil was encouraged by our laughter and sought to sustain it. "If I no good, Allah hit me good. Give me one right across here." To illustrate, he socked another of the kids in the jaw. "Allah strong man. Just like Muhammed Ali Clay."

The American fighter was another popular figure in Turkey: both a bruising Muslim and confirmed king of the hill.

"But what ve must wait for?" Rolf wasn't intimidated by anyone.

"For driver man. In there," Kemil announced at last. "That hospital. From our company. Badly injured yesterday. Must go to Erzurum. Driver is friend. This bus take him to Erzurum."

Kemil spoke without apology, but defused our protest. How could we object to a mission of mercy? Or whine because our bus was merely late instead of crashed? During Kemil's next long absence, other questions arose. Why didn't the bus company take care of this? How long had the man been there? What was wrong with him? And if his condition required urgent treatment, why were they taking so long to fetch him? Now a few of the Iranians claimed to have seen a crumpled bus ten miles back. The accident, rumors assured, took place yesterday, on the way back from Istanbul. Three passengers had been killed. The driver was lying in his own blood, in a bed with no sheets. Evidently, in Turkey, a man drove at his own risk.

"Dis ist still Asia!" Rolf proclaimed triumphantly, flailing wildly and kicking the last wave of challengers away from his knees. "Dis ist ze old way, ja? Dis ist not ze new way. Ve have not left A-zi-a!"

It was almost dark. He grimaced across the dimming dirt curb, still packed with he-men and Cinderellas. He looked to me for confirmation. I nodded.

"Ach! Der is no escape!" Rolf was exasperated, but also tickled to the core. With every curse, it became more obvious that he had no wish to leave this makeshift madhouse, this nonsensical and startling continent. Rolf needed a shove, and another shove from Asia, to turn the big tumblers of his compassion.

Our consumers' revolt was clearly at an end. We were not passengers anymore, but ambulance drivers. Kemil returned to organize the rescue party. Rolf and the cowhand were the first volunteers. They couldn't resist the chance to play heroes. Iris and I followed them over to the hospital. We wanted, at least, to supervise. Space had been cleared over the water cooler in the back of the bus. Still, we waited. While we did, the girls and boys raced off to a nearby orchard. They returned to the watch across from the hospital with armfuls of green apples. Each of us ate one to please them, though they were terribly sour. Some of the girls had not even bothered to pick them but had frantically torn whole limbs off the trees. The passengers held these tributes like opera singers holding bouquets.

The injured driver was hauled down te hospital steps, clutched at his ankles and shoulders by Kemil, Rolf, the cowhand and the bus driver. They looked like pallbearers. In the midst of this most unexpected mission, their sudden grimaces and mock determination suggested the participants had seen too many performances by Charles Bronson and Kirk Douglas. From now on would adventure try so hard to look like a Hollywood stunt? This couldn't have been a movie: in all these hours, they hadn't been able to locate a stretcher for the poor man. The flabby, balding fellow was still dressed in the clothes he'd worn during the accident. His shirttails were rigid with coagulated blood. He'd probably broken his back. And his rescuers bent his cracked bones all the way down the road and up the back steps of the bus. The passengers had reassembled like a polite audience after a long intermission. Everyone was concerned with the injured man's comfort, not their own. I had even lost my usual sense of urgency about arriving wherever it was we were hoping to arrive. But there was spontaneous applause when the engine was started again. Then, at once, the whole bus fell asleep.

Kemil woke us to announce a dinner break. Everyone groaned, except our extra rider, who was too far gone.

"Let's get it on, man! Ve don't need no lousy supper!"

Rolf was again the protest leader. We were over half a day

late and carrying a wounded man. But Kemil insisted, "Driver eats. Company rules."

We filed into a village tavern where the food simmered forever in giant pots. Each of the passengers pointed at the stew of their choice. While we ate, half-dazed, we saw the dim outlines of peasants lingering in the town's one cobblestone square. Hands jammed down their pockets, watch-chains showing from their vest pockets, pancake-shaped caps overhanging flesh-buried eyes, the men were submerged in silence. They seemed to be holding a tortuous vigil, waiting for a drawing of lots that would determine the next one to lose his crop, his land, his best mule or his wife. Or the next man to sneak away in the night for America.

Before reboarding the bus, while Iris searched out a toilet, I wandered off into the square. The night offered a sweet, sheep-herding darkness, though it was lit by stars plentiful as prophets' oaths. The villagers smoked strong cigarettes; they fiddled in syncopation with strings of sorrow-polished worry beads. I did nothing but drift, circle and watch. From the way their wide-brimmed caps shielded their weary faces, from their formidable recalcitrance, they could have been Sicilian Mafiosi. Any of them could have been my grandfather, a guarded and suspicious greenhorn, getting off the boat at Ellis Island. And I realized I was wearing my Mao cap from Hong Kong to the same effect: slung over same eyes, same anxieties, same gratitude for night. Hunched over, in their black vests, the Turks were coughing and whinnying and worrying. They carried the burden of the stars. In my homespun white vest, I whinnied and worried and hunched over, too. When I tried to turn away from my likeness with them, I noticed how all of them seemed to turn away doggedly from their common likeness. The turning away was part of the likeness itself.

Then Allah hit *me*. A genetic chill struck, more strongly than it had with the yiddisher mommas of businessmen on the bus. I knew that I was getting as close to my beginnings as I was ever likely to get. In silence, I communed with these brethren of mine, with a peasant's legacy of grieving and furtive strength that I carried in my bones. What difference did it make if I moved up and down these well-traveled routes from one hiding place to another? The planet spun and held me to it along with these crumbling walls and broken men. I would always be found in the village square.

Together, under the stars, under our thinking caps and our planning caps and our working caps and our yearning caps, clinging to our glorious separation, my colleagues and I brooded over the unyielding terrain we'd been placed on, and over our identity, which came hard, which also had to be sown and reaped, all of us pondering long journeys, and what purpose we might serve on this earth.

HIEROGLYPHICS

I N ISTANBUL, there is no story to tell. The best places yield no neat anecdotes. The best faces retreat into beehive enclaves, or vanish in the crescent shadow cast by widows' shawls. The best vistas are always around the bend. The best eats are served at a party to which the passerby is never invited. Our best feelings go unrecognized.

In Istanbul, the busses are equipped with television sets. Mounted at the front of the aisle, they wince with static at every bump. The drivers spend more time adjusting the picture than they do fiddling with the wheel. Iris and I watch bus-television, and the bus driver, as we cross the Kemal Atatürk Bridge over the Bosporus to end our half-year in Asia.

In Istanbul, everything is named after Kemal Atatürk. (Atta boy, Atatürk!)

In Istanbul, they put dogs and cats in the zoo. The dangerous species called "Boxer" is displayed behind bars, while standard household kittens scratch their whiskers against their cages all day. Yet black forest bears, led by gypsy trainers, strut on two legs down the most fashionable boulevards.

In Istanbul, doctors work the public parks, giving free blood pressure tests to patrons of rose garden benches. In Istanbul, dentists double as importers of English marmalade, display the jars around their offices as they fill cavities.

In Istanbul, there are Roman aqueducts, Byzantine gazebos, Sultanic palaces, Islamic mosques, Indian markets. In Istanbul, there are grubby Slavic neighborhoods made of row houses that are just enlarged chimneys. There are plenty of Eastern European people: broad women with their hair sealed in dark kerchiefs, blue-eyed laborers whose ruddy faces are covered with moles. They have daughters with unmined black eyes full of cabbage and lamenting. In Istanbul, there are Parisian manners, Parisian cobblestones, Parisian thunderstorms. In Istanbul, there is a beneficent Californian light, there is the eccentric hilliness and water-dappled contour of San Francisco. In Istanbul, there is German primness, German black suits and a former ally's regard for Germanic discipline. In Istanbul, there is Constantinople.

In Istanbul, there is an Egyptian obelisk. The Romans hauled it there, not the Turks. You can tell by the marble base carved with patrician profiles. The obelisk is an off-mauve dildo polished bright from screwing the sky. It's highly legible, as long as you respond to phalluses or know how to translate hieroglyphics. Cat, owl, eye, sea, jagged-edged ripsaw. A cat that can't eat the big-eyed owl. A disembodied eye that somehow sees. A saw that can't see. A sea that saws. In Istanbul, there are alphabets that no one remembers how to read.

In Istanbul, there are some viciously friendly people called Turks. A few of their ranks have been known to pull knives on those who refuse an invitation to their home. The quick temper appears defensive. It tries too hard to keep you from getting within range of some mass inferiority complex. In Istanbul, the Turks are still learning to read what now passes for Turkish. The language has only recently been Romanized. But a French "*merci*" always wins a formal bow. In Istanbul, the young Turks try so hard to act European that they show just how un-European they are. It's the same way Europeans fail at being American, playing at being disaffected cowboys through buying the right blue jeans. In Istanbul, the old Turks, who were once young Turks, don't give a damn what you call them.

In Istanbul, a few items are Turkish. There's Turkish coffee, Turkish delight, Turkish baths but no Turkish fez. That's been outlawed by the modernists. The Turkish coffee is brought to you each morning in munchkin cups on a worn silver tray by a man whose slicked-down hair is parted in the middle. The man never smiles, acid as the coffee. The Turkish delight quivers in blocks, sometimes hidden in sweet shop window wind drifts of confectioners' sugar. The baths are even more discreet. They're concrete igloos with skylights letting off steam all over the city. Everyone goes at least once. No one can resist, not even the pointedly unkempt hippies waiting in front of the Pudding Shop for the next "magic bus" to Nepal. But a Turkish bath is much better if you're returning from the psychedelic front. The universe of warmth offered you—hot towels, hot stone, hot vapors on tap—can then be appreciated as it must have been before the invention of the water heater. The baths' fire is purification, a caress, also a luxury item. The quiet, too, is part of the treatment: rented wooden sandals make the only clamor in the steam room. A muscular attendant, with genuine curl to his mustache, will be glad to give you a genuine Turkish massage. He stands full force on your spine until you want to cry Ataturk. He soaps you up and brushes you down. He opens your pores with a natural Brillo pad sponge, then points gleefully to the gummy ooze he's dislodged. Coming loose is the sap of Malayan rubber plantations, the soot of coal-burning Gangetic ferries, the caked-on sweat salt of Hindustani plains, the dust of central Asia kicked up by Mongol horsemen and all time's wanderers. It's a Biblical dust that never settles. Successive nomads must breathe it and eat it. Months of cold showers along the caravan do no genuine cleaning, but the baths' surfeit of heat is every survivor's reward. Istanbul is the end of the line.

In Istanbul, there are spice bazaars, covered bazaars, old bazaars, new bazaars, leather and gold bazaars, bazaars of carpets and meerschaum and inlaid boxes, bazaars of ancient coins and the bric-a-brac of fallen empires. In the back alleys and crowded stalls of the old city, Asia infiltrates Europe. Sales are concluded in the Asian way, all bluff and guile. Feuding cousins sell the same wares side by side through generations. Merger would mean mixed blood. Work is done in the Asian way, too. Men are still cheaper than machines and far more expendable. The Turks, a chef at a roadside kebap salonu tells us, do only two things: sleep and work. Sometimes three, he leers. Gofers and warehousemen crowd the waterfront with the day's loads harnessed to their backs. They crouch patiently, impersonating mules. They balance reams of paper, bales of cotton, even six-legged velvet sofas. The coolie lives! Produce depots that line the Golden Horn expel a file of human forklifts. They do vaudeville to entertain us, and themselves, their act consisting of piling crate upon melon crate atop the dependable hoist of their spines.

In Istanbul, there is the Topkapi Palace. Seat of the Ottoman Empire. Ottoman of the Seat Empire. Inner sanctum inside inner sanctum burrows toward some final, unbuildable space. The world has been brought indoors by rulers who preferred not to go out. Chinese porcelain, emeralds and the heavily secured dentures of the prophet Mohammed. The harems turn out to be joyless cells constructed with a binary touch. Corners within corners: nature reduced and codified until it's mastered. Fascinating, but where's the fresh air? Life is opaque inside the royal dungeons. In one of the deepest pits, a torture chamber padded in silk, the prince was kept from all outside influence until he was ready to take over. This sheltered upbringing seems to have made the line of Ottomans eager to acquire more loot, but unwilling to flaunt it. There was nothing consumeristic about it. The Sultans weren't "buying in," they were buying out. The Topkapi's greatest privilege was privacy. Its inhabitants gobbled their imperial candy in the dark and quickly flushed the wrappers down the harem toilet.

In Istanbul, there are waterways. There's the Bosporus and the Golden Horn and the Sea of Marmara all the way to the Dardanelles. Fingers of the Mediterranean encrusted with history. But where the hell is the Hellespont? I see hills of curlicue cypress, shimmering inlets, Draculaean castles above. Toward the horizon, a hint of Riviera, jagged skyline of cabanas creeping toward a tamed ocean. In Istanbul, the port is a cafeteria. Stop for a sesame-covered pretzel, halvah and fresh pickles or the trans-alliterated sandwich: sandoviç. Fresh fish is fried in giant pans that burn in rowboats tied to the quay. In Istanbul, there are too many sailors and too little sea.

In Istanbul, they take the "h" off hotel. Ours is the Otel Akdeniz. A five-story spiral staircase with rooms attached, including a couple tacked on to the roof. We're thrilled to get one of them: no heat, no running water during the day, but the best view in town. We're above the multitudes' crush for the first time since we lolled on the balcony of Macao's Bela Vista. This is better than the South China Sea; we can hang our Woolite-rinsed socks and chemises on a line against the backdrop of the mammoth Aya Sofya. Built by Constantine, later ringed with minarets that sit on the architectural launching pad like defused rockets, the Aya Sofya is the first church of Christianity. Its grandiose dome is a giant bald spot in the city. It radiates foreboding, like a fortuneteller's glass orb. Munching tomatoes and peaches and other raw fruit long taboo for us, we study this reminder of a time when Jesus was but another guru of some dark Oriental cult. Or we can turn our chairs and watch the sun drop behind the six turrets of the Mosque known as Sultan Ahmet.

In Istanbul, they call Sultan Ahmet the Blue Mosque. On the outside, it's really no bluer than Suleiman the Magnificent's, or any of the others. Perhaps it's just a touch bluer inside, where the azure tiles pulse with the changing light of the day. This retreat in grotto tones is so peaceful only warriors could have built it, so grandiose it must house the most intimate revelations. At dusk, we can hear the call to prayer from a loudspeaker atop one of the Blue Mosque's minarets. Farther off, there are the competing calls of downtown and uptown muezzins. In Istanbul, one always cheats on his sundowns so he can beat the others to the plaintive punch.

In Istanbul, the Otel Akdeniz is run by a gentle, beleaguered sandy-haired man who I can only think of as Mister Akdeniz, though Akdeniz means Mediterranean. He is the heir apparent to our vertical dive. When he smiles, he looks boyish. He's old enough to have a father with silver mustache, wool vest and beret, who reads the paper all day in the hotel office. The old man mumbles and assumes all his guests speak Turkish. Sometimes we catch him playing cards at the tavern or knocking the cobbles in the street with his cane. He taps the street like he owns it. He is a hard father to get away from. So his son rents the rooms, keeps the books, struggles with the toy Turkish telephones and is chef of the ground floor restaurant. Before each dawn, he exiles himself to the basement kitchen from which he brings forth the day's helpings for the steam table. Up the stairs to our rooftop come waftings of lamb stew, imam bayaldi ("the Sultan fainted"), broad beans and potatoes, yogurt with fresh dill, more eggplant, more mutton.

In Istanbul, we breakfast downstairs, and dine there, too. Akdeniz keeps his apron on until the last lamb sausages have been skewered and grilled. Then he brings out a bottle of raki and shares it with his friends. One evening, when the stuff takes effect fast enough, he urges helpings of firewater upon his guests. At the checkerboard-covered table next to ours, there's a brace of aging Austrian love birds, in knickers and feathered caps, hunters not hunted, who're no doubt touring Asia Minor in the footsteps of Schliemann. They beam at any smudge of local color: to them, all is *gemütlich* and tidy bliss. At the next table, a dozen French transcendentalists are ready to try anything that gets them in the nether state. And there's Iris and me, returning exiles, unused to the hard stuff and oddly fearful of it. Finally, there are the Turks, eager for some hard-nosed gaiety. Toasts of *"Prosit!"* are followed by army songs, probably anti-Greek, followed by more *prosits* and urgings for the foreigners to join in a ditty, this time about love. Innkeeper Akdeniz is radiant, though only a mock exasperation in his eyes and ruffling of his toupee let you know it. His face is not in the habit of happiness. Nightly, in Istanbul, he tries, with the help of a licorice elixir, to mix duty and pleasure, then raises his glass to their incompatibility. Akdeniz is both proud and melancholy in a way that is familiar to us. He is a modern rebel, and unlike his counterparts in the East, carries on his drudgery without the balm of faith. He is resigned to meaninglessness, not tradition—and we find this resignation far less inscrutable because it's the brand we practice. Also because this man has not entirely given up. As if to spite his hotelier's fate, Akdeniz needs, actively, for us to feel what he feels, live what he lives. He passes the bottle.

In Istanbul, Iris becomes the chief boarder of Akdeniz. Robbed of her characteristic pluck, she barely has the enthusiasm to sit out on our inadvertent rooftop terrace. Seemingly sated, she stuffs no more souvenirs into her perceptual kit bag. Worse still, brown patches appear on her forehead and her newly-grown locks fall out in the comb. In Istanbul, the diagnosis will be malnutrition. Strange, since she's overeaten the planet.

In Istanbul, we must sneak away in the darkness. It's Sunday, and Akdeniz has taken the day off. He's set up a café table near the railing on our roof. He and a drinking companion have their legs slung over the railing. On the table is a half-finished game of chess and a fully finished bottle of raki. The two of them appear to be holed-up and hiding from their dreary continuum. The blue trough of the Bosporus is going black with sunset. Only the Blue Mosque's tint is vague enough to remain eternally blue. O, blue that never was and blue that always will be! Iris and I are tiptoeing out, laden with our packs, our Afghan blankets, and sacks of baklava tied on with ribbons. We are spotted, and Iris approaches Akdeniz as closely as you can approach anyone when you're wearing a pack.

"Goodbye. We must go." I can hear my own fondness for the man in her voice.

"Goodbye!" he hollers back, almost vindictively. An extravagant sweep of his right arm follows. He looks like he's throwing salt over his shoulder for luck, but there's no salt. Akdeniz is a drunken good man who might have been, with a little luck, a drunken great man. I can just make out that he's looking up at Iris in the new moonlight. His expression is bemused and envious. If only he could do like us, just pay his bill and skeedaddle! "Farewell to you, children. 'Stamboul shall miss you."

Iris and he touch hands. It's my turn.

"We liked your hotel."

"Oh, you like my otel. Very good." He glances at his pal, then back up. "You like my otel. . . . But do you like *me?*"

I answer our friend in the affirmative, but I'm shamefaced. It's too late. The picturesque memories will be marred.

His question is somehow a very Turkish question. It implores, this need to skirt history and its mistaken identities. It is always a jab with the eyes, a push to get beyond, to squeeze and touch, or alternately, to fight. But I've learned to deflect such intensity, to aim for survival, no higher. I've come to see people as stepping stones, or potential obstructions, good so long as they don't do anything bad.

Where am I hurrying? Why this obsessional drive to get onward only to get back? I've got no particular obligation to job, community or kin—and the World Series will be played out. I should be stalling, if I'm smart, since our arrival means only that Iris and I will have to carry out our emotional suicide pact. Soon enough, we'll complete the last leg. We'll fly over continents, clouded as our intentions. Our journey continues westward, always westward, in the direction our white man's history has progressed. We follow the sun—but how progressive can that old star be?

And is it possible to be against progress and for history? That's the curious program which I've come to endorse. Some Marco Polos! Iris and I don't import gunpowder or silk or pasta proto-types, just more bad news that no one will want to hear. Also, we're developing a tender regard, bordering on mawkishness, for those foreseken lands we've just finished scorning. We return with a need to revel in each scrap of news that reaches us from such hot spots as Gilgit and Johore Bahru. More than anything, Asia stimulates in the two of us an obnoxious tendency to equate gains in consciousness with discomfort.

As for those notions of "seeing the world" with which I set out, I know now that at best I've seen a tiny bit of myself. In particularly, I've glimpsed those parts that a sheltered American upbringing left unrevealed, including: my capacity to bear anything and complain about everything; to squeeze ahead of fellow beings in a ticket line, or simply out-endure them; to skip dinner in Delhi or scratch up breakfast in Bangalore. I've proved a whiz at "getting through" Asia, but getting through something is not the same as being there.

It's all in the hieroglyphics: cutting knife, seeing eye, shining sun. Cultures are stronger than men, and men are not so weak as they think. At least, I'm not.

In Istanbul, the Orient Express leaves at midnight. (Sydney Greenstreet, where are you?) Strolling the cars just after we've pulled out of the station, we discover there'll be no food on board for two days. Luckily, a young Turk in our compartment carries a luscious black suitcase. His mamma has packed it with roasted chickens, loaves of fresh-baked bread, sacks of sweet tomatoes and dried apricots, pans full of the flaky cheese pie called borek. The Turk's a boutique owner taking his current best girl on a buying trip to Paris. He shows off for her by taking English lessons from us. He shows off for all by downing a full gallon of Johnny Walker he's bought tax-free in the station.

While he finishes the whiskey, Iris and I take our tutorial pay by finishing his food. It is his pleasure, the universal honor. To eat and to offer. To take and be taken. To help one another down the last mile. The more we gobble, the more the Turk slaps us on the back. Appreciative after five months' abstinence from the home-cooked, we devour everything down to the platters. Dish by dish, he disposes of them as quickly as we dispose of what's on them. He's modern, this Turk. His wink assures us all is under control. Somewhere between Istanbul and home, maybe Bulgaria, the young Turk tosses his mother's best china out the carriage window and onto the tracks.

NEAR HOME

THE TRAIL OF BLOOD

"To the dengue!"
"To the itching!"
"To the iodine drops!"
"To the bougainvillaea!"
"To the gamelan!"
"To Buddha's feet!"
"To Mack's bush jacket!"
"To curiosity!"
"To Ganesh!"

Iris and I were clinking glasses of Napa Valley champagne, not Singapore Slings. We'd reserved a table with harborview, white linen, fresh flowers, at one of San Francisco's oldest seafood grills. One of San Francisco's oldest waiters bore overgarnished blue plate specials. I made Iris ask him for a candle. And bring on the crab cocktails, the heels of hot sourdough! We gobbled salmon in hollandaise without checking for bones. No nasi goreng tonight, no curried yak. Our just desserts were baked Alaska and brandies.

"To the special cake!"
"To the rhinestone cowboy!"
"To Pappa Din!"

"And Mother Teresa!"

"To the dying destitute!"

"To the living resolute!"

Had the other diners overheard us, they could hardly have made sense out of these references. They were clues to a crime that only Iris and I had witnessed. No wonder we had to continue looking out for each other. "To the trick!" I wanted to cry out, but didn't. "To happy endings!"

For tonight, we could lay claim to several of those. Not only had we survived, with our critical faculties and colons intact, but we were starting anew. Iris' edict, uttered so many thousand miles back yet so close to where we once more found ourselves, had passed its expiration date. The trip was over, but we weren't. Instead of parting, we'd rented the all-redwood, if slightly aslant, bottom floor of a Victorian house across the Berkeley line into Oakland, where we planned to pool futons, rice cookers, catcher's mitts, libraries. Though we'd moved in little more than our bedding, there appeared to be enough nonmildewed space for me to set up a proper writer's office and for Iris to have a seamstress' workshop where she could begin turning her collected fabrics into the "robes" of her Indian woman. Maintaining separate flush toilets, individual surpluses of hot water, now struck us as spendthrift. Nor could either of us afford to sustain the emotional extravagance of "non-commitment." Perhaps we were just too exhausted to stage the tragedy we'd written. We couldn't get worked up enough to end things. And we still made such a good team: her stoicism and my complaints, her acceptance and my strivings, her trust and my anxieties. We were road buddies now, defying road's end. Having played house in a hundred cheesy rooms—forced, despite the hotel touts' claims, to make our own music in all of them—it was only natural that we should lighten our satchels under the same leaky California roof.

To spend our first night there, we had to get back across the bay in Iris' reclaimed VW. She was the only person I knew who drove better from booze. I steered the radio dial, searching out a year's worth of missed top forty hits. Let the music waft, turbines spark, traffic surge! More than ever, California was our spanking-new playpen.

Usually, when hurtling through the Yerba Buena tunnel, I had visions of a motorized gas chamber into which all six lanes were being led. Not this time.

"I must be content," I told Iris.

"Congratulations, sport. What does it feel like?"

Underneath us, Oakland began. It began in the water, the way all of us had begun. We slid down one long asphalt arm into our adopted home town: a pit where regional planners consigned the working poor, the non-working non-poor, the poor working.

"It's a basement," I had to admit. "We're moving into life's basement."

"How can you say that after what we've seen? You're such a snob."

But who could deny that this Oakland was an all-American heartbreaker? It possessed all the current qualifications. It offered freeway exhaust for air, telephone poles for trees, and schools where third-graders paid protection money to their classmates. It took your money and housed you in pasteboard fractions of long-sunken sea captains' cottages. It took your money and fed you in a hundred kwik-serv ways. It took your money but could not find you a job. Ravaged by white flight, Oakland was a modern ghost town, patrolled by Afro-cowboys in their customized stallions—where poverty was portable and could turn right on a red light, where nothing ever happened except accident or overdose. Hold tight in your seat; ride the signals' green wave. This was one drive-thru riot, breakdowns be damned.

Oblivious to anything sinister, Iris guided the VW past great tabernacles of coffee shops, where pimps, prostitutes and other sinners came to sip from the sleep-staving java. She ignored the creatures from a nightly Satyricon, showcased in hot pants and torn leotards, who strutted in motel driveways. Plenty of vacancies. Instead, Iris pointed with delight at the figures manning the office registers. I nodded. The motel owners were nearly all turbaned Punjabis. Only in America: the sons of the Golden Temple were running franchised whorehouses. When they wrote home, they undoubtedly called themselves "real estate magnates." Best Western Rajahs.

Just a few days prior, I'd given one of them an offhanded "*Namaste!*" It was here, in one "Golden Gate Motel," that I'd spent my first night back, having just finished the globe's encir-

clement with a transcontinental train ride: half a week's club car
piano rinky-tink and sleeping car porter's pillow-fluffing minstrel,
the space between the oceans hitting me like some sodden drug,
nembutol of Altoona asleep, hurtling past that small-town prairie
bliss sleep under swaying elms, Toledo and Oswego specks in my
eyes, Utah's desert of dried tears, Nevada a series of neon boots
in the air kicking me along to the promised land. Arriving home
a day early after nine months away, I'd awaited Iris' return from
a visit to her family homestead in a place that was actually called
Liberty, Texas. (With a stopover by the shores of Lake LBJ! Better
than the Vale of Kashmir!) Hardly missing a barefoot beat, she'd
studied, at her usual nonjudgmental distance, native behavior in
that plutocracy where life was doused with pride and pepper sauce,
where Phillips Oil was the sole arbiter of truth and Ramsey Clark
a convicted traitor. Hearing her grandma called her granddad "the
nicest man in the world," as she passed him another slice of cornbread, had pushed Iris farther toward renewing our couplehood.
But I'd sweated out the suspense of her decision in my sanitized
rubber room, strapped to a water bed that vibrated for a quarter.

Tonight, Iris and I cruised a few stoplights beyond. Just off
the strip, our new neighborhood looked evacuated. The only evidence of life in this lower-upper-middle enclave was the blue
flicker of televisions through doilied curtains. Could we take our
place in this quaint tomb? Draw the shades on public life like our
neighbors did? Keep the stereo going to drown out the freeway's
constant rubber gurgle? Once, before it was turned into just another exit ramp the street where we parked had been lined with
San Franciscans' summer estates. Now the false gables, rounded
turrets and screened verandas were being replaced with the concrete layers of efficiency apartments: no kids, no pets, all-electric
kitchen. The remaining "single unit" houses were defiantly unique:
squat stuccos with slant-eyes eaves, camp lodge brown shingles,
brittle and wan "painted ladies." One had red wainscoting, one a
Shinto rock garden, or lawn of painted concrete, or natural barbed
wire of overgrown cactus patch, or frontyard collection of ships'
masts, or windows barred in mustache curlicues of anti-burglar
iron.

Yet each was touching in its attempt to cram utopia onto a
single lot. Strolling toward our flat, every yard seemed to tell us
that this ordinary place was now ours as well to try and make

extraordinary. The forever-in-bloom six square feet Shalimars of the do-it-yourselfers were stuffed with cosmos, princess flowers and the crusty trim of the rosette succculents called "chickens and hens." Even under the yellow, anti-crime streetlights, Iris identified every garden variety for me, a bouquet of names retrieved from childhood memory. I was sharply attuned to her delight. My wanderlust was satisfied by this single turn around the block.

Wobbling arm-in-arm up our walkway, it looked like the hydrangia bushes had suddenly bloomed just for us. The flowers were white bubble gum wrappers.

"Home again, home again, jiggity-jog . . ."

Maybe the champagne was making me giddy, or it could have been our clothes. My Italian linen jacket and Iris' full-length Afghan dress were all wrong in Oakland. We were trick-or-treaters, disguised as ourselves.

"Home again, home again . . ."

The wiring in the night light was loose—a first repair job for Iris—so that she had to fiddle with the switch. She dug for an unfamiliar key in the crumby depths of her Nepalese purse. Blowing kisses in her ear, I waited for her to get the damn door open so I could sweep her across the threshold.

Looking down at the lock, Iris gasped. As I knew from many occasions, she was not one for unprovoked gasping. I peered over her shoulder and down toward the spot on the walkway where she was looking. Something wet glinted there. It had been poured, or gushed, down the middle, and stopped right at our doorway. Though the night light was dim, we could tell the stain was freshly made and red.

"It's blood," said Iris.

"From inside the house?"

"No, I reckon not. There's none on the doorstep."

"It comes to here and stops. Like someone was looking for help."

"I know. Look back . . ." The blood was dribbled down the walkway and out to the curb where it was lost in the darkness.

"I brought over a flashlight," Iris remembered.

"Maybe you shouldn't go inside. The police will take care of it."

"Sweetie! It's fresh blood!"

Iris crossed the threshold by herself. While she rummaged in her tool chest, I couldn't help thinking about omens. I didn't want to believe this was a calling card left by the wounded lands from which we'd retreated. It could just as well have been a voodoo rite, the Passover smearing of lamb's gore, offering protection. Perhaps we needed this vaccine to immunize us against butchery. Apparently, the geomancer's coins, still in our pockets, weren't good enough anymore. I pulled mine out and stroked the red sash. Red, the lucky color, was all over the front steps.

Iris returned with the flashlight she kept in case of earthquakes. Be prepared! I fell in line behind my intrepid scout, watching her track the trail of blood. It was a thick trail, with few breaks in it. I didn't want to touch it, but it looked hot. If we'd been bloodhounds, we would have been in bloodhound heaven. We wouldn't have needed our Eveready. Halfway down the block, the trail turned down a driveway that led to a garage at the back of a stucco apartment house. Iris followed it into the darkness. Her high heels skated on gravel.

"What if he's down there?" I froze on the sidewalk. So the thing at the end of my trail was a he! I couldn't speak the rest of my scenario. The climax had something to do with a dazed and cornered maniac raising his gun one more time at Iris. The killer was played by Richard Widmark. The moral was that this world was indeed a dangerous place, and that there was nothing like coming home to prove it. Why did this have to happen tonight?

"Iris?" All I could see when I squinted down the alley was the square and sullen silhouette of a Dempster dumpster.

"Not a trace. The track just turns around."

"Don't go anywhere without me again."

"I won't. But you're the one who stayed behind."

"Come on. Let's not argue. Look at this mess!"

We traced the trail from streetlight to streetlight. At the next corner, it was reduced to splotches, which branched in two directions. With Iris' permission, I went on a scavenging foray across our six lane street. There were hardly any cars at this hour, and certainly no pedestrians for miles. Except the one we sought. At the far corner, I stooped on one knee and dirtied my suit. I was a ridiculous suitor, proposing to the sidewalk. If there was blood down there, it could have been from some previous homicidal spill. I saw only the usual blemishes made by tar, motor oil and rain. There was plenty of writing, a city's notes to itself, left in the memo pads of wet concrete. "WIMMEN R POWERFUL," "PIGS EAT SHIT" and the less forthright but equally popular "CIA PUTA." I headed back toward Iris. She was combing every inch with her flashlight, as if it was a Geiger counter. We were two detectives in evening dress, Nick and Nora Charles scanning for traces of plasma. Wisps of Pacific fog were rolling in, right on cue.

"Shall we call out?" Iris asked.

"It's almost two. We'll wake everyone."

"What would we say anyhow?" she asked again.

A black Thunderbird slinked around the corner, slowing as it turned.

"I seen him!" cried the driver.

"Where?"

"I seen him!"

The car was gone before we could ask, "Who?" Still, Iris kicked off her shoes and began running barefoot. I stayed with her while she tried to stay behind the car. If the driver was trying to lead us somewhere, he wasn't doing any better job than the peasant boys in the paddies of Nepal. Two turns and no U-turns, then he peeled out. Several houses down the dark side street where we'd been lured, we heard chatter and approaching footsteps. This time, I grabbed Iris. We saw another flashlight, swaying like an altar boy's incense in the mist.

"Ahoy there!"

"Hello!"

We weren't face-to-face with the killer, but an elderly couple. Italian maybe, small but robust. The man wore a flannel parka and a knit Raiders cap with tassel on the end. Two curls of white hair crept toward his ears. He held peeled spuds of fingers to his forehead, shielding his eyes from the nearest light. He looked like an old prizefighter. His wife wore a white shawl and clutched her husband's arm the way I clutched Iris'.

"Are you on the lookout, too?"

"Uh-huh."

"Gee, that's dandy. . . . Does the path go down that way?"

"Uh-huh. But it backtracks to here."

"You folks sure now?" the prizefighter asked. "We better be certain. Better give it the once-over ourselves."

"What about your way?"

"Oh, it's nothing but dead ends," his wife volunteered. "The poor animal."

"Animal?" In this neighborhood, that could have meant anything.

"Yah, that's right. German shepherd. Purebred, wasn't he, hon?"

"Purebred."

"Goes by the name of Rajah. Awful nice fella, too."

"Is he yours?" Iris was nearly crying.

"Thank God he ain't. Belongs to the folks livin' next door to us. Awful good people. Colored, but honest. Real hardworking. They've been our neighbors for near thirty years."

The four of us looked at our feet while we talked. We weren't shy, just scouring the sidewalk for clues.

"So what happened to the dog?"

"It was the police. Some young officer came around, said he was investigatin' a burglary. Don't know where. He must have gone in their yard, you see. Naturally, Rajah was on guard. I don't think he would have done the officer any real harm. But a German shepherd in the dark . . ."

"He shot him?"

"I'm afraid so. He was just a boy, this patrolman. Kinda panicked, you might say."

"Is he out looking, too?"

"Oh, no. He took off. Had to keep the peace someplace else. Either that, or fill out some paperwork. Couldn't be bothered with a dog."

It was hard to look for the blood and shake our heads at the same time.

"Have your neighbors come home?"

"Not yet. It's gonna be a surprise for 'em. That's why we're tryin' to find ol' Rajah. Try to save him if we can. I don't know though. They seem to have a way of pulling through the worst calamities. . . ." I couldn't tell if he was referring to the dog or its masters. "Still, he's lost a lotta juice."

"Did you see where he got shot?"

"Didn't see him nor hear him. He must have gone a little crazy. Run six blocks, at least. He's been all over the neighborhood. Hope he's found what he's lookin' for."

"Damn cops," the wife added. She looked straight at me for the first time. Somewhere between sandbagged eyes, quivering lips and collapsed chin, I caught the outlines of a Walkyrie maiden. I couldn't imagine her ever being afraid of anything.

"Damn cops," I answered, saying hello.

The four of us worked together. We followed the trail back to our apartment, and retraced our steps down the dark driveway, and came to the block where the search had first merged, and weaved, eyes at our feet, around each stained corner, every glass-littered lot. Each time the blood thickened in solid globs, Iris ran faster, and I had to move to keep my arm around her. I had to admit that I was relieved when we didn't find this "Rajah," given his current condition. But Iris refused to turn back until the trail became indistinguishable from air bubbles in the pavement, street noumena, the flashlight's soft-edged mirages.

The old couple matched us step for step. The woman hippity-hopped in sneakers, worn under her housedress, though one foot dragged a bit. The man lugged an all-American gut that held too much beer and white bread. Yet they were models of stoicism and decorum. They were comfortable in this place. It made no difference that the government labeled this a "changing" neighborhood. It made no difference that it was the crime-ridden depth of night. Like us, they were on native ground, native asphalt, native astroturf.

They were hardly rattled when our search party was joined by a black wino in dark suit with the jacket pockets torn out.

"Hey, hey, now! What're you spooks doin' out?"

We told him, but each time we did, he'd just ask again, adding, "You wouldn't have a little taste, then? Something to keep warm off, bro'? Some way to get *full*. I'se full as a mother-fucker! . . . What you doin' out here, bro'? Lookin' for the Viet-cong?"

"For a dog."

"A dog! Let's go get some o' that Vietnam herb. Get full as motherfuckers. Real fucked-up. . . . What you'all lookin' for, any-way?"

He didn't want an answer. He just wanted to take up the rear. But where was the front? We kept losing the sidewalk's grisly directions. It was possible the bleeding had stopped, or that there was no more blood left, or that the dog had been picked up and taken to the Humane Society. None of our humane society wanted to be the first to give up.

"I'm slidin' on through. Catch your act later." Only the drunk had better things to do. "Ain't you got nothing to get full on, bro'?"

Starting the same circle for the fifth time, the old man pulled off his booster's cap and scratched his bald spot.

"We can't do anything more now. Maybe by daylight, we'll get him. Poor old boy. . . . You folks been awfully kind. You go on home to bed."

It didn't seem the right moment to tell him that we'd never gone to that home or that bed before. Our posse exchanged phone numbers and addresses.

"Thirty years on this street," the wife told us, smiling mightily all the while. "Lord, I wish I'd never seen this street."

And this was just our first night! Home sweet home! Welcome back! Watching the couple walk out of our life as calmly and bravely as they'd entered it, Iris asked, "Aren't they great?"

"They are. They make me feel like settling down isn't a compromise."

"I want to be just like them when I'm old. I want to make a habit out of being good."

Iris and I kissed. We'd forgotten all about Rajah. We never did call the old couple to find out what became of the dog. There was enough bad news in the world, in Oakland, without having to seek it out. In a week, we'd be walking over the blood stains, hardly seeing them, just like everyone else.

"At least, we tried. . . ."

"At least, we got to know two of our neighbors. . . ."

We were finally through the front door of our new place together.

"At least, it wasn't blood from a man. . . ."

At least, it wasn't blood from one of us. At least, the streets did not flow red with the juices of vendetta or massacre. At least, we'd found some purpose that made us claim those streets without fear. There were times when you could go on with "at leasts," whittling away at less and less, until there was so little left it was nothing.

Just as our lives were opening up, things "as they are" were beginning to close in. Backdrop became foreground. At least, having come around the world in our bad mood, Iris and I were determined that what we'd seen had to be more bleak than what was ahead. Our journey of ten thousand li was ending with this single significant step. But how far was a li anyhow?

At least—one last lessening—we could sniff our way back down the trail, following the scent of itinerant memory. Combing for clues while asleep, we were no longer out to solve mysteries so much as accept them: we didn't need to reconstruct the exotic, just reinvent. At dreaming's safe distance we would pay off the beggars, rehabilitate the lame, cool the eternally feverish, tip each waiter no matter how grumpy, believe every tout no matter how hyperbolic, tag along down every dark alley, swap our credit cards for clean knives on the black market, leave flowers at all the neglected shrines, go down on one knee before assorted idols.

Iris must have known just what I was thinking. In another musical room containing little more than our bed, sliding toward me across unchristened sheets, she exclaimed, "If only everyone was traveling all the time! . . . Then nobody could get hurt. Then there would be nothing for anyone to see."

Music:

THE REBELLION OF
THE CHINESE WAITERS

NO ONE CAN IMAGINE why it began. What made the rebellion of the Chinese waiters most remarkable was its emphatic lack of origins. If the uprising had its plotters, they proved loyal to the discretion of their trade. These architects left no conspiratorial blueprints for future generations of waiters to follow. They raised no demands unmet. Grievances? Like germs, grievances are everywhere and better left invisible. Facts? Sometimes a wave rises to rinse clean the safe harbor we call facts. Unless further evidence emerges from the gunpowder haze that clings to the Orient, we can speak only of the revolt's telepathic logistics, its unknown infrastructures, the stringent secrecy of its communicants.

It has been suggested they sent their messages by fortune cookie. It has also been suggested that dead Chinese waiters return to this world as Peking ducks: preserved in pancakes, honored with wreaths of scallions. We do know that one February afternoon, while the Pacific wept over Oakland, a waiter named Ng shuffled back and forth from the kitchen in his pointed black shoes with the laces missing. He trod effortlessly in rented black pants with black satin stripes down the sides. His bow tie sat properly and his hair was greased back. His golden vest, worn too short, buttoned in one place, as always, was stained with soy sauce. As always. When a group of roundnoses stopped spinning the dishes of their lazy Susan and asked for forks, Ng asked them, "What's a fork?" Everyone laughed, and later the cashier's father, who was the proprietor, laughed hardest of all. Ng continued to ask his question, without guile. He bore mustard and rice bowls and bill, but he would not go near a fork.

When Ng did what he had to do, or didn't do what he had to do, or had to do what he didn't do, the headwaiter of a fashionable dim sum house in the East End of London ignored a plea for chili oil from a party of sixteen Kuomintang traders. At the same time, at Wo Fat's noodle joint in Johannesburg, another waiter, in tan jacket, in bow tie, in pointed shoes, would not replenish the water in a pot of tea whose lid had been thrown open. At an American-and-Cantonese diner with grill vent shaped like the roof of a pagoda, in Raleigh, North Carolina, a thirty-year-man named Waylon Wong stood by the swinging, padded doors to the kitchen, without looking for the next order through the diamond-shaped cutout, and smoked a cigarette. In Taipei, a compatriot unloosed his collar. In Singapore, an entire staff spent the afternoon watching vapor rise from the bamboo steamers. In Harbin, and Mukden, and Chungking, in the basement courts of fraudulent emperors, from the smoky blue gorges of the Yangtze to the Great Hall of the People itself, the intransigence spread. Soon, messenger boys in knee socks were scurrying around the world's Chinatowns, trying to find replacements for the dinner service, discovering that the strange illness had struck wherever they were dispatched.

The waiter Lin was the first to be sent home. Others were led to nearby herbalists. Antler powder and ground butterfly wings did not do the job. Acupuncturists and necromancers were consulted. Confucian priests composed special prayers. In Hong Kong, the British rounded up all suspects. In New York, industrial psychologists did time-and-motion studies. The teamsters stood ready with their tire irons, unsure which way to swing them. Within three hours, every Chinese waiter in every Chinese restaurant in the world had gone on strike. But no one mentioned the word strike or even stoppage. Nothing could be offered to these men that could entice them to return. Return? They had not left. They simply smoked cigarettes, removed their rented trousers, and slipped deeper into their silent, black-haired anonymity.

How many of them were there? They were larger than any standing army. They lived in every third-rate port, and every trading post, where coolies hoisted bamboo cartons, where anything could be made for less and sold for more. They were everywhere Chinese were—which was every city on the earth. They had been breeding, and training, and shuffling back and forth with silver platters and lacquered soup spoons shaped like the hips of old prostitutes ever since the second Peking Man had ordered won tons from the first. They were enough waiters to serve every meal that has ever been served to mankind. They had made enough trips to and from tables to have marched across the South Sea archipelagos and trampled the Andes and stormed Europe's citadels. Counting the busboys and the broth makers and the cleaver wielders and the dumpling stuffers and the pot scrubbers and their cousins and their dependents, they were more people than they fed: the hungry feeding the full, so the full could want more and the hungry eat.

For nearly a week, the restaurants tried to remain open. Why, anyone could take orders, set places, refill tea pots, cart trays, point to the house specialties on Column A or Column B. But no one could. The messenger boys didn't know how to fold the linen properly. The owners' relatives were too feeble. The cashiers got the dropsies. The broken enamelware alone was enough to fill the gaps in the Great Wall. Slabs of pork butt festered. Greens wilted. Signs went up on restaurant marquees: "Closed for Unique Chinese Holiday," or "Closed for Untimely Death in Family." As though a Chinese restaurant ever closed for such a thing! Some signs even read, "Closed in Honor of the Great Proletarian Cultural Revolution." Bosses everywhere tried to save face.

Little was recorded about what the waiters were doing. They had so much time now. That must have proved overwhelming to these ordained couriers who were used to thinking only so far as the next course. It appears that most of them were as inactive as possible. It was observed that, once in their tenement homes, with their families, the waiters broke their trances, dropped their glares, emerged from sullenness. Some were seen staring out their back windows toward far-off water towers and smokestacks, skinny as overworked mules in white undershirts, reaching for more cigarettes and comic books and straw hats. A few of the waiters went to mahjongg parlors and the racetracks. Many more held their children out of school. The waiters were seen leading sons and daughters by the hand toward zoos and sweet shops. Some did nothing but go to Kung Fu movies. One shrieked and tried to leap over the three-story U.S.-China Friendship Association, but he died on the way down. Some waiters painted their houses red. Some walked by the waterfront, and wore slippers, and loose happi coats, and threw skipping stones across the water. When they passed restaurants, the waiters were seen pulling mirrors from their pockets and using them to shield their eyes. A few plastered up wall posters. They read, "Let a thousand napkins bloom . . ." Others erected shrines in back alleys to their patron saints, prayed to gods with no mouths, gods with no stomachs. None feasted.

Seven times seven days gone, the waiters took a deep breath and went back to work. The proprietors, who pondered raises and made offerings and finally sulked away to their lairs, hid their great joy. They tried to hand out bonuses, but when such gestures were received impassively, the owners gave up. They decided it was best not to speak of what had occurred unless the waiters themselves spoke of it, which they never did. The restaurants refilled like goldfish ponds. There was the renewed clamor of skillets, belches and bargaining, the smell of jasmine and burnt garlic, the exchange of paper money beside the statuette of a fat and sassy Buddha on every counter beside every cash register and the toothpicks. Tips increased. The family associations lowered their interest rates by one percent. A new holiday was established: that cold day in February when Ng forgot the shape of a fork became a day off forever. No one gave the holiday a name or discussed the meaning of the observance.

In a few dark places, where fish were cleaned and protection enforced, it was whispered that a gear had momentarily slipped, refused to catch. That the world has sighed. That an old debt had been repaid. In Vancouver, and Bahrain, and Cincinnati, and Zanzibar, by the shores of the Hooghly and the Straits of Malacca, at Kweilin and Canton, in the Great Hall of the People itself, the waiters returned to their model decorum. The shiny, pointed black shoes pinched their feet. The rented pants itched. The bow ties felt like chokers. The gold vests fit like strait jackets, always too short, making the waiters look like circus clowns or trained monkeys or, worst of all, bellhops. Beneath the itchy scalps and the clear foreheads and the cheeks full of pallor and the dry lips and the peculiar folds of eyelid that forever marked their superiority, the waiters' black eyes saw only what they were required to see. Yet all eyes look two ways. The waiters did not laugh when the foreign devils placed the most preposterous orders. They brought banquets to overstuffed merchants, and forks, and were content to gobble cold soup at the end of their fourteen-hour days. They swept, and made deliveries, and took out the garbage, and covered thirty tables to a man. Many scalded their fingers with sizzling rice and none were given a yuan upon retirement.

Grievances? To want something more is the beginning of an end to all happiness. To want nothing else is the end of all beginnings. Facts? We can state unequivocally that the rebellion is now at an end. Poke your head in any door and you may see. The waiters are busy carting hot pots and duck sauce, shark's fin and sea slug, chow fun and strange taste chicken, into the new millennium.

❖

THE DESCENT

DAY FIVE. Maybe those village boys have the right idea. Off
with wristwatches! I'm learning to tell all the time I need
by the colors in the icy confluence of rivers: orange pastels for
day's end, pink ones for daybreak. Around six AM, Anno Domini,
a split second after we left California and before we returned, Don
and Iris and I cross the bridge out of Taramarang. Our now dog-
eared charts, crowded with smudged whorls of incline and decline,
show an unscenic route toward civilization—longer but flatter than
the way we've come. If we'd taken it in the first place, we might
still have been going in the right direction. Having given up on
the high country, we have nowhere to go but back. A twenty-mile
day will get us to a town on the main highway toward China. Our
last day of trekking is inevitably more rigorous than the first. We
must push ourselves harder to get out of the Himalayas than we
did to get in.

Such are the misadventures of travel: seemingly random and
impersonal, yet bearing a pattern that is persistently ironic and
one's own. This morning, our headstart in the race against daylight
and compulsions is immediately sabotaged. Just over the bridge,
a lone figure in oversized military woolens flags us down. Then

we notice his unobtrusive guardhouse. At first, we suspect that this is simply another, more official invitation to tea. But there's a second frowning sentry inside, dressed like a Czechoslovakian mailman. He sits behind the only furniture in the guardhouse's one room: a desk no bigger than a sewing machine. The legs of the desk buckle under the weight of a carbon black ledger. The officer dips his pen in an honest-to-goodness inkwell. The sun rises through the one glassless window onto the open pages of his never-ending list. This is a checkpoint. Our "permits to trek" are required after all. But the Nepalese have again devised a way to confound the digital orderliness of the modern registry of persons. Taramarang's designated clerk does not merely note the numbers on the cover of our booklets. That would be too succinct. He copies down every bit of information on the inside so that all the district will know that my eyes are brown; that Iris' place of birth is Houston, Texas. With his partner standing at attention all the while, it takes the keeper of records an hour to process us. What is time but a color?

Iris has finally chucked her rented boots, trading them for the sandals in her knapsack. She's become a hiking Apollo, swooshing over the remains of a road that once allowed jeeps to struggle up one side of the latest river we're following. Not even Don can keep up with her slavedriver's pace. I'm further handicapped by blisters that have turned into gashes. At one tchai-stop, taken on a bench beside the open kitchen of a town's master brewer, I can only get back at Iris with teases about her determination to escape the cherished wilderness. Soon after, we spot another group of Westerners, ponytailed and horribly sunburned in their BVD's, floating down one of the river's deepest, coolest channels. Iris trudges ahead, untempted.

The villages remain more intriguing than the landscape. In these huddles, made of one soft, somber wood piece that, unlike Kathmandu, is uncarved, gargoyleless, each house appears to support the next, so that if one were removed, the rest would surely lurch over. Big deal. The reluctant urbanites could then go back to farming or trapping or combing the hills.

Few inhabitants show an active interest in us; their mountain wariness serves them to the end. By mutual consent, we stay safely behind a one-way mirror. On the other side, the *dramatis personae* of public life exit and enter: tireless porters, bickering traders, an infrequent spate of burros, the odd tribesmen in checkerboard caps who either work for Ralston-Purina or have dropped in from the fifth moon of Saturn. Everyone in sight is a bit player, each takes a radiant character role. Center stage, before stacked pyramids of tinned merchandise, a short order chemist struggles over scalding pots and wood fire to bring forth beverage. In Nepal and India, tea-growing nations, one tastes in every sip the bitterness of underdevelopment. No wonder the populace takes it with so much sweetening! All the real stuff is exported; the dark-skinned man loses out to Lipton's and Twining's. He concocts what he can from "tea dust," the scrapings of the bushels, boiling it through a sieve, then reboiling it with sugar and curdled canned milk, decanting the goo scientifically from pot to pot; then aiming it as it froths toward a glass, where the mixture sears tongues and fingertips but stirs legs and imaginations. Tea dust to tea dust . . . these people have known little else.

The trail stretches on. We try not to calculate how much might be ahead, but occasionally allow ourselves the gauge of a glance back. Over our shoulders, one last irony: on the day we've given up reaching our goal, the heavens have unclouded to reveal it. Where the curve breaks right, we get the vista of a white summit, like the top of a question mark, like a misshapen snail, like the seductive eye of the All-Seeing One. There they are! Sizzling mirages in the Ektachrome sky, also known as *Los Himalayas, Les Alpes D'Inde, I Dolomiti.* But showing themselves for the first time, we're able to see how many rifts and ravines separate their heights from lowly us. There's just no way to cheat and sneak up on these suckers. (Fly directly to Everest Base Camp, do not pass go and you get the bends.) This ultimate range undoubtedly appears unapproachable right up to the moment one's world turns to rock and ice. These postcard visions have to be illustrations of Plato's "ideal form" of peak. A thing to be scaled, a working definition of the unattainable. Annapurna and Kachenjunga exist as perpetual destinations or not at all. Trekking isn't required to plant a flag on them.

Such legends are just as readily claimed by climbing up one's closed eyelids while lying in bed. Or by daring to look back in the midst of one's retreat. For it is only in retrospect that I allow myself to be amazed at where I've been.

The river widens and so does its belt of delicate, round staircases of rice. In their eye-enveloping progression, these paddies remind me of Michelangelo's Spanish Steps, Bernini's oval *barcaccia* at the bottom. Here land dictated design, the farmer is draftsman, and the result's as pleasing as anything man might have wracked his brain to achieve on his own. We pass stocky peasant girls who smile as they sow seed, look up with a sway of pigtails. They make suitably bovine portraits, posed against a pastoral canvas of grain. The contented beaming grows less frequent as we close in on the twentieth century's asphalt arteries. The towns are dustier and more raucous, a collection of spatting in-laws forced to bed down with one another; the tchai-shop regulars become ever more diffident. Envy creeps into the woodwork. For several miles along a deserted ridge, two beady-eyed Indians, toting umbrellas and perhaps something more lethal, stay awfully close behind the three of us. By the way they're assessing our packs, we get the feeling, which remains unconfirmed, that we're in the presence of genuine brigands—those cutthroat highwaymen of yore.

It's the children, always so many more children than adults, who change the most. They seem out of kilter, wandering in undisturbed valleys that no longer suit their level of disturbance. Unruly and unattended, they band together near mudholes on the outskirts of villages, not so much playing as brooding. The sight of more huffing, overtaxed trekkers holds little amusement; their response is to shoo us angrily on toward the world of our forebears. They don't whine for Hershey bars or Chiclets, but insist on cigarettes. Is this the first word they learn, barely out of the crib? Spanky and the gang are eager to get started on that cough which is Nepal's fatal trademark. When we don't come up with death sticks, we're stoned—or, really, just pebbled. We are stung less by the showering than by this sign of corruption. It's not so much the appearance of false desires, or plain greedy cravings, that's so telling. We can see our beloved modernity at work in the itch for self-betrayal, that shows in the children's unwashed countenances.

Dodging their latest barrage, I catch myself thinking: If only everyone could be given what they crave! Distribute the Chesterfields and the lollipops! Is that so much to ask? If only the world could be forever into a good mood! I'm just tired enough to imagine individual solutions transforming the group when, unfortunately, it has to work the other, more circuitous way around.

And still, our downhill day offers one more variation of mishap. Fifteen miles along, I start having sharp pains in my groin. It's not appendicitis, I know that much, but an old prostate infection aggravated by prolonged dehydration. I can get some relief from wearing a jockstrap, which I've brought along, on doctor's orders, for such an emergency. But where do I change into it? Beneath the trail is one steep drop to the river, above the path is an equally unnegotiable rise to the top of the canyon. Don and Iris join me in a fanciful strategy session. To strip or not to strip? The condition worsens. I have to rest every hundred yards or so. And though Don keeps urging me to do my undressing, I'm hesitant about breaking any local taboos. Has anyone seen a nude Nepali? No, Don counters, but why would we? As a self-appointed spokesmen for all attitudes Indian, he assures me that the human body doesn't go on exhibit in these parts because it's considered standard, anonymous. I don't have to worry about appearing lurid. Anyway, who's looking? Porters pass infrequently, and when they do, hardly take note of us laggards.

I take his advice at the next bluff I can climb, which leads me off the trail but toward a spot that's high above the river and visible for miles. At least, it's at the kink in one very long curve, so I'll be able to see anyone coming in either direction. Of course, just as I get my pants down, and begin working them over my big boots, a whole caravan appears. Frantic to finish before they get too close, I catch the bands of the jock around my ankles. I've roped myself, I'm vulnerable as a stuck pig. Bearing down are ten hefty porters trucking baskets of firewood held by stirrups across their foreheads. I'm indecent by any community's standards; Don and Iris cry the customary *"Namaste!"* to distract them. But this time, they get more than a cursory reply. The whole crew stops dead and wants to chat. None of them seems to see me, though they must notice that Iris and Don are laughing so hard they can barely stand up. I manage to get my jock in place and waddle farther up the hill with my jeans around my knees. The porters, it turns out, are fascinated by Don's camera. They've seen plenty of penises, but never a Nikon. They peer through the wrong end of the lens. Don takes their picture and they take ours, once I'm put back together and ready to pose. The caravan moves on without shedding light on the Nepalese definition of obscenity.

We chug through one final dip, a hollow dominated by a still pond and accompanying crown of reeds. In the water, evening is giving hints of its approach, so we use this Xanadu just for a breather, comb our hair and tuck in our shirts with the help of the pond's mirror. The last stretch to the highway isn't indicated on our maps. Naturally, it's all uphill; strangely, it's through our first pine forest. The terrain turns recognizably Nordic, therefore picturesque. Iris reaches the road and waves like Balboa discovering the Pacific. Don is next. The two of them mush on toward town while I kneel to kiss the Chinese-laid blacktop: harsh, hissing home.

The settlement along the highway is no more prosperous than the ones we've already seen. It looks like an enlarged body shop, one failing livery stable, mostly boarded-up, no Denny's or Ramada Inn or Mobil Station, not even a "Himalayan Happiness" lodge in sight. But a government bus is approaching and rumbles to a stop. Out the back door of this overheated apparition, this aluminum lady bug, leans an adolescent jockey, calling, "Kathmandu!" Instinctively, Iris and Don run for it. As I catch up and board, I notice that the pains in my groin are already diminishing.

If we don't watch out, we'll be in the big city sooner than we think. Don plunks himself down in front of us, suddenly just another passenger, and amazingly eager to while away the commute with conversation. He immediately gets just that from a pair of pudgy Bengali tourists beside him. "And what are your qualifications?" they begin. Don knows just how to answer, with the name of the institute run by his caffeinated guru. Soon, he has his listeners marveling over the thing Indians loved to marvel over most, which is Don's praise for all things Indian.

Iris and I lean in a daze against our packs and each other. She whispers that we should stay on the lookout for an outpost to stop at along the way, so we can try for another peek at Everest and company in the morning. But it's getting too dark for us to inspect each stop for hotels. And it's Iris who mentions that, if our timing's right, we may be able to get the management of the Kathmandu Guest House to turn on their one water heater for us. Silently, I calculate our accomplishment. We've walked sixty miles in five days and, for all that's gone wrong, there's no way I'm going to call our journey a failure.

The bus rockabyes, easing up and around slow, grinding passes. A deep lavender fog envelops our motorized cradle. We float, atilt, through banks of alpine mist; only the red taillights of another bus up ahead guide us over one hurdle, down the next. When the twists break right, we catch the line of famed pinnacles quivering in the twilight. The mountains are rigid petticoats of snow; they are biceps pink with the strain of bench-pressing Tibet; they are a row of stalled cement-mixers; they are decapitated bits of ice cream stuck in scoops of raspberry sherbet; they are anything but what they are, damn rock. Then, all at once, the curtain drops. The bus plummets through a genuine night that's broken only when we reach the first terminals of electrification.

So quickly, we're back in the web. Death-like "Western Civ." encircles us, and the globe, with its tentacles of promise, its asphyxiating cycles of debt, its billboards and radar and inexorability. For those of us who are both the pawns and beneficiaries of industrial power, trying to escape—at least in ways that travel brochures promise—is like trying to escape death. We know that we can't really do it, but that all the meaning we'll ever find will be in the effort.

We are falling fast into the Kathmandu Valley. The fluorescent stanchions along the broad approaches to the capital whip past the bus with stroboscopic fervor. These boulevard approaches, meant for phalanxes of army tanks or Oldsmobiles, are ludicrously empty. Only this time, we see the quaint city, our Hamlin, as a Nepali peasant must see it. Compared to the one-shack hitching posts of the trail, Kathmandu is New York, Rio, and Osaka all in one. The signs are in English, invasive tongue. Broad arrows point and point toward the future.

The bus winces over the uneven driveway of the main depot. The hawkers and touts are waiting. Once we've angled our packs through the door, rickshaw drivers besiege us. Iris and I trade frantic pledges with Don. We will see each other again, soon. We will travel together again, soon. The appearance of that scourge, that invention called choice, divides us for now. Don is hankering after anything curried for his long-postponed restaurant meal, while Iris and I have been dreaming of Tibetan dumplings. We clamber into separate carriages, let two different rag 'n' bone men pedal us off. We wave to one another from under the cabs' drawn hoods that shield us from the blue streetlights. We peel off in different flows of klaxoned traffic. Our last glimpse of Don, merging with the shadows, reveals a winking, coping sahib.

So long, accidental companion! Goodnight, crush of a world's wisely insatiable mob! All is illusion. The Hindus, or whichever holy men first said it, are right. Operationally speaking, they—those other four billion out there—aren't all that necessary. Yet those phantoms have something we want, everything we want. Like light into matter, we go to them, until we're trapped. Laying my head on Iris' shoulder, I close eyes and ledger, still nowhere near my right time, my right place.